SICK FROM WORK

Sick From Work

The body in employment

PAUL BELLABY
University of East Anglia

Routledge
Taylor & Francis Group

LONDON AND NEW YORK

First published 1999 by Ashgate Publishing

Reissued 2018 by Routledge
2 Park Square, Milton Park, Abingdon, Oxon, OX14 4RN
711 Third Avenue, New York, NY 10017, USA

Routledge is an imprint of the Taylor & Francis Group, an informa business

Publisher's Note
The publisher has gone to great lengths to ensure the quality of this reprint
but points out that some imperfections in the original copies may be
apparent.

Disclaimer
The publisher has made every effort to trace copyright holders and
welcomes correspondence from those they have been unable to contact.

A Library of Congress record exists under LC control number: 99073631

ISBN 13: 978-1-138-34550-8 (hbk)
ISBN 13: 978-1-138-34551-5 (pbk)
ISBN 13: 978-0-429-43784-7 (ebk)

Contents

List of Figures

List of Tables

Acknowledgements

The work drawn together in this book has been carried out over a considerable period, and so I have many debts, some to referees' reports on papers that have been or are about to be published:

(1986)'Please boss, can I leave the line?' A sociological alternative to stress and coping discourse in explaining sickness at work. *International Journal of Sociology and Social Policy* 6: 52-68.

(1987) The perpetuation of a folk model of the life cycle and kinship in a pottery factory, In Bryman, A., Bytheway, W., Allatt, P. and Keil, T. (eds), *Rethinking the Life Cycle*, Basingstoke: Macmillan.

(1989) The social meanings of time off work: a case study from a pottery factory, *Annals of Occupational Hygiene*, 33: 423-38.

(1990a) What is a genuine sickness? The relation between work-discipline and the sick role in a pottery factory, *Sociology of Health and Illness*, 12: 47-68.

(1990b) To risk or not to risk? Uses and limitations of Mary Douglas on risk-acceptability for understanding health and safety at work and road accidents, *Sociological Review*, 38: 465-83.

(1992) Broken rhythms and unmet deadlines: workers' and managers' time-perspectives, In Frankenberg, R.J. (ed), *Time, Health and Medicine,* London: Sage.

(1999) Spatiality, embodiment and risks encountered in the making of pots, *Social Science and Medicine*, 48: 1321-32.

(1999) (with Felix Bellaby) Unemployment and ill health: local labour markets and ill health in Britain 1984-1991, *Work, Employment and Society*, forthcoming.

Mildred Blaxter, as medical sociologist, and Theo Nichols, as industrial sociologist, were kind enough to provide comments in quick order on the almost completed manuscript of the book as a whole. My thanks also to Barbara Bellaby, Jill Maguire and Hazel Taylor who made it read better and sound more sensible. My valued research colleagues include Felix Bellaby, Sheila Cleverly, Diana Gilbert and, perhaps above all, Judith Sidaway. Mildred Blaxter and Ronnie Frankenberg encouraged me to write. All field workers depend on people who selflessly allow themselves to be observed and questioned. Though they must remain anonymous, I dedicate the book to them.

List of Abbreviations

ACAS	Advisory, Conciliation and Arbitration Service (UK)
ADA	Americans with Disabilities Act 1990
AWOL	Absent Without Leave
BCMF	British Ceramic Manufacturers' Federation
CATU	Ceramic and Allied Trades Union
DDA	Disabilities and Discrimination Act (UK) 1995
DIY	Do-It-Yourself
ESRC	Economic and Social Research Council (UK)
ESSP	Employers' Statutory Sickness Payment (UK)
EU	European Union
FEV	Forced Expiratory Volume
GHS	OPCS (ONS) General Household Survey
GP	General Practitioner (Medical)
HALS	Health and Lifestyles Survey (GB)
HMSO	Her Majesty's Stationery Office
HSE	Health and Safety Executive (UK)
HSWA	Health and Safety at Work Act (UK) 1973
ICD	International Classification of Diseases
ILO	International Labour Organization
JCC	Joint Consultative Council
LFS	Labour Force Survey (EU)
LS	OPCS (ONS) Longitudinal Study
ONS	Office of National Statistics (UK)
OPCS	Office of Population Censuses and Surveys (UK)
PMS	Pre-Menstrual Stress
PSSI	Personal Social Support Index
QC	Quality Circle
RGSC	Registrar General's Social Class
RIDDOR	Reporting of Injuries, Diseases & Dangerous Occurrences Regs
SEG	Socio-Economic Group
SES	Socio-Economic Status
SMR	Standard Mortality Ratio
SWD	Single, Widowed, Divorced
TTWA	Travel to Work Area

Introduction

'When you come to a patient's house, you should ask what sort of pains he has, what caused them, how many days he has been ill, whether the bowels are working and what sort of food he eats.' So says Hippocrates in his work *Affections*. I may venture to add one more question: What occupation does he follow?
Bernadino Ramazzini, 1633-1714 (1940, Preface).

In his *Discourse on the Diseases of Occupations*, Ramazzini claims to identify the mark left by each occupation. For example, a middle-aged tailor is known by his bent back, crooked legs, and short sightedness, produced by sitting cross-legged over his sewing in dim light. So exact is the correspondence between impairment and occupation that a physician might shortcut a diagnosis if he first finds out what a man's occupation has been.

At the turn of the second millennium, occupations seldom leave such clear footprints. The same ground has been trodden by many factors - among them, upbringing, adverse life events, housing and environment outside work and individual health-related behaviour. People who might have shown the mark of their occupation may not survive long enough in that job for the effects to develop, or may have the stigmata, but display them misleadingly, in a changed job. Discerning the effect of a specific occupation involves sifting evidence to distinguish between many contributory factors. It is the task of epidemiology.

Ramazzini's cases seem to have been own account workers or journeymen in small workshops. In his Padua in the seventeenth century, large employing organizations were rare and, when found, usually impermanent. The exceptions were military, such as the Venetian fleet and, in England, Cromwell's 'new model army'. The industrial revolution that began in the next century and eventually overtook the world, brought together large numbers of producers in factories, mines and mills, divided their labour into detailed tasks, subjected gangs, hired and led by foremen, to direct employment, and established management hierarchy to coordinate and supervise producers (Pollard, 1968, Littler, 1982, Best, 1990, Grint, 1991). In short, it extended to industrial production what the military had pioneered. Distribution, banking and government were similarly developed on a large scale.

Organizations produced their own diseases and impairments or else gave rise to old ones in new ways. In place of Ramazzini's tailor, is to be found an

1

employee 'burned out' by stress, or with circulatory disease caused psycho-socially. Many occupations, especially manual, continue to display the effects of exposure to physical hazards. Psycho-social factors have added another layer to what was already a complex relation between work and health.

There are yet other layers that have been relatively neglected. The extra concepts in *Sick From Work* are derived from combining a return to Marx's theory of alienation with engaging in contemporary debates in medical sociology and social anthropology. So far, few attempts have been made to apply either approach to work and health, much less to combine them, perhaps because the field has fallen into the gap between the sociology of work and the sociology of health. However, Nichols (1997) focuses on the parallel issue of injuries that arise in work, and sets them in a Marxian political economy of capitalism, while Navarro and Berman (1983) draw together a collection of papers that take a similar approach to health at work, and Navarro continues to lead in this direction. Nichols draws on his original research as I draw on mine in this book. My sources are varied, from participant observation in one workplace, which I am able to describe in depth, to smaller studies in other settings, interpretation of official statistics and secondary analysis of data collected by other researchers.

The main concepts are as follows. First, employment is an asymmetrical relation of power, on which both parties depend, but for contradictory reasons - employers must exploit labour power to draw profit and employees must conserve it to carry on earning a living. Workers are usually forced to comply with what employers demand by economic interests, but the relation also gives rise to conflict and resistance, some of it involving health and safety. Second, workers not only *have* bodies, which might be exposed to differing hazards to their health and safety, they *are* embodied selves, who have been shaped to perform useful labour of some kind. This implies a process of selection for fit with occupation, which would accentuate qualities appropriate for the purpose in hand and suppress others. The process might be conceived as one of natural selection, but I pursue the alternative view that the selection is social, and draw on the evidence to criticise the natural selection approach to health, disability and employment. The social model implies that there are real choices as to who gets what jobs and survives in them. Further, as embodied *selves*, workers seek to accommodate to the demands of their jobs, and become, partly through disciplines imposed by employment, 'docile' as well as just potentially useful labour. This 'making of the worker' is the subject matter of Part I.

However, the way the worker is made is also the basis on which specific forms of ill-health flourish. When learned ways of coping with normal demands break down, ill-health develops. The incidence falls either where qualities have been accentuated to fit the job or where qualities have been suppressed that are not required by the job. The vulnerability to ill-health that is embedded in jobs is addressed in Part II, where two other themes are taken up. The first concerns how workers, as embodied selves, *experience* ill-health. Generally, epidemiology and the psycho-social approach to health and work are concerned with disease, physical or mental, as the outcome of a determinative process. Here I focus on how distress, discomfort and pain are felt in the course of work. At first, I relate these not so much to the physical or organizational properties of the work as to the meanings that workplace culture attaches to both bodies and the spaces in which they are put to work. However, the relations of employment and the labour market conditions in which they are embedded influence workplace culture.

The second theme in Part II is how the otherwise individual experience of illness is *made social* and others witness it, react to it and may be ready to give the sufferer leave from normal obligations. Medical practitioners are sometimes involved at this stage. Their view of the condition that is presented to them is necessarily partial and my account helps complete it. Another issue is how relations of employment might make absence for sickness more or less frequent.

Part III engages with epidemiology and the psycho-social approach, rather than the experience of 'illness' and the social process of 'sickness', and views disease and injury as an outcome of determining factors in work and employment. Aside from factors outside work, the bodies that workers have are at risk from their own actions, physical and organizational aspects of their occupations and, finally, the labour market. Instead of seeing their own health-related behaviour as an alternative cause, I suggest that it arises from the relations of employment and the cultures of risk that tend to develop around them.

I also seek to show that many occupations do leave a physical footprint, even today. I would argue that psycho-social explanations have been unduly inflated, especially in popular discourse, and so would restrict their use to where they are clearly relevant, and substitute a more sociological account or a physical one in other cases. The idea that employment is a relation of power, which is asymmetrical and tilted in the employer's favour, runs through the sociological account and is elaborated in the last chapter, where the effect of labour markets on the health of working age populations is put to test. Here the implications for health of the current trend to 'flexible' labour markets are considered. Finally, the concepts that sociology can bring to this already multidisciplinary field of work and health have implications for the approaches that other disciplines take. There is scope for a productive division of labour. At the same time, I challenge the medical and psychological approaches by reordering some of the basic premises in the field of occupational health research.

Before any of these substantive issues can be tackled, some ground clearing and foundation digging is needed. This is undertaken in Chapter 1.

1 The Body and the Relation of Employment

..at the beginning of 1863 twenty-six firms owning extensive potteries in Staffordshire.. presented a petition for 'some legislative enactment'. Competition with other capitalists .. did not allow them to limit the hours worked by children voluntarily. 'Much as we deplore the evils before mentioned, it would not be possible to prevent them by any scheme of agreement between manufacturers.' (Children's Employment Commission, First Report, 1863, p.322).
Karl Marx (1976, pp.381-2, footnote 82).

The aim is to produce a distinctively sociological approach to health in paid work. This involves an understanding of social relations in work and how work is valued and represented, especially in this late modern Western culture. It also demands a concept, in similar vein, of the many dimensions of health and ill-health. Finally, these have to be connected together, in order to see how health may be explained by work. These are the tasks of this chapter.

One explanation for the relation of employment, work and health is gaining ground and is my point of departure.

Autonomy and Control and Health

In the occupational psychology literature and in work by epidemiologists that draws upon it, the view has emerged that autonomy and control in work reduce stress and thereby ill-health arising from jobs and how they are organized.

However, there is not just one tradition. There are two in which autonomy and control feature with health and work. The first is Marx's materialist rethinking of the Hegelian concept of *alienation* (Marx, 1975, Ollman, 1976). The second is North American pragmatism, and the psychology of *self-realization* that has arisen from it. In recent years, alienation theory has been coopted by self-realization theory, as in Blauner's (1964) reconstruction of Marx's concept.

Marx is concerned with how humans not only manufacture useful objects but also make themselves through labour that transforms what nature has to offer.

4

Humans produce individually but cooperatively, in social relations. They are fundamentally social beings. Yet their cooperative labour may produce consumables in abundance, while stunting their potential to become fully human. In the language of our own times, human beings are *embodied* as various forms of useful labour. In Marx's Hegelian terminology, their material being is thereby alienated from their *species being* - that is, what they could be.

Marx insists that the potential is given by the varied technology, knowledge and skills available in a given epoch. Progress in knowledge and skills, science and technology, enlarges the possibilities for humanity. The potential for becoming fully human is not universal, neither innate nor immanent in human nature, but a function of the labour of each generation added to that of its predecessors. When Marx speaks of 'alienation', it is as the denial or negation of the historically specific potential of human beings.

Alienation is accounted for by the specific forms under private property that relations of production have taken in the history of civilizations: masters and slaves, lords and peasants and capital and labour. Quite different forms, based on collective ownership of property, are required to realize human potential. Individuals cannot realize themselves in isolation. The dis-alienation of each person involves the emancipation of the propertyless as a class, from control by the propertied.

While the accent in Marx lies on control - on power relations - in self-realization theory, it lies on autonomy. In the latter, control tends to be conflated with autonomy - as if it were merely control of one's immediate situation rather than control by or of another class. Moreover, autonomy is treated as a universal need. Often it is represented as if it were pre-given. If so, resistance or at least resigned acquiescence is to be expected of anyone who is the object of someone else's attempt at control. Or, as Maslow (1970) claims, autonomy may be immanent, in which case self-realization is the apex of a hierarchy of needs, activated only when lower level needs are met - such as food and shelter and security.

In this perspective, the individual and his or her relationships are treated in abstraction from society. For Marx, by contrast, the individual is the nexus of social relations, the varied character of which in time and place produces different selves and different meanings for individuality itself. Study of the individual must be set in a context of social relations and culture, with particular emphasis on what shapes individual working lives - labour markets, employment relations, technology and work organization, gender, ethnicity.

Marx's emphasis on the relations of production accords better with the sociological perspective adopted in the present study than does the concept of autonomy and control in work deployed by many psychologists. It does not follow that Marx's ideas are relevant throughout this book (they were after all conceived for a society now past) or that the large body of research by psychologists in this area can be neglected.

Embodiment

Another key concept in the book is 'embodiment'. Embodiment has implications both for the medical model of disease and for the sociological model of illness and sickness (Turner, 1996, Fox, 1993).

Humans not only *have* bodies. They *are* embodied. It is as embodied humans that we know ourselves and our environment, though we habitually use our bodies and minds to explore what lies beyond them and, in doing so, tend not to be aware of either (Leder, 1990). Embodiment is produced, not so much by individuals as cooperatively, and what is learned is often handed down to later generations. Thus, what an athlete can do at the end of the twentieth century is of a different order than could be done in a similar event in the past. Athleticism of the highest order is necessarily rare, but athletic pursuits are now common. At the same time, abilities that not only gifted people but also many of their ordinary followers once had - such as transcending the body and the conscious mind in shamanistic trances - have become scarce. Embodiment is, thus, not the fixed legacy of nature, even of the stage to which *homo sapiens* evolved by mutation and natural selection in the stone age, but the joint product of an ever moving interplay of nature and culture.

The production of space *outside* the human body - of 'the environment' in which humans live, including workplaces - is similarly a joint product of nature and culture. Arguably, at no point in the history of the lived environment can a steady state be identified, far less a state that would have been so had humans not been involved. Humans have made, and continually remake, the bed on which they must lie. In producing the space in which they live, humans also imbue it with meanings and react to the meanings as well as the physical properties of the space they encounter.

Embodiment cannot be reduced to culture and social relations any more than it can be reduced to nature. 'Bringing the body back in', where it has long been neglected, implies serious attention to nature. Thus, in today's administered market economy, employment helps define what people need to be capable of, and, therefore, what it is to be disabled. At the same time, bodies and minds tend to be naturally impaired in varying degrees and qualities, becoming so from birth or in the course of life. Today's able-bodied may yet be invalided out and are likely to fall temporarily sick. Society disables, but so does impairment

(Shakespeare, 1998). Even the able-bodied cannot do everything they imagine, for there are limits to what any human can do unaided, and, in any historically given state of the art, to what humans can do with the tools they have invented to overcome the limits of their bodies. Moreover, the bodies humans have are exposed to varying risks, from conception throughout life, which we may or may not be aware of. We may incur risks, knowingly or otherwise, or they may be imposed upon us

Without the concept of 'embodiment', much thinking in the social sciences, environmental sciences, psychology and medicine alike, relapses into dualism (Bendelow and Williams, 1995). Bodies are treated as if separate from minds that control them. Both are separated from selves, as if the self merely had a body and a mind, rather than consisting of body and mind in a dynamic interplay with self. Selves are separated from social relations and culture, as if agency made sense without socio-cultural structure or pattern to guide it, and social structure could exist without human agency. Finally, the environment is treated as if distinct from the human activity that constantly transforms it, and so merely a determinant of that activity, rather than its product.

Control of What and Why?

The guiding concepts then are not just autonomy but control - the relations of power in employment - and not just having a body which is at risk but being embodied in a way that is shaped for and by employment.

The relations of power are contradictory - that is, typically, the two sides are mutually dependent and thus gain from cooperation, and yet they also have opposed interests and tend to struggle with each other for control. Potential for conflict arises because the employer has to profit from the effort employees make, whereas employees need to conserve their labour power in order to continue selling it for a living.

The object of control is not general on either side of the struggle, but limited to specifics. For instance, employers have an interest in when employees take their holidays, but not where and how. Employees have an interest in whether a new machine is going to make them redundant, but not in who supplied it and what it cost. Typically, two objects of control which have implications for health and safety are contested by employers and employees:

- useful *labour power*
- the *effort* involved in production.

Labour power is the human resource - physically and mentally fit people, who are equipped to enter into the contract of employment. Their capacity must be reproduced day to day, over a working life, and from generation to generation. Employees not only have to be in place but also motivated to perform to their abilities and in tune with the demands of their jobs. There must be inducements for them to put in the necessary effort, and punishments if they fall short. Among these, wages and salaries are clearly of major importance, since people without capital must earn a living. The effort due for given reward is contested terrain between employers and employees (Baldamus, 1961). Figure 1.1 suggests how differently the two sides, employer and employees, approach reproducing labour power and producing effort.

Figure 1.1   Control of labour power and effort in production

		AGENT	
		THE FIRM: ITS LABOUR FORCE	THE EMPLOYEE: BODY & MIND
	LABOUR POWER	Reproducing labour power by recruitment, training and exit of the unfit	Maintaining fitness or passing as fit in order to get and hold jobs
OBJECT			
	EFFORT	Regulating labour force by means of close supervision, bureaucracy, technology, wages	Acquiring know-how and rhythm required for doing jobs painlessly

Control of Time

Control of labour power and effort may be analytically separable, but they combine. The key is a contest between employer and employee to control *time*. Time varies in meaning in this context from the pace of work at this instant, to security in the rest of an employee's life or the future of the employer's business.

Reproducing able bodies is cyclical process: whether it is a matter of an individual recovering energy with sleep or a nation state encouraging high fertility. In motivating effort, the accent falls on linear time, for incentives and disincentives are goals towards which one works.

The moral basis of capitalism is using time to add value rather than 'wasting' it. This gives rise to a distinction between work and play (Turner, 1982). Play can be valued indirectly - as a rest from work and opportunity to renew spent labour power. Even when play is preferred for its own sake, it is by virtue of its opposition to work. Individuals distinguish what is happening *inside* the place/time-span where work is carried out, from what would be happening *outside* it if they were not working. A long journey by train is a useful analogy. Here one engages in activities that at least pass the time. However, while the journey is happening, time elapses that could have been used in some other way (Canto-Klein, 1975).

The completely autonomous worker, if there were ever such a person, would be able to control their own time, external and internal alike, that is, to determine what proportion of their life, their year, their week and their day were devoted to work and at what pace they worked. William Morris, and others who sought to revive the craft tradition, knew that craft autonomy was incompatible with the relation of employment (Boris, 1986).

However, even independent producers for the market are constrained by what Marx called the 'fetishism of commodities' - the socially accepted illusion that what the market will bear is an objective, even natural, determinant of human conduct (Marx, 1976, Chapter 1.4). Independent producers are free only formally, not substantively. The division of labour between producers is an invisible network of power relations. Each has to produce and exchange the product with others to make a living. The effect is that they are likely to work long hours and sacrifice leisure-time for work-time, becoming what their businesses or professional careers demand of them.

While employees of all kinds, and even workers who are their own bosses, fall short of complete autonomy in significant ways, there are substantial differences in how much control those who hold jobs have over their effort. In many employing organizations, lower grade employees have more autonomy in time *external* to work than do higher grade, whether managerial or professional. This difference is marked symbolically by the provision of paid overtime, which compensates lower grade employees for giving up their leisure to work extra hours. The absence of paid overtime for higher grade employees implies that they have less right to keep their leisure time intact from the employer.

In time *internal* to work, managers and professionals, the higher the grade the more so, are more likely to given latitude to pace their work (Zerubavel, 1981), but are also expected to exercise *responsible* autonomy. Friedman (1977), in a study of the car industry, found that this, rather than real subordination to the employer in matters of detail, characterized jobs in areas where processes were relatively unpredictable, such as the repair of machine breakdowns. Managers and professionals too, must cope with the unexpected. In an ideal world, employers control their effort by setting objectives and enabling the means to reach them. Managers in production refer to this as 'responsibility', but the reality of it is not only having latitude to make decisions, but also being held to account for outcomes one may not be able to control.

By contrast, lower grade employees are likely to be controlled in some detail. Technology may dictate what they do in each moment of working time, and, if not technology, then rules and procedures or supervision or these in combination. Of course, they will be held responsible if they break rules or disobey orders, but not (legitimately) if machines break down or supplies fail to reach them. Variations in employees' control of time in the course of work arise even within these limits. Thus, the person who has a work station on an assembly line, the flow of which dictates the precise interval at which an operation is repeated, is line-paced. By contrast, a worker on his or her own bench, even with a machine as a tool, is likely to be able to pace their effort. Self-pacing is a far from negligible feature in jobs that would otherwise appear to be highly subordinated.

Effort in internal time and time elapsing while at work will have different values depending on parameters external to the model:

- Among people in or seeking employment, the status of the labour market in which they compete for jobs is significant: is it a buyer's or a seller's market? In a buyer's market, the employee will have less control of external time than he or she would in a seller's market. When jobs are at a premium, employees tend to work all the hours they can get. It is when jobs are plentiful that they are more likely to choose one that fits in with their commitments or interests outside work. They are also more likely to avoid a reputation for taking time-off when there is high unemployment.
- The strategy of the employee's household will affect how many hours he or she might work and how they are distributed in the day, week and year; obviously the labour market will have a large bearing on whether the individual can do as the household's needs dictate.

What is Health?

Health has both positive and negative meanings. The positive meaning attaches to *well-being*, having or believing one has a quality of life that fulfils one's needs and ambitions. It also attaches to fitness, including fitness for work. These are not to be confused: it is perfectly possible to be well and yet be unfit for work. Nor is a person who is able to do a job necessarily fulfilling their needs and ambitions in that job. To these two independent positive dimensions of health, must be added disease, illness and sickness, for health may be conceived as the absence of one or other of these. Thus it has to be acknowledged that health is not the one-dimensional, pre-theoretical phenomenon that it is widely accepted to be. On the contrary it has many dimensions, each of which is saturated with theory.

Disease

The predominant medical practice is to treat health as absence of disease. Disease in a biological and medical sense is a process within the organism that threatens its survival and/or impairs one or more of its functions, whether temporarily or permanently. Disease is almost always seated beneath the surface of the body and conscious mind. It may be visible by lesions in living bodies to the surgeon and in corpses to the pathologist, but has to be read by the physician or psychiatrist from symptoms and signs, and confirmed by tests. Where health means absence of disease, its measurement is even more problematic than is that of disease, for examining everyone frequently in the detail required to eliminate all possible diseases is hardly feasible.

Where screening is done at all, it is targeted on specific diseases that are prevalent, have high case fatality and are clearly preventable. However, expert judgement may also be used to determine an individual's fitness for work. This is so when a firm insists that new recruits fill out a health questionnaire, and commissions medical examinations to assess claimants for sickness severance or injuries compensation. It also applies - far more commonly - when one who is absent from work through sickness must refer to a medical practitioner. In current UK practice this is after seven consecutive days of absence - prior to that, an absentee may be required to certify their own reason for absence.

The relation between physical and mental conditions has been represented in several ways in medicine. The Cartesian dualism, which separates the body as machine and the mind as reason and will, is now considered *passé*, but its shades remain in a tendency to deny reality (that is, disease status) to 'new' conditions, on the grounds that they are 'in the mind' and so merely apparent, for instance (in recent years) myalgic encephalomyelitis (ME) and repetitive strain injury (RSI), and (in the First World War) 'shell shock'. The concept of psycho-somatic disease proposes in place of this dualism, that the body and the mind interact in producing ill-health. The concept of mental illness (as disease) proposes that the mind can of itself suffer ill-health. Such counter views insist that when mind is implicated, disease is just as 'real' as when body alone is involved.

It appears from this brief discussion that disease, though but one dimension of health, is more conceptually problematic and in practice more difficult to observe than tends to be suggested by the positivism that still often dictates the representation of medical science.

Illness

The concept 'illness' refers to individual experience and behaviour - to suffering and restriction of normal activity. Distinguishing illness from disease is familiar in medical practice and indeed necessary to the processes of taking a history and making a diagnosis, which require that the individual's account (verbal and visual) be analysed and reconstructed to help point to the disease beneath the illness with which he or she presents. Illness is not necessarily correlated with disease: one may suffer or be restricted without having a disease. The converse also applies: individuals with disease may not be aware of anything abnormal.

Illness is the conscious aspect of ill-health. Thus, it is illness, not disease, that drives people to seek treatment. The concept of disease is commonly applied either to individuals, who are dealt with as clinical cases, or to aggregates of people (populations). The concept of illness applies to individuals as persons. The role of mind in illness is uncontroversial, unlike its role in disease. It is accepted that illness may be physical or psychological or both at the same time. Thus patients may present to a General Practitioner with a sore throat or nerves, and again with persistent tiredness, in which physical and psychological elements are combined. The treatment depends not only on the diagnosis, but crucially on how the patient responds to the advice the GP offers.

The person is the seat of illness, but culture mediates that individual experience. Whether people suffer pain, far more so whether they consider that it incapacitates them for work, depends not wholly upon their individual characteristics but also on ideas, values and beliefs that they have acquired from others early in life or in their occupation or workplace. For instance, Zola (1966) showed in a classic study that, among North Americans, those of Irish ethnicity were more reticent and stoical about illness and its discomforts than, say, those of Italian descent. These were cultural not racial differences, and they overrode the variations in individual thresholds of pain that may be expected.

Given that illness is conscious, it invites dismissal as wilful fantasy, perhaps for secondary gain, such as care and attention from others, or to give a justification for failure. Without denying this possibility, it is necessary to treat illness as a reality in its own right, on a different level than disease. It is also important to recognize that illness is not likely to be wholly in the individual's control. This is partly because diseases frequently produce pain and discomfort, distress and depression, and indeed specific symptoms presenting as illness; partly because social relations and culture constrain the expression of illness (Alonzo, 1980).

Sickness

'Sickness' is a less familiar concept. It refers to the distinctively social dimension of ill-health. The pioneering discussion of this is by Talcott Parsons (1954, 1958). Parsons describes what he considers the normative model in American society of the sick role. Occupancy of that role entitles the individual to leave from their normal obligations, including work. However, the role is temporary and access to and exit from it is in the control of doctors from whom patients must be willing to take advice. Indeed, patients are obliged to be genuine in their claims for sick leave and to try to get better. Thus, doctors control what would otherwise be open access to social deviance: to reneging on normal obligations at home, school and work.

In this context, doctors' ability to identify disease authorizes them to decide whether the illness that the individual experiences, merits leave from work. Of course, what matters is that doctors should have the credibility to make this decision, not that they should actually be able to find disease.

Parsons' seminal idea has been built upon, but also criticized. He emphasizes that his model is culture-dependent and normative: that is, it is a description of how things were supposed to work in America in the mid twentieth century, not of how they actually worked there, far less of the social relations surrounding ill-health in the world as a whole throughout history. Accordingly, one can follow Parsons' lead and contrast the sick role in different cultures, and also study the problem of implementing the sick role in any given culture.

Sickness absence in Britain is morally ambiguous, because while absence infringes work-discipline, the claim to be unfit for work seeks the indulgence that is thought to be owed to the sick. Sometimes, other people, including managers, take the absentee's reason on trust; sometimes, they reject the reason. A doctor's note plays an important part in determining attitudes to absences of more than a week. That there is such a note tends to dictate payment of sickness benefit and to prevent the absence from becoming a legitimate ground for dismissal from employment. But the sick note may not quell all doubts, and repeated sick notes may confirm doubts. Furthermore, the production of a doctor's note is part of the negotiation of a 'genuine' sickness with the employer. Absences lasting less than a week tend to be 'certified' by the absentee's own stated reason. Neither this nor an appeal to external authority amount to a statement of absolute truth.

How Disease, Illness and Sickness Relate

It is clear from the discussion to this point that sickness, illness and disease are independent dimensions of ill-health and yet interplay. A sick person may not think they are ill, though it is likely that those who coerce them against their own beliefs into stopping work, do so because they think that they have a disease. Conversely, a person who feels ill may be prevented from entering the sick status to which they think they have a right by an expert judging that they have no disease. Figure 1.2 presents some of the probable consequences of the relation between the three dimensions for understanding the behaviour of employees where their health in relation to work is involved.

Figure 1.2 Disease, illness and sickness - their combinations

	SICK		NOT SICK	
	ILL	**NOT ILL**	**ILL**	**NOT ILL**
DISEASE	medically certified absence	coerced into taking time off	unknown disease - stoically endured	disease unknown to self & others
NO DISEASE	time-off with malaise	malingerer	judged to be hypo-chondria	healthy

Fitness for Work

Work covers a great range of different activities - manual and mental; heavy manual and light manual; involving great or little knowledge from experience or learning; and so on. When health is taken into account, a person can be fit for one type of job, say behind a desk, but not another, say in the front line in battle or on the shopfloor. Determining fitness for work is a responsibility often imposed on health professionals, such as General Practitioners. Larger employers may employ physicians and nurses to do this for them. However, the potential conflict of interest previously referred to between employer and employee often surfaces when employed professionals judge another employee's fitness for work (Walsh, 1987).

There are two other issues to address under this heading. The first is the extent to which people are selected for employment and remain in jobs because of their health. The more this is the case, the greater the *healthy worker effect*, which gives the impression that so far from paid work being a risk to people's health, it is associated with better health than not being in employment. The second is how *disability* might affect fitness for work. Disabilities are grounded in various kinds of 'permanent' impairment - locomotor (unaided movement), sensory (sight, hearing), learning (intelligence, dyslexia), neurological (epilepsy), among them. These may be more or less severe in effect on what the person can do. They may not preclude employment. Moreover, while disability is sometimes associated with long term (chronic) illness, it is not necessarily the case that disabled people are in ill-health. Thus the disabled may be fit - in the sense of healthy - and fit for work too. The issues are: how far are people with disabilities excluded from employment, and are the reasons for exclusion actually not being fit for work or a form of discrimination against them?.

Well-being

The World Health Organization defines 'health' in terms of well-being, that is, not merely freedom from disease, but also a state of fulfilment - physically, emotionally, economically and in social relations. Well-being is famously subjective. In comparatively recent years, St Teresa of Lisieux (1873-97) sought to infect herself by drinking the sputum of TB patients she was nursing for the sake of her immortal soul, because, in the tradition of Christian asceticism, the suffering that accompanies ill-health has been an opportunity to share in Christ's suffering. Still more recently, but in a materialist vein, attempts have been made to measure the variable 'quality of life' of individuals and groups in terms of what the world's production capacity makes possible for them. There is vast inequality across the globe between north and south and within each country, developed and developing alike. To achieve for all standards of well-being considered the minimum acceptable in Britain, not only here but elsewhere in the world, would of course involve a massive redistribution of resources between the developed and the developing countries, and between social classes, genders and ethnic groups within countries in both sectors.

Mechanisms Linking Work and Health

Given that work and health are each multidimensional, the link between work and health cannot be simple.

Figure 1.3 seeks to clear the ground of the confusion, which arises if no distinction is drawn between whether work is the site on which ill-health happens, the cause of ill-health or merely affected by ill-health. All these possibilities are of interest to a sociology of work and health, and, since there are overlaps, it is convenient to represent them by a Venn diagram. Each of the possible combinations is represented by a letter and the ones involving an overlap between two or three factors are as follows:

Figure 1.3 Work as cause, effect and site of injury and disease

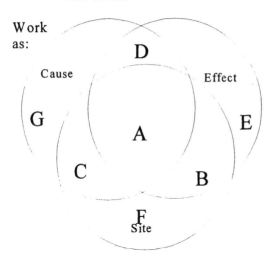

A) Where all three overlap, industrial injury and disease that incapacitates the employee for work are found.

B) Where ill-health happens on site and affects work, but is not caused by work, a disabling injury caused externally may be found.

C) Here lies ill-health that happens at work and is caused by it, but leaves work unaffected while the employee soldiers on.

D) When work causes ill-health, which in turn affects capacity for work, the individual may take time off for it and suffer the effects at home.

In three cases, only one of the possibilities arises:

E) Employees have illnesses that are not caused by work and do not happen at work, and yet lead them to take time-off from work.

F) Alternatively, a stoical employee may bring a condition like this to work, but not allow their performance to be affected by it.

G) Finally, the condition may be caused by work but affect leisure, leading to a weekend or paid holiday in bed.

While the examples stress temporary ill-health, long term health may be treated in a similar way. It is easy to see that the concerns of the law and medical opinion affecting an employer's liability for industrial disease and injury occupy a narrow range of the relation between work and health. For instance, the assessment of damages for pneumoconiosis arising from employment falls into A). It is never an issue until the disease disables the victim for work, and the question that must be resolved by expert evidence is how far the present condition can reasonably be said to stem from each earlier employment, for pneumoconiosis is a degenerative disease that may manifest only years after it began and when the victim has retired or moved to a different type of job.

Health-related and risk behaviours may also be mapped onto the Venn diagram. Alcohol use may account for injury at work in some circumstances, but may itself be caused by work factors, even if drinking is not allowed in the workplace, and so fall into D). Taking risks with moving machinery falls into A) in so far as factors such as production pressure, shift patterns, long hours, lack of discretion and repetitive work are involved.

While the term 'cause' has been used freely, it has to be said that links between work and health are only in rare cases specific. It is more productive to consider health as a matter of multiple causes, or to speak of a 'mosaic' of risk factors. This is not, of course, unique to the problem of how work and health may be linked: it applies to much of the field of health as a whole.

There are several types of causal link between work and health on which sociological analysis can throw light:

- stress, which may arise from work or be brought to work from the household or community
- the control of effort and labour power and their implications for maintaining rhythm or meeting deadlines
- social and cultural variations in the sick role
- the imposition of risks to health and safety upon employees by employers
- employees' taking risks to their health or safety.

Stress

'Stress' has wide currency in lay discussion of ill-health. The prevailing ideas help form *illness* today - how individuals experience ill-health and make sense of it, and also *sickness* - for, in justifying lapses of performance in social roles, a connection is often made between what work and commuting to work involve, the stress they engender and health. By this route, ill-health is made social, and stress comes to be seen as the distinctive pathology of modern life (Herzlich, 1973, Herzlich and Pierret, 1987). Young, A. seeks out the relations of power that sustain this view, both in the wider context (1980) and in the specific setting of the treatment of post-traumatic stress disorder (1993), a modern pathology of the armed services. There may be a parallel between the shift from physical to stress explanations of ill-health in a work context and the shift from explanations based on poverty to others based on consumer lifestyle (affluence) in a community context (Bartley, 1985). If so, the traditional Marxian interpretation would be that both are 'ideologies' which represent real relations in a distorted way (see Eagleton (1991) for a wider discussion of the concept).

In particular, the lay view is that stress is suffered not by manual but by non-manual workers, especially executives. The presumed incidence of stress is allied to the division between mental and manual labour. Stress is thought of as a state of mind, which may well have secondary consequences for the body. The potential for interplay of mind and body in the production of ill-health is conceived as ranging from what Breuer and Freud (1974) called 'hysterical conversion', in which the mind causes the body to mimic physical impairment (such as paralysis), to a 'holistic' model, in which many diseases, that would otherwise be considered physical (such as heart conditions and cancers), are construed as malfunctions of the person. Often, treatment of stress is seen as a matter of education. *Coping* with stress tends to be seen as an essential property of people in executive positions, not only for the sake of the organization, but also for their health, and this skill, it is assumed, can be taught. Lay views of stress, thus, borrow from medical and psychological discourses, and there are many professional practitioners whose conceptual frameworks merge with popular beliefs.

The study of such ideas and of the social relations on which they rest and which they engender is part of sociology's mission. However, it is one thing for the sociologist to bracket off the truth value of a concept, in order to examine its social usage, and another to deny its truth value. The experience of *distress* is part of the human condition and its reality cannot be denied. Distress belongs with illness, and so pain and discomfort. Stress also has a meaning that derives from natural science rather than everyday usage and is linked to disease rather than illness. First, there is now a substantial body of epidemiological evidence (for instance, from the Whitehall studies, which are discussed below), which disputes the lay assumption that stress-related disease is confined to executives. Karasek and Theorell (1990) take the contrary view, and locate stress where jobs demand much, but provide the occupant with little freedom to determine how the demands are met. These conditions often apply in lower grades, rather than among executives. Second, there is a counterpart to this 'job strain' model for locating stress in organizational structures, which seeks stress in psycho-biological systems, much as civil engineers do in roads and bridges subjected to constant use. 'Stress', in this context, extends from the potential for fractures in bones that arises when they are subjected to bending or twisting motion, by stages, to how heightened blood pressure, aroused by mental strain, may damage the tissues of the cardiovascular system (see, for example, Brunner *et al.* 1996). At base, the more complex of these models may still reflect the premise that the way humans live in an industrialized, urbanized environment is out of joint with nature: under shock, it is natural to run away or turn and fight, but modern living and its disciplines inhibit both responses and so causes mental strain, leading to stress and thus damage to the organism (Selye, 1956).

In what follows in the book as a whole, I shall continue to discuss separately, at intervals, lay beliefs about stress in employment, scientific explanations of disease that draw on stress in some form, and, finally, the part that *distress* - the experience - might play in linking patterns of work to illness and sickness. It is to the last that I turn first.

Control of Time and Health

There is another way of approaching the interaction of felt *distress* and health than psycho-social explanation. In employment, the body has to fit the requirements of jobs and produce acceptable effort. Employees accommodate to this by developing rhythms. Employers try to enforce their requirements by watching over employees and giving incentives to comply. Should the employee's rhythm break down, he or she will experience discomfort, and failure to regain rhythm under pressure can cause distress. Alternatively, distress may start the process rather than finish it. Thus, a row with a supervisor or with one's partner at home can affect work rhythm, leading to discomfort. The distress may well be amplified by the process that has already been described.

Disease and injury may enter either in the process or as the outcome. Thus, loss of rhythm, for whatever reason, makes a manual worker, word-processor or data-entry clerk vulnerable to strain injuries. Disease may also be the outcome. Conversely, disease or injury may cause loss of rhythm. For example, 'flu makes people slower in their reactions and less capable of concentration. The rhythm which enables one to maintain the required pace can no longer be sustained. If there is no decision latitude on the job itself, the person with 'flu has little option but to take time-off. If he or she stays at work and tries to soldier on, it is at increased risk of accidental injury.

Health-related behaviour may be keyed in with work and in turn affect health. Ageing and inexperience alike may make injury more likely. Health-related behaviour conventionally includes smoking, drinking, exercise and diet. Drinking alcohol to excess, or perhaps even at all, slows reaction times and reduces concentration, and so can initiate a process ending in sickness absence, injury or long term disease, related to work. Ageing makes it difficult to maintain rhythm in high-paced work, and inexperience makes it difficult to develop rhythm in any job.

In Figure 1.4, the first column concerns broken rhythm and the second unmet deadlines as sources of ill-health and possible sickness absence. When

Figure 1.4 Broken rhythm, unmet deadlines and health

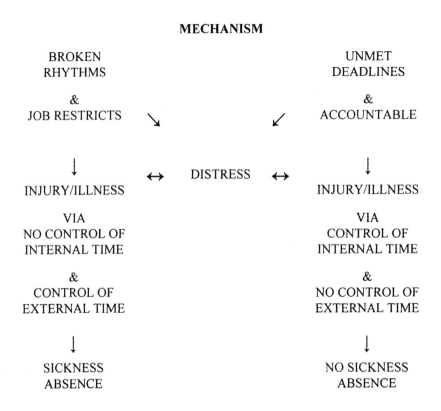

rhythm is broken, restrictive job design - like the assembly line - makes recovery of rhythm difficult and distress is likely to be engendered. Distress in turn makes illness or injury probable, or aggravates it if it was originally the cause of broken rhythm. Sickness absence is likely to occur if the worker is denied relief by supervisors or fellow workers, but the path to it may be blocked if the employee lacks control of time external to work - for example, fears that taking time-off will jeopardize his or her job. It is probable that if the employee repeatedly finds relief at work or in absence from work blocked, illness or injury will be aggravated, until a relatively prolonged period of absence becomes necessary for treatment or the person wastes from the job.

The second flow chart, on the right hand side, deals with a type of job in which the employee has decision latitude, but is accountable for meeting targets set by superiors - a common situation in management and among employed professionals. Failing to meet deadlines, it is presumed, causes distress, as does broken rhythm on restricted jobs, when superiors are unforgiving about those failures. However, the manager's or professional's latitude enables them to get relief from the immediate pressures while remaining at work: for instance, they can hide in the office and take the phone off the hook. Repeated failures to meet deadlines exacerbate distress. Stress and coping discourse is used by managers, professionals and their superiors to describe the situation. Ironically, the discourse can contribute to the distress (while relieving superiors of any blame for causing it) because the individual is expected to learn to cope with the problems that gave rise to the initial failure.

Cultural Variations in the Sick Role

The model just outlined resembles stress theory in at least one respect: it is (in principle) cross-cultural. However, there are striking cultural differences in several aspects of health. Of interest to medical anthropology are the varieties of explanatory models, often radically different from biomedicine, that are to be found both in literate and in oral traditions (Kleinman, 1980).

Sickness involves the social relations into which one may enter in ill-health. Frankenberg (1986) has characterized it as a 'cultural performance'. This appears in a contrast between how contemporary Japanese and contemporary Americans perform in sickness (Ohnuki-Tierney, 1984), for where Americans, like the British, feel that they should soldier on through minor illness, the Japanese take minor illness seriously and cosset themselves and indulge family members and colleagues at work when they are ill. This does not, however, imply a more relaxed view of work discipline and sickness absence on the part of the Japanese.

Within each culture there is likely to be a family resemblance between the performance required of men and women, young and old, and elite and non-elite, which is distinct from that of other cultures. Even so, variations are likely to be required of people occupying different statuses. This is a particularly fruitful ground to explore in a workplace where men and women, young and old and managers and workers are all likely to be expected to perform differently when in ill-health - even to give different pretexts for leave from work.

Risks Imposed by Employers

No occupation (nor indeed any condition in life) is free of risk to health and safety. Employment, like crossing a busy road, entails some risk. Accidental deaths at work may be considered relatively hard evidence of the effect of work on health. They may be partly attributable to factors outside work (e.g. alcohol use, family stress), but are almost always avoidable by measures taken at work, and the injuries, unlike chronic illness, will arise immediately or in a short time, rather than gradually over many years.

On the face of it, the probability of accidental death at work is low by comparison with that in the home and on the roads. In Britain there are roughly 10 fatalities at home and 10 on the roads for every 1 at work. But there are several reasons for considering that fatal accident rates give a misleading impression of the relative health and safety of work:

- people who are employed are of a less vulnerable age than children and elderly people, who have disproportionate numbers of accidents at home
- during the hours in which most people are at work, they are likely to be more alert than when at home, commuting, or in leisure pursuits
- accidents are less likely to occur where activity is relatively organized and supervised, as in most workplaces, than where it is less so, as in the home
- a significant proportion of fatalities on the road are work fatalities, such as those involving commercial travellers, and drivers of lorries, vans and buses
- work may contribute indirectly to deaths on the road or in the home involving employees, for example, when people commute or when they return home tired after work.

Moreover, fatal accidents are but the tip of an iceberg, whatever the context - work, home or the roads. Hidden beneath the surface are accidents causing non-fatal injury and diseases that are occupational or work-related and may be fatal after chronic illness. Many of these are much more probable at work than in the home or on the road: such as poisoning by exposure to toxic chemicals and strains caused by lifting, repetitive motion or remaining seated in a bad posture.

Employers impose risks on employees, but not because they want to do so. No doubt, some employers (like some employees) are more concerned about health and safety risks than others. But arguably it is the social, economic and political/juridical structures of capitalism, not individual motivations, that take the lead in making for safer workplaces. For instance, firms compete to sell their products, and must make a return on their investments. This may involve direct competition between production costs and health and safety at work.

Employees' Risk Behaviour

Jobs differ, of course, in how hazardous the substances, machines or environment are: that is, how much damage to health or safety, and to how many people, would be caused by exposure to the hazards. However, catastrophes, like an explosion in a nuclear power installation, may be a low risk, because the incidence has been zero or very infrequent and, other things being equal, remains improbable, while modest threats to health and safety, like cutting a finger while peeling vegetables at home or in a catering establishment, may be a high risk, because of past frequency and likely recurrence.

How employees behave frequently increases or decreases the likelihood of their being exposed to hazards. Workplaces tend to develop safety cultures, shared views of what is unsafe and why, which accentuate some risks and neglect others, and may sanction, say, neglect of respirators or helmets where regulations require them. It is to be expected that low risk catastrophes will receive disproportionate attention, and high risk low threats will be minimised. This is not necessarily irrational. All life is risky: even inactivity is bad for the health. Aversion to catastrophes, even if they are improbable, makes more sense than being paralysed by fear of trivial threats, even if they are frequently encountered.

Work groups play a part in reinforcing safety cultures. They are likely to disapprove of or even ostracize those who (for whatever reason) tend to have accidents that are considered serious, while discounting other accidents: thus, for example, strains to backs, shoulders, wrists and elbows may seem to fellow workers insufficient grounds for time off work. However, safety cultures are not likely to be self-standing. Habitual practices and the meanings attached to potential hazards reflect past experience and present circumstances. For instance, if workers neglect respirators, it may be because they impede them in trying to work at the pace that technology or management imposes.

Another form of risk behaviour common in work is health related behaviour. This is so called because of epidemiological, clinical or laboratory evidence that the behaviour has consequences for health, usually far distant in time. Smoking tobacco, cigarettes especially; consuming alcohol above certain safe limits for men and women; eating a diet low in fibre and high in saturated fats; and taking little exercise, especially no vigorous exercise, are the four health related behaviours most commonly referred to in public health literature.

It is debateable how much weight health related behaviour, rather than employment and work, should have in explaining health. A greater association of ill-health with employment and work than with lifestyle choices, and a link between health related behaviours and employment and work patterns, would favour the view that choice of behaviour was of minimal significance. For employment and work are major constraints on individual freedom, even in a political democracy.

Conclusion

In this chapter, it has been argued that 'health' and 'ill-health' are multidimensional - they do not just have many synonyms. Being embodied entails experience of the pain and discomfort of *illness*, when it strikes. Having a body exposes humans to risks to normal biological and psychological functioning, that is to *disease* and injury. Both disease and illness tend to be made social, as *sickness*. Ill-health is typically experienced through culture, not idiosyncratically. It is typically analysed and explained with cultural categories, in which even biomedicine - originally Western, however cosmopolitan it may have become - remains embedded. Becoming a sick person entails entry into a web of social relations, which both empower (one can set aside normal obligations and claim the indulgence of others) and subject the actor (one is required to become a good patient and demonstrate genuine cause for absence from paid work).

Employment is an asymmetrical relation of power, in which employer and employee are interdependent, but also divided because the one must extract profit from use of labour, and the other must conserve his or her power to labour, so as to be able to make a living. Control of time, both internal and external to the workplace, is crucial in this division of interest. However, before they enter the contest to control time, people have to be 'made' useful labour, and how they are selected and processed with this in view has implications for all aspects of their health. This making of a worker who is fit for employment is the subject of Part I, which follows.

PART I
MAKING THE BODY
FIT FOR
EMPLOYMENT

2 Fit Bodies: Selected by Nature or Social Process?

We will now discuss in a little more detail the struggle for existence.
Charles Darwin (1809-1882), *The Origin of Species* (1859, Chapter 3).

The main question is, 'how do jobs affect health', but the answer may be obscured by the extent to which only healthy and/or able-bodied people survive in jobs. Whether one is fit for a job is connected with the relevance of what one can do, but health and disability often affect capacity to sustain effort, whether permanently or temporarily.

There are two conceivable ways in which people might be excluded from employment by ill-health or disability. The first is 'natural selection'. Natural selection of the fit by the labour market is conceived as having two modes: intergenerational and intragenerational. In the first mode, ability and aptitudes are transmitted genetically from parents to child. In the second, survival in employment in the course of a life-time depends on continued fitness. Free markets involve decisions by numerous buyers and sellers, but, where knowledge is perfect (a prerequisite of the free market), the interests on which decisions are based are determined by the laws of supply and demand. Thus individual choices are apparent not real. When economic activity fluctuates, so does the volume of employment. As demand for labour rises, more of those hitherto marginal for employment find work or remain in it. As demand falls, so do the numbers of marginal workers who remain in employment.

The second way in which people might be excluded from employment by ill-health or disability is 'social process'. In this view, choices do count. Interests shape choices, but only interests as perceived by actors who face a relatively uncertain future, not interests as determined by any hidden hand of the market. There is a greater or lesser element of discrimination which, instead of treating each according to his or her merits, stereotypes people, drawing on commonsense or even expert knowledge to overgeneralize the consequences of age, chronic illness or specific disability for capacity to work. The outcome of this social process of selection may resemble what the natural selection model predicts, but the fact that real choices are involved is revealed by the imprecision and wastefulness of the allocation of people to employment and specific occupations.

The natural selection model is implied in the epidemiologist's 'healthy worker effect'. The social process model resembles Oliver's 'social model' of disability (1996a,1996b), who would call natural selection the 'medical model'. However, I allot a role in fitness for work to disease and impairment, and so imply that disability is grounded in nature as well as being a social construct. In this, the social process model is similar to the significantly modified social model of disability of Crow (1996) and Shakespeare (1996, 1998).

If selection for employment is a social rather than a natural process, decision-makers, who try to fit people with the requirements of particular jobs, can be expected to accentuate certain abilities and suppress others. Thus, what counts as 'unfit' will be defined in terms of the demands that jobs make. Natural selection may be said to sort those already goats from those already sheep, whereas a social process may be said to *make* working bodies, or at least complete nature's work. Moreover, imperfect shoe-horning of people into jobs may produce maladaptation, and thus specific types of ill-health and injury that arise in the course of specific jobs.

There is more to the difference between natural selection and social process models than can be resolved by evidence. However, the present purpose is limited and it is with evidence and its interpretation that I am mainly concerned. Is the evidence consistent with natural selection? Is there anything to show , on the contrary, that discrimination takes place in employment - in particular, that socio-cultural factors rule some groups out of consideration for employment, however fit they are for the job?

The Evidence and its Use

Most of the sources of evidence are medical. The proponents of the social model tend not to have large surveys to back up their claims. Nevertheless, official statistics leave no doubt that the chronically sick and disabled are *marginal* in labour markets. The statistics are also open to either interpretation: in principle, one could be marginalized by natural selection *or* by social processes.

There is no entirely clear-cut test of either interpretation. A view will have to be taken on the balance of probabilities. If discrimination occurred on grounds of race, creed, gender, age or sexuality, the probability of gaining and keeping a job in the UK would be higher, say, if one were white, Christian and Protestant, male, young and/or heterosexual. Since chronic illness and disability do not always *prevent* someone from working, discrimination might be tested for by comparing the chances of employment for the sick and impaired, who can work, with those of the healthy and able-bodied. Should the result be negative, a large part of the argument for discrimination on grounds of health and disability falls. Admittedly, not all the case falls, for the sick and disabled might have concluded that they were unable to work because of their past experiences of discrimination. However, if there were no current cases, discrimination would have become a dead issue and there might be weak grounds for saying that it had happened in the past.

On the other hand, it is possible that the sick and disabled are like marginal land - used by the economy only when demand is at its height, for their productivity is lower than that of the healthy and able-bodied (they may produce less per head or they may cost more to employ). If that were the case, their chances of gaining employment would increase in the expansion phase of the business cycle. If it did not do so, discrimination would be indicated.

Finally, of course, one should look for more direct evidence of discrimination, though whatever is found is likely to be for small segments of the total picture, and so can be used only for corroboration of a larger case.

There are several official sources that allow the wider picture to be developed, though they differ in whether they distinguish the effects of disability from those of long term ill-health and ageing. The Office of Population Censuses and Surveys (OPCS) Surveys of Disability do so and therefore will be my focus (Martin, Meltzer and Elliot, 1988, Martin, White and Meltzer, 1989). Arguably, they give a reliable account of the distribution of 'disability', as defined by the WHO, in the mid 1980s in Britain (Bury, 1996). To update and extend the account the Surveys of Disability give, I shall draw on Labour Force Surveys for the 1990s and Census data for several decades. There has been disagreement about the definition of disability used in all these sources, but not enough to invalidate them for my purpose.

The Marginality of Disabled People in Employment

The OPCS Surveys were grounded in concepts borrowed from the World Health Organization International Classification of Impairments, Disabilities and Handicaps (World Health Organization, 1980). The WHO approach, distinguishes three facets of disablement. The first is 'impairment':

> any loss or abnormality of psychological, physiological or anatomical structure or function.

In some cases impairments are congenital, in others the outcome of injuries or diseases acquired in the course of life. The second facet is called 'disability', but used here in the specific sense of:

> any restriction or lack (resulting from an impairment) of ability to perform an activity in the manner or within the range considered normal for a human being.

Finally, the WHO definition distinguishes from both 'impairment' and 'disability', a third facet, 'handicap':

> a disadvantage for a given individual, resulting from any impairment or disability, that limits or prevents the fulfilment of a role (depending on age, sex and social and cultural factors) for that individual.

Sometimes, as in the case of facial acne, an impairment may become a handicap, even though it is not a disability (in the specific sense above), because it may make a person's appearance seem unacceptable to others (Hawkesworth, 1998). On the other hand, disabilities are not handicaps unless what a role requires is beyond what the disabled person can deliver in the circumstances. For instance, not being able to walk is no obstacle to home-based work with information technology. The demand that is made and the accommodation that others allow in performing it have a major impact on whether disability becomes handicap.[1]

The original WHO model claimed neutrality, though it has been revised following debate that is both technical and about ideology (Chapireau and Colvey, 1998). By comparison, the political purpose of the social model is overt: it is to make people with disabilities independent, thus 'normalizing' them. This involves changing the physical, economic and socio-cultural environment that makes a disadvantage of disability, and, in effect, detaching disability from impairment. When impairment is taken to be the main factor in disability, the solution appears to lie not in *justice* but in correcting the fault or training the disabled person to live with it. As noted earlier, there is room for shades of opinion about the weight that impairment has in influencing disability.

Following the medical rather than the social model, the OPCS did four separate surveys: two of children, two of adults, and one of each in private households and in communal establishments. The information was gathered in a four stage process and was based on representative nation-wide samples. In the

---

1   The term 'handicap' has long had derogatory implications for disabled people. Ironically, it came from racing, where handicap *equalizes* opportunities. It may be reconceptualized, as in the present account, as social disadvantage.

first stage - for lack of a reliable list of disabled people in Britain - the OPCS team screened private households and communal establishments with a self-completion questionnaire, seeking those who were disabled to any degree. In the second stage, they briefly interviewed the group generated by the first stage to eliminate those who did not meet a threshold of slight severity.

The third stage involved a full interview designed to determine details of the impairment and how severe a disability was associated with it. The crucial final element was consensual judgement by a panel of how cases should be sorted into levels of severity (in ascending order from 1 to 10). Each panel consisted of professional experts on disability, researchers into disability, disabled people, carers and people from voluntary organizations for disability.

Figure 2.1 (below) shows the employment status of people with disabilities of varying severity, compared with that of the mainly able-bodied of the general population. For present purposes, there is special merit in the fact that the Surveys of Disability separate being unfit to work from severity of disability. It militates against the danger of generalizing from particulars of disability (e.g. cannot walk) to employability in all types of job.

Figure 2.1 Disability and employment status:

Great Britain 1985-8 and 1991

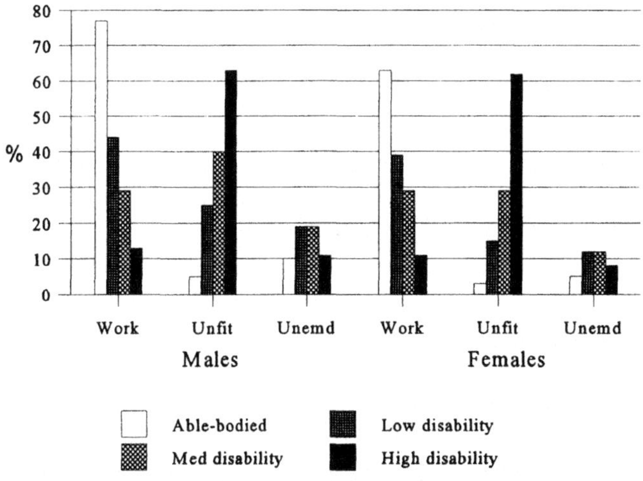

'Able-bodied' = General Population (1991)
Severity of Disability: Low=1-2; Med=3-6; High=7-10 (OPCS 1985-8)
Unemd= unemployed

Source: *OPCS Surveys of Disability in Great Britain, Report 4: Disabled adults: services, transport and employment*, HMSO 1989, p.69; Census 1991: *Economic Activity*, HMSO, 1994

A smaller proportion of disabled people have paid employment than of the 'able-bodied'and it declines sharply as disability becomes more severe. The major difference is how many are unable to work. This is consistent with the natural selection argument.

However, the results can be turned on their head. Among people with disabilities, slightly under two thirds of men and over two thirds of women of working age were *able to work*. Even at levels of severity of 7 and higher, almost two fifths of men and women were so. Unemployment rates suggest that the disabled might be overlooked by employers. For those who were economically active, unemployment rates were much higher among the disabled than the largely able-bodied of the general population - for the general population, they were 11% for men and 7% for women; for all the disabled, 34% for men and 28% for women; and for the most disabled (severity 7-10), 46% for men and 42% for women. Nor is unemployment the only form that exclusion from paid work might have taken. Disabled people who were able to work were also more likely to be economically inactive than counterparts who were largely able-bodied - in the general population, they were 11% for men and 31% for women; for all the disabled, 21% for men and 42% for women; for the most disabled (severity 7-10), 32% for men and 55% for women.

In short, when disabled people whom the OPCS survey found to be able to work sought employment far more of them failed to get it than was the case for the able-bodied. Moreover, far fewer sought work than their disabilities allowed them to do. This is substantial evidence against natural selection, derived from a survey conducted on the 'medical model'.

There is also an obvious gender difference in employment which cannot be accounted for by relative levels of disability among men and women. Fewer women of pre-pensionable age - whether able-bodied or disabled - take part in the labour market than do men. This is a social more than a natural difference, even though women's participation is lower and more often part-time when they have dependent children than when they have no children or none that is dependent (Martin and Roberts, 1984), for though only women can bear children, it is social convention that they should look after them more often than male partners do.

Conversely, much higher proportions of men who are outside the labour market are officially 'permanently sick' than of women. This and the fact that among men this is more prevalent before retirement than after it, are accounted for by social practices - one cannot draw incapacity benefit when of pensionable age and, because they often lack the necessary contributions to qualify, women draw it much less often than men.

Still another way of looking at the findings of the OPCS Surveys is to estimate the prevalence of disability in the population at large. It becomes more probable with advancing age, as Figure 2.2 shows. This relation too is statistical. It certainly does *not* imply that everyone who is over retirement age is disabled, far less unfit for employment. This is brought out by the reciprocal, representing the prevalence of disability in the population.

Figure 2.2 Able-bodied and disabled by sex
and age: Great Britain 1985-8

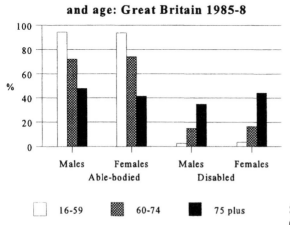

Severity of Disability (OPCS Categories): Med/High=3-10

Source: *OPCS Surveys of Disability in Great Britain*, Report 4, HMSO, 1989, Table 3.7 (resident in private households only)

Plainly, many women of pre-pensionable age who are outside the labour market are so not because of disablement, and the same applies to many people of both sexes who are pensioners. From the evidence that has been reviewed, retirement at a fixed age seems likely to consign many who are able-bodied to a time of life in which they are not expected to work gainfully and, if they choose to work, are likely to have to do so either voluntarily or for payment that is well below their qualifications and experience (McKay, 1998).

In the full period since the Second World War, this marks a major change, for, at the beginning. a higher proportion of men over retirement age were in employment. As Figure 2.3 (below) shows, more people responding to each successive decennial census of England and Wales since 1971, have defined themselves as either early retired or permanently sick. The effect is particularly pronounced for men. Labour market participation fell with increasing age after about 50 for women as well as men, though women's economic activity increased overall.

Figure 2.3 Intercensal changes in the level of economic activity, permanent sickness and retirement in England and Wales 1971, 1981, 1991

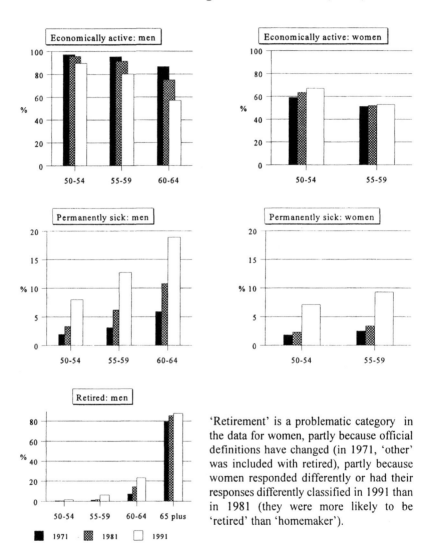

'Retirement' is a problematic category in the data for women, partly because official definitions have changed (in 1971, 'other' was included with retired), partly because women responded differently or had their responses differently classified in 1991 than in 1981 (they were more likely to be 'retired' than 'homemaker').

Source: Censuses 1971, 1981, 1991, *Economic Activity Tables*

More recent evidence from the Labour Force Survey shows that the economic activity rate of women of 16-59 has continued to increase - it rose from 69% to 71% between 1987 and 1997 - while that of men of 16-64 has continued to decrease - it fell from 87% to 84% in the same period. Women with children under 5 are less likely to do paid work and more likely to do shorter hours than those without, but their participation in the labour market rose far more sharply than that of other women - from 42% to 55% (Sly, Thair and Risdon, 1998). Again, it is not natural selection that accounts for this trend, nor does the business cycle have any bearing on it, for it is a long term trend that has no intelligible relation to fitness for work.

What Jobs Require and Bodies Can Deliver

Difficulties with locomotion affected more than half the disabled adults of working age in private households in the OPCS Surveys. Thus, manual work can be expected to be more problematic for disabled people than non-manual.

Indeed much higher proportions of manual than non-manual workers become permanently sick in the course of their careers, notably so when males of 60-64 (18.7% manual males at 60-64 as against 6.8% non-manual). In a labour market where manual jobs are hard to find and wages are low for the unskilled, permanent sickness is likely to be preferred to unemployment (Haynes *et al.*, 1997). If there were discrimination in this particular context, it might be a matter of medical practitioners *denying* access to incapacity benefit to unemployed people with ill-health or disability.

Yet, contrary to what natural selection suggests, disabled men and women workers, both full time and part time, are more likely than the general population to be in manual than non-manual jobs. Even when in non-manual jobs, they are more likely than the population at large to have junior posts. A higher proportion of disabled men are in semi-skilled or unskilled than skilled work than are men as a whole. Fifty-three percent of disabled women work part-time but only 44% of women in the general population.

These findings suggest that disabled workers find it harder to get employment than the able-bodied, and when they get employment, they are more likely to get lower status, lower paid jobs than the able-bodied.

How Competitive are the Disabled?

I am in process of qualifying the natural selection account. However, even negating it would not be the same as proving discrimination. For instance, qualifications and experience might make someone who is fit though disabled uncompetitive, as might any extra cost to the employer of making adaptations to the pattern of work to accommodate the disabled worker.

The quarterly Labour Force Survey is a source of further, more up to date, information on disability and employment in the working age population (Sly, Duxbury and Tillsley, 1995, Cousins, Jenkins and Laux, 1998). It relies on self-reports of limiting longstanding illness. Since the winter quarter survey of 1993/4, it has specified what 'longstanding' means (at least a year), and that its focus is whatever affects the amount and type of paid work respondents can do. In the winter quarter of 1994/5, this method yielded a higher estimate of how many were unable to work who were of working age than did the OPCS Surveys of Disability of 1985-8 (11% as opposed to 8.4%), but a lower figure than for limiting longstanding illness in the 1985 General Household Survey (16%).

The LFS confirms that the disabled are marginal in employment. It also shows that they tend to be less well qualified than the able-bodied. Two fifths of the disabled had no qualifications, but less than half that proportion of the able-bodied. The non-disabled were also one and a half times as likely to have qualifications beyond A-level as the disabled (Sly, Duxbury and Tillsley, 1995). Does this imply that employers reject disabled applicants because their qualifications are uncompetitive and do not discriminate against them?

The OPCS Surveys of the mid 1980s produced the same observation (Martin, White and Meltzer, 1989, Chapter 7). They also developed statistical models to assess the independent contribution of qualifications and a range of other attributes to the chances of disabled persons having employment (though they did not compare their situation with that of the able-bodied). Qualifications did appear to contribute to having a job, and lack of them to being permanently unable to work, but crucially - in view of the suggestion of discrimination in the high rate of unemployment among the disabled - lack of qualifications did not make unemployment more likely. Among the disabled, as in the general population, manual workers were less likely than non-manual to have jobs, and more likely to be unfit for work or unemployed. However, severity of disability and age (being over 50) were the strongest predictors of ill-fortune in employment. The authors do not suggest that this is remarkable, yet severity is *insufficient* to account for how many disabled people who sought work failed to get it, and how many of 50 and over were excluded from the labour market. In other words, while severity of disability and age account for more variation in position in the labour market than other factors considered by OPCS, they appear to leave much unexplained.

The OPCS Surveys also have material of interest about how often employers tend to make provisions to help disabled workers to do their jobs. The costs of such provision as had been made were not addressed. It is unlikely that they carried no costs, but provisions were not often made, even when, as in two thirds of cases, disabled employees said that their disability affected their current job. Then, 40% of men and 30% of women said that their employer had made provisions for their disability and a further 8% and 11% respectively that there was no need to do so. More than half of each sex said that the employer had made no provision at all.

It would seem that qualifications and the cost to employers of making special provision for the disabled are unlikely to account significantly for the disadvantages of disabled people in labour markets. This leaves a space which discrimination is likely to fill.

Discrimination? The Case of Ethnicity

Is there persuasive evidence that discrimination takes place in labour markets? Employers might not knowingly discriminate. They might do so by default, because it did not normally occur to them that someone who was older, a woman or disabled might be suitable for a specific job. This is 'institutionalized discrimination'.

Discrimination has often been documented against ethnic groups. The Census asked a question on this ethnic group for the first time in 1991, having previously asked only about country of birth. Figure 2.4 (below) shows how economic activity, the risk of unemployment and the likelihood of becoming permanently sick vary for men and women of 16 and over in the five largest ethnic groups. In 1991, these were, in order of size: the white majority (42 million of 16 and over) which, in turn, contains the largest ethnic minority - those born in Ireland (800,000); Indians (600,000); black Caribbeans (400,000); and, finally, Pakistanis (270,000).

Economic activity is uniformly higher among men than women in these major ethnic groups, but women are much more likely than average to participate in the labour market if they are black Caribbean and much less likely to do so than average if they are Pakistani. This reinforces the point that gender differences in employment status are by no means reducible to how fit for work men and women are. They are social. A comparison of Labour Force Survey results between 1984 and 1995, corroborates the impression that the Census of 1991 gives on this point (Sly, 1996, p.262).

All ethnic minorities appear disadvantaged in unemployment by comparison with majority whites. In the Census of 1991, unemployment was assessed by International Labour Organization (ILO) criteria, not registration or claiming employment-related benefit: one is unemployed if one does not have a job, has been looking for work in the last four weeks and is able to begin work in the next two weeks. On this basis, unemployment rates in 1991 are highest for Pakistanis,

Figure 2.4 Ethnic group and employment status of people
of 16 and over in Great Britain 1991

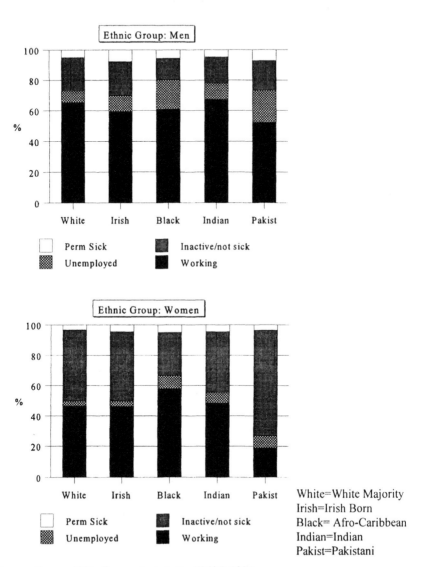

Source: Census 1991: *Economic Activity*, HMSO 1994

male and female, among whom almost 3 in every 10 who are economically active
are out of work. In general, when inactive economically, men are far more likely
than women to be defined as permanently sick or incapacitated for work.

However, men in ethnic minorities are more at risk here than are majority white men. The risk is highest for Pakistanis and black Caribbeans and for women among black Caribbeans.

According to the OPCS Surveys of Disability (Martin, Meltzer and Elliot, 1988, Table 3.10), of all ethnic groups majority whites have the highest number with disability among those of 16 and over. West Indian (approximately black Caribbean) and Asian (in large part Indian and Pakistani) minorities are assessed disabled much less often. However, the white population is older on average than the populations of the other ethnic groups. Indeed, when the three rates quoted for ethnicity are standardized for age, they become indistinguishable. Even with this qualification, it is clear that average levels of disability do not explain why men and women of ethnic minorities are more likely than majority whites to find themselves unemployed when economically active and (if men) permanently sick when economically inactive.

A group of papers based on the US Health and Retirement Survey (Bound *et al.*, Santiago and Mushkin, Wray - all 1996) seem to show that the greater tendency of black Americans to become unable to work in their fifties than American whites accounts for their low participation in the labour market. However, black Americans also *defer* retirement to a later age than whites with comparable health. The various authors argue that the same factor which accounts for their health also contributes to their putting back retirement. They are poor, something much connected to how insecure their employment is and the low pay that the manual jobs they tend to get provides. A similar story could be told in Britain of black Caribbeans, Pakistanis and Irish-born.

However, there is British evidence to suggest that discrimination for employment on grounds of ethnicity is involved as well. The Labour Force Surveys for 1984 to 1995 show that, while, for white men (including Irish), economic activity rates fell from 88.5% to 85.9% and unemployment rates fell, step by step, from 11.3% to 9.7%, among men in ethnic minorities, economic activity fell by much more - from 80% to 76% - and unemployment by much less - from 22% to 20% - if indeed at all, because it was not a consistent trend. The corresponding data for white women are a rise from 66.8% to 72.9% in economic activity and a sharp and consistent fall in unemployment rates from 11.2% to 6.5%; whereas for ethnic minority women they are a steady state in economic activity rates and a very modest fall in unemployment rates from 21% to 17% without a consistent trend (Sly, 1995).

In the period of reconstruction of the economy following the sharp fall in manufacturing employment of the early 1980s, labour markets have become more flexible. The LFS data on ethnic minorities and employment suggest that greater flexibility might allow discrimination to pass unchecked.

Discrimination? The Case of Disability

The LFS evidence corroborates the data analysis so far for a sample ten years later than that of the OPCS Surveys of Disability, showing, for instance, that around two and a half times as many people with disabilities were unemployed - seeking work, not necessarily claiming benefit - as people without disabilities. There is also a whiff of the discrimination in flexible labour markets that the same survey seems to reveal against ethnic minorities. Between the LFS sweeps of winter 1993/4 and winter 1994/5, economic activity rates fell among men with disabilities from 46.6% to 43.9%, and among women with disabilities from 37.8% to 35.4% while among men and women without disabilities they remained steady (at around 90.5% for men and 74.6% for women). Economically active men with disabilities also benefited much less than their able-bodied counterparts from the fall in unemployment over the year - their unemployment rate fell from 25.5% to 24.5% (a proportional decrease of 4%), while that of able-bodied men fell from 11% to 9.6% (a proportional decrease of 13%).

Macroscopic statistical analysis alone suggests probabilities but does not prove or disprove discrimination by employers against people with disabilities. Microscopic studies of discrimination tend to be conducted by means of 'laboratory' simulations abstracted from the real life situations in which discrimination would normally occur, and often focus more on attitudes than behaviour. Perhaps as a result, when disability has been the topic, the results have divided almost equally between studies which show that discrimination occurs, and studies which show that it does not occur. However, a field study in France (Ravaud *et al.*, 1992), using an innovative method, seems to demonstrate that employers do discriminate against people with disabilities in real life situations.

The authors sent fictional job applications to a sample of employers of differing sizes, some purporting to come from well qualified people with disabilities, others from the same who were able-bodied, and still others from modestly qualified people, some of whom were disabled, others not. France has shared in the trend to equal opportunities policy. Because of this, the authors expected employers to be particularly scrupulous about replying to applications from people with disabilities, but they proved to be no more likely to answer their letters than those from the able-bodied, though larger firms, presumably with personnel departments, were more likely to respond to all applications than smaller. However, able-bodied applicants were significantly more likely to get a favourable response than the disabled with similar qualifications. Surprisingly, perhaps, larger firms were more likely to discriminate against the disabled in this way than were smaller ones.

Discrimination was also identified in a British study (Glozier, 1998), in which personnel officers were given CVs of job applicants who were identical in every respect except that one had chronic diabetes and the other depressive mental illness. Far more of the respondents considered the employment prospects of the person with depression to be poor than considered those of the person with diabetes to be poor. This was not because the first was expected to lose more working days than the second, but because the mental illness was thought to have a greater effect on performance at work. Since there is no evidence to support the personnel officers' belief - if anything to the contrary - this seems a case of 'institutionalized' discrimination, based on the stigma attached to mental illness.

Summary

There is no doubt that the disabled are marginal to employment. The issue is whether the disabled are selected out of employment as a 'natural' function of free markets or are discriminated against.

So far as disability is concerned, natural selection appears to play a part in the following ways:

- disability affects employment status among those who are pre-pensionable, regardless of age and sex, the more so the more severe the disability
- it is manual workers who tend to be permanently sick and unemployed, which, given the preponderance of locomotor disabilities among the disabled who seek employment, suggests that the effect of disability is specific to abilities that jobs require
- the disabled are less competitive in labour markets, because less often qualified than the able-bodied and because there are often additional costs in employing them.

Yet the health worker effect plainly cannot explain many regularities in the relation between disability and employment:

- why, among those assessed as disabled but able to work, a much higher proportion fail to find work than among the able-bodied
- why among the disabled who find work, a disproportionate number are in manual jobs and, in general, jobs of lower status and pay than among the able-bodied, even when many of these jobs are ill-fitted to the locomotor disabilities that they tend most often to have
- why women - whether disabled or able-bodied - remain less economically active than men
- why men are more likely than women to occupy the permanently sick status

   if of pre-pensionable age
- why many men and women of pensionable age and even below do not work, for disability is not often implicated
- why proportions of men retiring and becoming permanently sick before pensionable age have increased since the late 1950s, at the same time as the proportion of women in employment has risen
- why qualifications do not affect the likelihood that disabled people who can work become unemployed, and why employers make special provisions for less than half the disabled people they employ, and so incur extra costs in employing them than able-bodied workers.

Is there evidence of discrimination? It can be discerned in areas other than disability:

- ageism is institutionalized, and operates independently of actual disability
- sexism similarly, though perhaps a diminishing force
- there is evidence of discrimination against ethnic minorities
- finally, there is direct evidence for discrimination against the disabled by employers.

The more flexible labour markets of the late 1980s and the early 1990s have increased the marginality of disabled people, even at times when unemployment has been falling. The best direct evidence of discrimination suggests that it does occur, but it is not plausible to claim that *all* the marginality of the disabled in employment can be attributed to discrimination, for impairment plays a part.

Why does 'Natural Selection' only Approximate the Truth?

What sense can be made of the fact that natural selection appears to operate, but only imprecisely? There are two possibilities: first, free markets would put natural selection into effect, but actual markets are *imperfect*; second, the selection that takes place in labour markets is not natural but *social*, and the choices involved are typically fraught with competing interests, poorly coordinated and prone to error.

Are Labour Markets Imperfect?

On the first view, markets might put natural selection into effect, if only freed from monopoly, subsidies, taxes and other sources of imperfection.

Discrimination may be counted among the imperfections. Arguably, its removal would ensure that - among people with equal ability to undertake a job - only the seriously disabled or unhealthy would be left out. However, removing discrimination would not give anyone the *right* to work. People in employment would be rewarded according to their ability and effort and not have security. Those who were excluded from the free labour market would have to have a separate claim to a living, based on their needs.

The 'imperfections' would include employment protection. Under the Conservative governments of 1979-97, and, so far, under that of Labour from 1997, there has been emphasis on normalizing employment for disabled people and removing many of the protections that were first put in place when soldiers were demobilized at the end of the Second World War. Claims for contributory benefit from those who have become incapacitated for work have risen steeply in number and cumulative cost (Department of Social Security, 1992). Access to benefits has been considerably tightened from the mid 1990s and the Labour government is, at the time of writing, committed to finding normal employment for as many of the disabled as possible.

In a study of 92 disabled workers during 1993, Hyde (1998) has thrown light on the contradictions in this policy. With the UK Disabilities and Discrimination Act of 1995, individuals can sue employers who discriminate against them in the meaning of the Act, but much of the collective provision introduced in the 1944 Disabled Persons' (Employment) Act has been repealed - in particular, the rule that all but small employers should take on a quota of registered disabled persons. Within Hyde's sample, 60 respondents were employed in sheltered workshops and 32 in supported placements (introduced from 1985). Both groups saw benefits in the relative security they still had. At the same time, most regretted the extent to which working practices were being brought into line with normal industry, for they felt too little allowance was made for their disabilities. Hyde concludes that recent policy is designed to make labour markets more flexible and that this benefits the employer rather than the employee.

The movement in UK policy parallels (or perhaps imitates) that in US policy. In the USA, legislation for disability equality was introduced in 1990 (the Americans with Disabilities Act), deregulation of markets became policy from Reagan's presidencies, and welfare reform characterized a Republican Congress under Clinton's presidencies. The US trend contains contradictions as does that of UK. Blanck (1995) cites a case of low back pain under the ADA in which the employer accommodated the pattern of work to the needs of one employee, not because there seemed to be direct economic value in employing the person with disability, but because the legal cost of not doing so might be high. Moreover, the employer could not deal with the case individually. An effective trade union obliged the employer to organize the accommodation that was provided for the disability to all able-bodied employees.

Blanck's observation shows that employers do not necessarily benefit from disability equality measures. Hyde's view has also to be tempered by recognizing how few disabled people of working age registered disabled under the provisions of the legislation superseded by the DDA. The OPCS Surveys of Disability (Martin, White and Meltzer, 1989, p.85) found that only 20% of men and 8% of women had registered. This suggests that few saw benefits and many may have found costs in the shelter offered by the old arrangements.

Nevertheless, what can be seen in both US and UK contexts is the extent to which provision of employment for the disabled implies their marginality in labour markets, and how attempts to 'free' those markets from discriminatory tendencies can have unintended consequences, whether for the disabled workers themselves or for employers.

Is Selection Social?

There is no doubt that there *are* social arrangements for selecting people for employment. Cadres of highly trained professionals are employed in the process.

It should be noted that personnel selection is only the tip of a large iceberg of arrangements that contribute to both forming and selecting people for jobs, starting even from infancy. In an analysis of the National Child Development Study, a cohort of those born in 1958 throughout Britain, Savage and Egerton (1997) take issue with the idea that it is inherited ability, rather than the advantages and disadvantages of social class of origin that determines where people are placed in the occupational hierarchy by their early 30s. Cultural and economic capital are both involved, as many studies of the relation of class, gender, family and school have shown (among them, Willis, 1977, Griffin, 1985, Bates, 1993).

There is no obvious way in which these varied institutions are coordinated, though it has been argued that 'society' (or else 'capital') has its own imperatives, and that in order to survive, society (or capital) must reproduce its pattern of relationships and its culture from generation to generation. This 'system' is supposedly *self*-regulating, like central heating or the free market as conceived in Walrasian economics. A more plausible view of both social reproduction and the operation of markets focuses on the distinctive properties of 'social action'. Society and economy are strategic arrangements which work in a rough and ready way so long as those involved comply, whether out of self-interest, duty or habit. Human monitoring is responsible for continuity and change in strategy, not the system's needs (Giddens, 1984).

Large employing organizations have codes of practice about publicly advertising vacancies, the composition of appointing committees and reporting the gender and ethnic breakdown of short lists. These 'equal opportunities' codes have been developed in response to state policy or law against discrimination. If a firm adopts an equal opportunities code, it is under an obligation to monitor how well it works, and to adjust its practices accordingly. Yet the policy may founder because of competing interests - for instance, those in charge may prefer to appoint internally, so that they can reward loyal protégés.

If free markets selected 'naturally', administrative arrangements would be unnecessary - worse, they would reduce the efficiency of the hidden hand of the market. Yet, left to themselves, markets would not ensure what most would consider fair outcomes. They have to be constrained by institutions to do so. Modern hiring practices grew out of rejection of both nepotism *and* casualisation - nepotism where fathers spoke for sons or employers promoted from within, and casualisation where men were hired on the day for the day's work, cash in hand (Kumar, 1988). More than this, it can be argued that markets are themselves institutions - a mix of pre-given and recently negotiated or enforced elements, to which the parties have to comply if trade is to take place (Polanyi, 1957).

Transactions in the market, such as hiring labour, involve decisions on both the demand and the supply sides. If the parties had perfect knowledge of the possible outcomes, institutions might be redundant. Each would know how to act in his or her best interests. There would be no risks, and, on some views, no profit or loss either. However, even small degrees of uncertainty may require institution-building - for instance, the invention of banks to advance credit, the pooling of risks in mutual insurance schemes, and, not least, the establishment of personnel departments.

It follows from this view of economy and society, that selection for employment by health happens - to the extent that it does - because of a strategy followed by employers, and is imperfect - to the extent that it is - because there are competing interests at stake. The various elements of the strategy are ill-coordinated, and decision-makers often act slowly and make mistakes.

The Sciences of Employment

Foucault (1977) claims that the human sciences (psychology, medicine, economics and sociology among them) have developed in synergy with the 'techniques of power' that characterize specific modern institutions. Thus, occupational psychology and medicine, for example, establish ways of classifying and measuring the capacities required for jobs of differing types in the division of labour. Practitioners use these sciences to select those who fit, to design training to make then fit better, to promote those who prove themselves to be best fitted, and, if necessary, to remove people who become unfit in the course of their careers.

One approach to how ill-health may arise from employment takes fit between person and job as its starting point. The psychologist, French (1982), argues that ill-health and injury are probable outcomes when the fit is poor. Like other psychologists, he focuses on mental stress to bridge the gap between poor fit between person and job and ill-health, but a similar argument could be mounted in which physical mechanisms are the mediators. French's idea allows the strategy of selection for employment to be monitored. One of the tests of its success or failure would be the health of people that the process had meant to fit to the jobs in its charge.

French's approach can be criticized for seeking to fit the person to the job, rather than the job to the person. Ergonomics (Pheasant, 1991, 1996) takes the opposite tack. It has a more sympathetic ring for those who tend to be excluded from employment, especially on grounds of disability.

Whatever direction the sciences of employment take, they contribute to a process by which some qualities of body and mind are accentuated and others suppressed for work. The process resembles livestock and bloodstock breeding - the very strategic action from which Darwin developed his discussion of natural selection. It is true that humans have rarely been *bred* for positions in the social division of labour, but humans are *reared* to fit specific social roles including types of job. If humans (and indeed other animals) were infinitely plastic, breeding or rearing for particular qualities would have no ill effects, but there are species-specific limits and abilities, and exceeding the one and undershooting the other may threaten health.

In the case of humans, the limits and abilities are cultural as well as natural. At any given time, there is a stock of tools and skills available which allow most to perform up to a limit. What had previously been limits to what humans could do, have, at different times, been passed without ill-effect by inventing tools and by innovatory use of the hand. Thus, the disabilities of one age might become irrelevant in the next, or vice versa - abilities once redundant may become functional, so creating new disabilities among those who cannot perform them.

Moreover, jobs which, for instance, require constant repetition of one motion with the arm and wrist and no mental involvement beyond steeling oneself to continue with that for several hours at a time, are likely to test normal ability to the limit in one specific direction and suppress its use in many other directions at the same time. However well the psychologist or physician had fitted a person to that job, it can be expected to produce characteristic pathologies with untypical frequency - such as tenosynovitis (inflammation of the tendon sheaths) for over use of some abilities (Thompson *et al.*, 1987), heart attacks (Alfredsson *et al.*, 1985) and depression and anxiety (Stansfeld *et al.*, 1995) for under use of others. Conversely, the more a job allows human capacity to be used near to, though not beyond, its cultural and natural limits, the healthier and longer lived its occupant is likely to be (Evans *et al.*, 1994).

Conclusion

In this chapter, it has been argued that industrial medicine, occupational psychology and ergonomics are the sciences that correspond to the 'techniques of power' for fitting labour to jobs and jobs to labour. The natural selection model is in tune with them. Yet there are many contradictions between the evidence and the model, and the selection process is more appropriately characterised as social than natural.

It seems that the healthy and able-bodied tend to survive in employment, while the unhealthy and disabled tend not to do so. Thus, the broad outline of the *healthy worker effect* must be allowed for in studies of how employment and work affect health. However, it cannot be treated as an explanation of how jobs come to be allocated. Rather, like social Darwinism before it, the idea amounts to an *ideology* rather than a scientific account of modern employment, and lends itself to invalid use to justify excluding the fit, but disabled or older worker.

The social process of selection for employment can be seen as an integral part of *making* the body fit for employment, for embodied selves are disciplined and self-formed to match niches in the division of labour. Though human bodies are unfinished by nature and so malleable to a degree, the process is highly unlikely to produce perfect fit, and the limits to which bodies can be made and remade over and again are likely to give rise to situations in which jobs accentuate some qualities and suppress others in individuals. In due course, in Parts II and III, I shall suggest that this makes workers vulnerable to illness, sickness absence, disease and injury. My first concern, however, is how workers come to accommodate most of the time to the jobs for which they are selected, and perform them without at least immediate ill effect.

3 Docile Bodies:
The Making of the Worker

..discipline produces subjected and practised bodies...it dissociates power from the body; on the one hand, it turns it into an 'aptitude', a 'capacity' which it seeks to increase; on the other hand, it reverses the energy .. that might result from it, and turns it into a relation of strict subjection.
Michel Foucault (1977, p.138).

Who *is* the Potter, pray, and who the Pot?
Omar Khayyam, *The Rubiayat*, translated by Edward Fitzgerald,
(1859, 1st edition: lx, 18).

Once a 'fit' workforce has been put together, are they ready to be put to work? They are not ready merely because they are fit or even appropriately skilled. They have yet to become 'docile' bodies, who will attend during the hours of work and put in the effort required by the employer.

Being selected as qualified and fit and made docile, embodied selves are tuned to the requirements of the occupation they follow. This enables people to sustain the effort required without ill-effect, at least in the short run. However, the tuning accentuates certain qualities of body and mind and depreciates others, so rendering workers vulnerable to ill-health and injury. That possibility is investigated in the next chapter, the making of the docile body in this one.

Bodies become docile and thereby useful for labour for several reasons. First, the wage or salary is an important incentive and should certainly not be underestimated, but people are not born to be economic actors - they are made so in the culture they share with others in a late modern capitalist society, even before they draw their first pay. Second, social relations affect the outcome - workers and managers are constrained by the asymmetry of power between employers who have capital that they can deploy elsewhere and employees who must sell their labour to live. Third, institutions imposed on the free labour market shape the docile body at various levels - from the welfare state to the private firm. Fourth, firms and occupations generate their own cultures and form their own patterns of social relations which help put the finishing touches on the docile body. Finally, each worker learns ways of accommodating body and mind to the demands of the job and carries them out with varying degrees of success, but they tend to be not idiosyncratic but typical of those who do the job, and are keyed to the meanings of the spaces in which people work and live.

It is difficult to grasp the significance of the forming of the docile body without giving a full amount of it in a particular socio-cultural context, that is without what Geertz (1973) calls 'thick description'. Therefore, I shall introduce it through an anthropological-style field study I did in a single factory in the pottery industry of Britain.

Introducing Masspro - a Pottery Factory[2]

Between 1983 and 1985, a span of two and half years in the midst of recession, the author made a close anthropological-style study of health and work in a large pottery factory (over 1000 employees) in Stoke-on-Trent, the centre of the British ceramic industry (Bellaby, 1985, 1987a). Several methods were used, and, among them, intensive studies were made of four areas of work, in each of which one of two investigators (Judith Sidaway (JS) and the author (PB)) spent three months as a full-time worker, with the knowledge of management, trade unions and shop floor colleagues that we were researchers. The four work settings were as follows:

- once-fired making, decorating and glazing: machine lines and women at work
- twice-fired glazing: machine lines and men and women at work
- kiln-emptying: self-paced work and men
- selecting and packing: self-paced work and women.

Both researchers were around 40 years of age, two or three years above the average for both sexes on the shop floor. Our jobs on the shopfloor were temporary and were of course done in a different context to that of fellow workers. We could not rely wholly on our own reactions as evidence. Nevertheless, we could make a virtue of our marginal position as novices to this work and ask fellow workers how to do the job and whether they experienced it as we did.

---

2   This factory was studied in two phases, each the recipient of an ESRC grant (F1225 0001 and F0925 0036). Apart from Judith Sidaway, Sheila Cleverly was a key member of the research team. The directors and employees of ' Masspro' were generous in their support.

Our aims were to discover how fellow workers experienced their work and its management, coped with the demands it made upon their bodies and minds, and acted when, temporarily, they could not cope as a result of illness or injury; and to investigate the reactions of fellow workers and managers to illness, injury and absence from work. Daily field dairies were kept by both investigators of conversations and observations for each of the areas over three months. Even three months proved long enough to reach the point at which new findings were becoming rare in each shop floor area.

This participant observation was balanced with other methods that are more widely used in investigations of work and health: for instance, absence records and sickness certificates were collected for samples of the workforce over a run of years; mortality by cause was examined for occupations in the industry; and structured interviews were carried out with random samples of workers and managers. A follow-up study enabled us to put some of our findings to critical test by altering aspects of work organization and monitoring their effects on productivity and absence from work. This triangulation in our observations serves to offset the danger in participant observation of going native against the danger in more formal methods of failing to ask the right questions and getting bland answers.

Each of the four work settings in which fieldwork was done had its own character. Their implications for ill-health, sickness absence and risk behaviour will be compared in succeeding chapters, and discussed in the larger context of the Masspro workforce as a whole.

Material Incentives

While slaves and press gangs are driven largely by violence and volunteers look for intrinsic rewards in the good works they are performing, those who are paid for their work are distinctively motivated by what the payment allows them to buy in the consumer market.

Pottery workers were acutely aware of the price of everything in their contracts, how the wage compared with what they might earn elsewhere and what their money would buy in the consumer market. Our shop floor work was not paid for by the firm, because our 'real work' was research under contract to the Economic and Social Research Council. We did not want to be compromised by becoming employees of the firm we were studying and we had to be supernumeraries, not replacements for people who would be employed if we were not there. However, we were occasionally surprised to find that the ESRC grant was taken to imply that we were working for government. Shop floor colleagues continued to puzzle about why we were not paid by the firm - more than that, they became angry with the firm for not paying us. On reflection, the key to this response is that, far from feeling debased by being paid for what they did, our subjects saw being paid as their *raison d'être* as pottery workers, and our unpaid, supernumerary role as an affront to this.

Money is a *symbolic* as well as a material incentive, and so its effect on behaviour presupposes a range of understandings. It is symbolic on two levels. First, in the strictly economic sense that it is a medium of exchange, not in itself goods and services that can be put to use. Second, and more importantly, in the sense that the wage or salary represents the value of the job. Both are embedded in culture, the product of a specific history. This can be glimpsed in an account written late in life by Charles Shaw (1969) who began work as a child assistant to a master potter in the 1840s. He describes how master potters took off 'saint Mondays' after heavy drinking, and then worked their hired assistants late into the night at the end of the week, to complete the quota of 'best' pieces for which they would be paid by the employers to whom they were under contract. Assistants were paid in turn by the master potter - Shaw implies that this typically happened in a public house, where the master potters drank away more than their share over the weekend. More pertinent is that, by the end of the century, this had become a cautionary tale, and that Shaw, as a good Methodist and now a retired pottery manager and local notable, had a particular motive for telling it. Potters had for the most part become direct employees by now rather than gangs under sub-contract. Methodism had played its part in the transformation, by making regular attendance at work on the six weekdays and at Chapel on Sunday, a standard to live up to and - to a large extent - habitual practice. It had also helped transform payment for work into a 'family wage', that unions bargained for, individuals sought in order to fulfil their felt responsibilities, and the community recognized as a token of one's value, not only as a worker, but as a citizen. In the eyes of a Methodist like Shaw, alcohol put that under threat and represented the return of all that was irregular in the past life of potters. Potters henceforth conformed to what Weber called, at much the same time, the 'iron cage' of industrial capitalism's culture.

Relations of Power

The circumstances that are of interest here to begin with are entirely to do with the 'free market', not with any legal, political or administrative regime that is imposed on it. How much freedom one has depends on the extent to which one can afford to leave or not to enter the market. Having capital (a store of wealth) provides a cushion against having nothing but labour or its product to sell and having to sell it to live.

The employment relation is not master-slave, but neither is it equal. Once employees have entered into a particular contract of employment, they are obliged to obey their employer, subject to the law. They are employed on condition that they fulfil their contracts and they neither own their jobs nor have any right to them beyond what the contract specifies or statutory employment protection provides. Redundancy - no longer being needed by the employer - is almost always a legally accepted ground for dismissal. Employers have considerable, unaccountable power, even in modern democracies and even over managers and professionals and skilled workers who have some autonomy in employment.

Rank and file workers - manual and non-manual - are still further subordinated. An illustration is that one person, with whom I worked closely in a manual job, asked me who was my boss. I said that I did not have someone who told me what I should do, but he found this unconvincing. I tried to reframe my answer by suggesting that I was accountable at some future time for what I had done in this research project and would be judged on it. This was a state of affairs approximated by managers, the more senior the more so.

The reality of the employer's power was illustrated by a takeover of the firm. It was impending during the study and much discussed on the shop floor. The firm was founded by two brothers. They continued to be executive directors, working with others day to day who were professional managers. By the time our study began, the firm had gone public. The PLC's probably under-priced assets attracted the interest of other capitalists, including an outsider to the industry who sought a mass production pottery firm to complete a mixed group. Word was that the brothers were about to betray their employees by selling their shares. The brothers sought to reassure people that they were fighting the take over, but in the end did sell out to the outsider. Masspro employees knew there was a threat to jobs, because - in the early 1980s - more than a quarter of jobs in the pottery industry were lost, and, after the long, steady run down of both coal-mining and steel production in the area, there was talk of the largest single employer, Michelin Tyres, pulling out of Stoke.

Masspro personnel records were examined for the 1970s to the mid 1980s. There was a downturn in the crucial American market for tableware in 1978, which precipitated a recession in the industry that lasted into the 1980s. Prior to that, there was high voluntary turnover, when there was plenty of managerial, skilled and semi-skilled jobs on offer. This gave way to a combination of redundancies and dismissals on disciplinary grounds. Workers who had jobs now held onto them.

The interests of employees are to some extent the same as those of the firm when both can prosper. At the same time, employees have an interest in giving only as much effort as they can gain reward for, and in conserving their labour-power for the future rather than damaging their health or safety now. Managers are employed (in part) to control employees' day to day conduct by surveillance and the use of incentives and sanctions, for the employer seeks, through these agents, to get as high an addition to the value invested in production as possible.

Social Institutions Imposed on the Free Market

The outcomes at Masspro in the mid 1980s were products of a 'free market'. How might institutions 'imposed' on free markets affect the issue? It has been argued that the welfare states built after the Second World War 'decommodified' labour, and varied in the extent to which they did so (Esping-Andersen, 1990). 'Decommodification' means that benefits cover all or almost all of normal earnings in employment. For instance, a pension that enables retirees to maintain the standard of living that they had when employed gives them the freedom to retire if they wish to do so. Similarly, unemployment benefit that covers normal earnings allows the unemployed to wait until they find a job comparable to the one they have lost. When there is no unemployment benefit, only relief should one become destitute (as in the USA), and when unemployment benefit is much lower than most earnings (as in the UK), the freedom that decommodification brings is all but absent. Instead the 'free' market coerces into employment those who have to sell their labour to live.

However, even in the most decommodified welfare regimes, access to benefits is usually conditional. For example, on reaching pensionable age, the worker loses protection against unfair dismissal. Again, one who leaves a job voluntarily or will not seek further employment may not draw unemployment benefit (as in the UK), and one who becomes unemployed may be obliged to enter retraining and/or relocate to find new work (as in Sweden, a regime of much higher decommodification than the USA or the UK).

As both workers and managers, pottery employees who lost their jobs had the same regime of state benefits to contend with. Many also benefited from another institution imposed on the free market in labour: the 'internal labour market' (Doeringer and Piore, 1971). Internal labour markets shelter employees and employers alike from competition external to the firm and, from an economics point of view, rather than allowing supply and demand to match the wage or salary to the marginal productivity of labour, try to achieve this effect administratively, using wage structures, career ladders and promotions. At Masspro, such a scheme provided relatively secure employment with one employer and better pension and sickness pay than the welfare state. Internal labour markets have developed where welfare states do not decommodify labour much (for instance, in Japan, the USA and the UK). Their value to employers lies in retaining skilled and experienced workers and encouraging them to use their skills flexibly. However, if all employers provided such schemes to all employees, the relative advantages would be lost.

In the insecure conditions of free markets, trade unions often seek internal labour markets for their members, and individuals are often prepared to trade higher wages for the long term benefits. Such was the case in the pottery industry. From April 1983, an agreement came into force which gave full-time hourly employees of two years service four fifths of the basic wage for two months of temporary sickness. Earlier Masspro had introduced an employers' superannuation scheme as well, with union approval. Employees must elect to enter this and make contributions, but the employer also contributed. The prime beneficiaries were full-time employees of long service, and relatively few of these were women. While the sickness scheme was industry wide, the pension arrangement was not transferable should the employee move to another employer.

Both the sick pay and the pension schemes also tended to favour managers and others described as 'staff' who normally received monthly salaries by cheque or credit transfer to their bank accounts, rather than weekly payments in cash, as did the hourly paid shop floor workers. For instance, staff were paid their normal salaries beyond the two months limit imposed on hourly paid sickness payment. They also became entitled to extra days holiday *pro rata* of their years of service. Finally, to around two places down from managing director, they were entitled to use of a company car, the model of which, as is the custom in Britain, was precisely determined by status.

The more extensive internal market provision for managers was reflected in the way their salaries were determined. Shop floor workers were paid on industry wide rates and even bonuses were publicly known. Managers were assigned to grades, but these gave no indication of their salary, so that no manager but the most senior seemed to know what others were paid. In this way senior management was able to reward not only productivity but also loyalty, and retain the most valued managers.

Organizational Culture - Tacit Understandings within Contracts

From Durkheim (1984), sociologists have stressed the extent to which contracts are fulfilled (and sometimes broken) not because of the formal terms that attach to them but because of what is tacitly understood between the parties. In a classic study of industrial work in the immediate post war period in the USA, Gouldner (1954, 1965) demonstrated how the understandings built up between a retired plant manager and his workforce were violated by the incoming manager and his 'loyal lieutenants' and by head office, which put the new manager under pressure to tighten up what they believed to be a lax regime. The violation led in due course to a wildcat strike. A wage demand was the ostensible basis on which the trade union spoke to management and tried to regain control of their members. However, Gouldner found the less manifest cause to be the breaking of unspoken agreements arrived at with the previous management. These agreements had secured what other commentators have called 'trust' (Fox, 1974). As often, the importance of this to habitual working relationships was only apparent when it had been broken.

Trust is rooted in the moral order and, thus, 'responsibilities'. In the widest sense, responsibility comes in two forms, both with consequences for obedience in the workplace. The first is almost ubiquitous, but particularly marked for men and women with families to care for, that is, 'external' responsibility outside employment for which income is needed and other services have to be provided, such as health care. The second is more unevenly distributed. It is 'executive' responsibility within employment. Employers have much of this, but also delegate it, especially to managers and professionals.

In the collectivized context of a large workplace, employees generalize rather than particularize what they expect of the employer. A fair day's pay is what enables a typical worker to discharge their external responsibilities. For a long time in the history of collective bargaining and the development of the welfare state in Britain, this has been considered a 'family wage', earned by the male head of household. As dual earner households have become more common, working long and 'unsocial' hours and taking holidays may have become more of an issue. Typically, pottery kilns call for round the clock and weekend work, because the main type (the tunnel kiln) has to be fired, fed and emptied continuously. Masspro employed a significant number of men of South Asian origin, most of them Muslims, in this work. One of the kiln managers said that they were prepared to work two shifts end on if required. Among those we interviewed, partners were seldom employed. The men were the quintessential 'family wage' earners, and the manager - a longstanding kiln worker - felt white workers, of the next generation to his, rejected unsocial hours unjustifiably.

Middle managers must be sensitive to their subordinates' external responsibilities, while at the same time holding executive responsibility delegated by and accountable to the employer. Much as the mesh of external responsibilities is seldom formalized in the employment contract, so much of the executive responsibility of employers' agents remains tacit. It is quite usual for employers to expect managers and professionals to exceed their narrowly contractual obligations. In Masspro they were often expected to work overtime, but rarely paid for it, so waiving their external responsibilities in the employer's favour. They were expected to feed information up to the employer, but to respect confidences when information was fed down to them.

When understandings are not coded and remain tacit, they are open to the play of power. Trade unions have long understood this, and seek to write as much as possible into collective agreements and individual contracts. The most bureaucratized of organizations are also those in which subordinates have the greatest protection and right of appeal against superiors. Middle managers and professionals are typically enmeshed in tacit executive responsibilities that belie the claim that they have autonomy. Employers, on the other hand, are the better able to evade their executive responsibilities when these are unwritten.

Organizational Culture - Making the Workforce Behave 'Responsibly'

Much of what goes into making the docile worker is unspoken. However, in the mid 1980s, Masspro's senior management was engaged in a highly vocal campaign to make its workforce 'responsible' for the company's performance in the product market: first, arguing that the customer was the arbiter of what was produced in what volume, and the standard it must reach; second, seeking to improve flexibility in production methods; third, pressing employees to be involved in team briefings and quality circles; finally, trying to channel employees' grievances away from industry-wide adversarial bargaining towards enterprise-based joint consultation and develop identification with Masspro.

Realising these in Masspro at the time was constrained by what managers in general considered backward attitudes among workers, and senior managers considered inappropriate attitudes in middle management. However, there were contradictions between policy and practice.

The customer is always right The 'customer' was in practice one of several supermarket or department store chains or a household name in food and drink who wanted to use coffee mugs or cereal bowls in a promotion. Masspro was a volume producer of earthenware despatched in bulk direct to the retailer, in arresting colours and varied decoration.

There was sometimes tension between the employer's and the employees' concept of what the customers wanted. When lines that were market-researched failed to make a profit, employees needed less persuasion to agree that the customer mattered, than to agree about what the customer might want. Many employees would buy china in preference to earthenware, especially dinner and tea services. Some were not keen on many of Masspro's colours and prints. Finally, many professed a sense of what 'real quality' was and tended not to include Masspro's products. These attitudes were plainly seen when the company offered 'seconds' for sale to employees.

Flexible production The firm was especially noted for having developed 'once-fired' products. Traditionally, ware has been fired at least twice in the course of production: first, while newly pressed or cast, when still 'green', to make 'biscuit'; and then again after the application of liquid glaze, to make 'glost'. Once-firing was Masspro's main contribution to flexibility.

Masspro used the twice-fired system in producing flatware and hollow ware (plates, saucers, bowls and so on), but developed the once-fired method for making beakers (coffee mugs). The significance of once-firing was that it removed the slack that biscuit firing allowed. Once biscuit, ware could endure minor knocks and could even be stacked on pallets, each layer bearing the weight of those above it, to await a subsequent stage. Once-firing was a just-in-time method, for ware had to complete the full cycle of production in one move.

Once-firing turned a large part of pottery manufacture into an assembly line. It was more 'Fordist' than 'post-Fordist' (Kumar, 1995). On the other hand, by switching moulds in the automatic making machines, by changing the colour of glazes and by varying decoration, a relatively wide range of different products could be made by the same production lines. The amount of tooling required for these variations was small and the changeover time short, but batches had to be large to avoid high unit costs of production, especially where variation in shape was required rather than decoration.

Improve quality 'Quality' was contested terrain between managers and workers. This should not be misunderstood. Employees were not championing a craft tradition against mass production. Despite its public image, even the upper end of the pottery market was mass production not craft based and had started on this course with Josiah Wedgwood I (McKendrick, 1961).

The contradiction between quality and quantity in Masspro arose from mundane practicalities. Managers must meet orders within the limitations of the available production facilities and workforce. When orders were hard to get, as they were in recession, managers were often obliged to accept tight deadlines. Sometimes compromises had to be made simply to meet the deadlines. These invariably disrupted established procedures. Nowhere was this more evident than among women selecting ware as best, seconds and pitchers (rejects). They were sometimes obliged to adjust their standards or even re-select ware they had previously deemed seconds, so that the order could be filled from the ware produced within the time limit. Though this is an extreme example, it illustrates a wider principle: that consistent quality depended on production being predictable, and that in turn on demands from the sales department.

'Quality circles' were introduced to address questions of waste, inefficiency and poor quality. They involved workers and managers directly engaged in a particular area of production. One QC that was successful in its own eyes was criticized by workers at the next stage of production for solving its own problems at their expense. Employee involvement in quality circles was coupled with quality control inspections by peripatetic officials, who (contrary to the spirit of QCs) often seemed to be looking out for pretexts to criticize.

The personnel department contended that building the trust needed to involve employees was a bootstrap operation. Initiatives like quality circles and joint consultation would give workers a voice and show that management valued them. Employees should be kept informed about the company's order books, and each production line about its weekly performance. A company-wide bonus scheme would teach employees that higher earnings depended on profits.

However, the continuing social distinction between and rank and file workers and management made this objective difficult to achieve. Staff privileges, such as preferential sick leave and service holiday arrangements and company cars were often known to and disapproved of by workers.[3]

The apparent democratization of the running of the company also drew criticism from middle managers. This was because the new arrangements by-passed them. For instance, joint consultation committees enabled workers' representatives to bring up complaints about conditions in their departments, where senior managers also sat. Middle managers felt that - if they had decided that these complaints were groundless or they had been seeking a remedy for them - their leadership would be undermined.

The solution might have been to remove managerial hierarchy. However, both the organization of production and the system of industrial relations presupposed it.

Company first, not union Collective bargaining that affected wages, basic hours and holidays at Masspro was carried on between the unions (the main one between CATU - the Ceramic and Allied Trades Union) and the employers' federation (the BCMF - British Ceramic Manufacturers Federation). Agreements were usually reached annually in March. Individual members were represented in grievances or in a disciplinary action by plant representatives. It was the personnel director's role to put the company's side.

---

3   As was revealed in a 1985 BBC2 TV Open Space programme: *Breaking the Mould,* based on the factory and produced by Jeremy Gibson.

District officials and committee members and at least two of the three plant representatives in CATU suspected the motives and doubted the practical value of the employee involvement strategy. It seemed to them calculated to undermine attachment to the union and divert into joint consultation what should be negotiated in collective bargaining. They felt that members were too canny to be taken in by this. However, union consciousness was not widespread among ordinary members, and, when questioned in an ACAS (Advisory, Conciliation and Arbitration Service) survey about team briefings, quality circles and joint consultations, they appeared to accept them.

'Involvement' would be a misnomer for most workers' orientations to both company and union. The immediate pressures of work and home life engaged their attention to a much greater extent. Monthly team briefings were attended, because that was a company requirement, but seemed either to engender frustration - 'they only tell us what they want us to know' - or be treated as a break from work - 'a chance for a joke and a smoke'. Union branch meetings were district not plant based and as poorly attended as any. A dispute over pay between CATU and BCMF in March 1984 revealed rank and file disaffection towards both company and union. When agreement was reached on a much lower rise than the union had claimed initially, the union sought ratification from members. Over the industry as a whole, the vote was in favour of acceptance, but in Masspro the vote went against.

Following managerial fashions enhanced the reputation of the personnel director and the credibility of the PLC in the capital market They were used in company publicity, including articles in the Financial Times and a personnel journal. British companies depend heavily on financing investment from share issues and bank loans. Boards of directors are also vulnerable to takeover should real asset values be known to exceed money share values. In such a climate, favourable publicity is by no means a negligible factor.

The Embodiment of People as Workers

Everyday experience from infancy induces a rhythm over the year, over the week, over the day, minute by minute that enables the person to be a *docile* working body. Industrial and, no less so, post-industrial forms of work require a rhythm which over-rides the seasons and even the difference between day and night. Global commerce and financial dealings are even more demanding in this respect than local shift working. These work patterns are as much at odds with the agricultural cycle that preceded them as that in its turn was with the hunting and gathering economy of the stone age (Sahlins, 1974). Most bodies most of the time are in tune with what contemporary work demands. It is this embodied aspect of the formation of the worker that tends to atrophy when people are out of work for long periods, for it rests on continually repeated disciplines (Jahoda, 1982).

On top of this relatively passive ground of 'rhythm' is built an active 'project', which is most evident among managers and professionals. It resonates with a belief in responsibility for one's own health, and also with appropriating stress and coping discourse as a lay explanatory model (Bellaby, 1986). In this lay form, mental strain is assumed to relay external threats to the internal body. By using the same route in reverse, individuals can be taught to 'cope' with this stress, developing substitutes for fight and flight. From a manager's point of view, a capacity to cope with stress in having to meet deadlines is the equivalent of rhythm in repetitive manual work. It enables one to survive in employment. For those who employ managers, coping with stress is a criterion for recruitment and promotion, and failure to do so a sign that the manager is out of their depth.

Both rhythm and coping with stress are strategies for rendering the body docile in employment. They must be learned and are typically handed down from experienced workers to novices. They are cultural products, even though experienced viscerally and emotionally. Both are effects of discourses that have developed alongside the requirements of work under capitalism, the one, that of rhythm, belonging with an earlier history of manual crafts, the other with a later history of bureaucracy. The discourses of rhythm and stress and coping play a similar part in making people docile for employment as does the discourse of natural selection in legitimating access to and exit from labour markets.

Body and Space - the Docile Body in the Workplace[4]

Power relations lurked behind the struggle for hearts and minds in Masspro, but they did not exist in thin air. In general, power relations are inscribed in the spatial arrangement of work, whether physically in the factory or the office or in the virtual space that connects the home PC of a teleworker to the employer's centralized server. Individual embodiment is also spatial. The body occupies a unique space. In moving from an understanding of how workers acquiesce with employment to how their bodies become vulnerable to injury and ill-health in work, one has to locate the worker's body in the workplace.

Lefebvre (1991) helpfully distinguishes three spatialities - real, imagined

---

4   An extended discussion of embodiment and spatiality in the pottery factory will be found in Bellaby (1999a), part of which forms this section of the present chapter.

and lived, and it is instructive to seek out examples of each in the pottery setting. Real and imagined spatialities are imbricated, in the sense that, like the tiles of a Roman roof, they overlap to form one surface - lived space.

Real space Real space, Lefebvre argues, is no less social than space imagined or lived in. Nor does it simply happen, as do the works of nature. Rather it is produced by 'labour' in the Marxian sense of transformative activity.

In a factory context, this is in part to do with making the building and equipping it with plant. It is also to do with how the people who work within modify the space by use. Masspro was developed on its current site from the early 1950s. The firm established three virtually self-contained units, because over a period of years it moved its subsidiaries - employees and equipment - from their old premises, retaining their separate identities and granting them considerable autonomy to develop their own business plans. It is to these plans that I now turn, for they are part of imagined space in the pottery context.

Imagined space There are several representations of the space of pottery manufacture, which include those of epidemiology, law and controllers of capital.

Employers design an arrangement of human bodies in space and, in a strict time-frame, seek to make of it a production system that will return a profit. They can only realize this by gaining the compliance of employees, because the product is made by the effort of those they employ, even when machinery is involved. At the same time, the bodily reserves from which effort comes have to be renewed. Every entrepreneur has to pay attention to reproducing labour power for the future as well as to using labour power effectively now.

Other representations of space are those of epidemiology and law. Epidemiology seeks clues about the causes of specific diseases and injuries by determining in which working bodies, in what places and at what times they occurred. Evidence of this kind is not only of scientific importance. It is also crucial in law, when courts and/or lawyers arbitrate employees' claims that their employers are liable for causing their ill-health. Law and biomedicine share a particular perspective on work: they observe from without. Their observations are of course not just sense-data, but laden with theory. In the case of biomedicine, theory posits biological structures of disease and assumes that the organism is causally affected by its environment. In the pottery, the most celebrated work of epidemiology in the past concerned respiratory disease and its link with the 'free silica' dispersed in air in the vicinity of such, now much altered, operations as fettling the seams of moulded ware and placing ware for firing in the kiln.

In the law, theory proposes that human agency is the final cause of injuries, whether the agent is the employer or the employee. Actors are assumed rational, and expert witnesses are adduced to explain how one person's action typically leads to their own or another's injury. Thought experiments are conducted in which the tragic outcome is preventable not inevitable. In the pottery, the most notable current actions in law concerned 'repetitive strain injury', which has only very recently become generally accepted in English law as an industrial injury, having previously been a grey area between the unobserved physical and the presumed psychological. The courts that sit on cases of employer's liability seek understanding of the motive in order to apportion damages under the law of tort or to decide guilt under criminal law.

Lived space   The forgoing are interested observer perspectives. Participants in lived space necessarily have different perspectives.

Of course, participants may well draw on medico-legal or capital discourses to help form their accounts. This can be expected to happen, because medico-legal and capital discourses carry authority, and employees who want to make a case against the employer are obliged to frame it in these terms. However, a claim against the employer is not an everyday affair. In everyday life, employees may offer accounts that are at variance with medico-legal discourse. The evidence I shall present below supports this. Taken together, shop floor workers offer a quite coherent account of how working bodies are vulnerable to the hazards that vary from place to place in which production is carried out.

Middle managers and supervisors are accountable to seniors for the performance of the teams of shop floor workers that they lead: for meeting production targets and for remaining within budgets for labour and materials. They are trained in health and safety regulations are and how to implement them. They hold rank and file workers responsible for keeping within regulations, but are themselves blamed by their seniors for any breach, especially if it leads to injury. Middle managers and supervisors are thus immersed in the medico-legal and capital discourses by the relations of power in which they find themselves. On the other hand, health and safety is only one of a number of priorities and is truncated to form just part of the wider management field.

The production of embodiment   The manager's and the worker's parts in producing and reproducing embodiment in the workplace can be summarized by adapting Turner's (1995, 1996) typology of the relations between the female body and a patriarchal society. First, I shall take a mirror image of Turner's model, which makes the relation of class its central concern rather than that of gender. This is masculinist, and so maintains an ideal of *disembodiment*, as if appearance, sensations and emotions had no relevance. It therefore covers half the picture at best.

Figure 3.1 Managers' and workers' parts in production and reproduction

	Manager	**Worker**
Reproduction	Personnel functions	Discipline, coping
	Incapacity	*Chronic Illness*
Production	Regulation and surveillance	Presenting self as fit
	Malingering	*Stress*

In each cell of Figure 3.1, following Turner's example, I have introduced pathologies that afflict employees (in their own eyes or those of employers) when the imperatives of reproduction or production cannot be met. While they involve the body willy nilly, they are essentially problems of performance and the appropriate response to it. For instance, when productivity fails to reach targets, employees' claims to be injured or ill often seem untruthful to employers. The solution to this malingering appears to be a tighter regime of regulation and surveillance. Correspondingly, employees are likely to perceive the employer's mistrust of their motives as stress. The solution in their eyes is to improve the way one presents for work, to appear more committed and capable. When the employee has a chronic condition, keeping the job depends on digging deeper into one's reserves and developing ways of coping with acute episodes that will prevent the employer from concluding that one is no longer capable of doing the work. The employer, on the other hand, wants to identify incapacity in the workforce and overcome it, if necessary by retiring the afflicted. Employers' liability insurance and occupational pensions are devices that may enable the interests of the employee and the employer to be reconciled in such a case.

Figure 3.2 (below) amends Turner's original model less aggressively, by focusing on gender relations not class. This restores embodiment to centre stage. As Iris Marion Young has suggested, where disembodiment is the ideal: 'women suffer workplace disadvantage .. because many men regard women in inappropriate sexual terms and because women's clothes, comportment, voices and so on disrupt the disembodied ideal of masculinist bureaucracy.' (Young, 1990, p.176). In short, women are out of place at work, and there is a variety of ways in which risk to the health and safety of women is implicated, a few of which Figure 3.2 captures.

Figure 3.2 The control of women's bodies in production

	Female Work Force	Individual Women
Temporal	Recycling of generations	Restraint
	Disorders of pregnancy	*Anxiety/depression*
Spatial	Regulation and surveillance	Presenting self as fit
	Time off for family problems	*Obesity*

Like textiles, the pottery industry has long employed substantial numbers of women and depended on women employees to reproduce the next generation of potters (Duprée, 1995, Whipp, 1990). Even a hundred years ago, medical observers complained that women jeopardized the health of their babies by working in pregnancy and returning to work soon after birth. The individual woman, as Turner suggests, is expected to show matronly restraint, and the corresponding disorder in this was once 'hysteria'. Equivalents today in the pottery context would be anxiety and depression. Complications of pregnancy, and anxiety/depression, are both viewed as temporal disorders, tied into stages of the life cycle, the latter with the menopause. The other imperatives and the disorders associated with them are spatial rather than temporal. For management, there is a particular problem in disciplining women who take time off for domestic duties, such as care of a child or elderly relative, for this is popularly viewed as legitimate, more so than absence for personal sickness. McDowell and Court (1994) found that presentation of self was critically important (and problematic) for women in financial services employment. That it was an issue for women on the pottery shop floor was evident from the disdainful view they had of female office staff, because of their long nails, high heels, dress and comportment, and their disapproval of two women who had allegedly flaunted themselves to attract in one case a manager, in another a fellow worker's husband. Failure to conform to rules of matronly conduct threatened to undermine positions won for women against management and male employees.

Symbolic meanings of lived space   Thus embodiment took on a variety of meanings, different for women than men, varying also by situation. Lived space also had many meanings. To capture these, I have drawn on the concepts of *boundaries* and *lines* developed by Douglas (1970, 1982, 1986, 1992), which make an explicit link between embodiment and spatiality.

It is a typical finding that encounters at boundaries and lines seem incongruous to those involved in them, and in the pottery this was often made manifest in a habitual joking relationship, though at other times avoidance behaviour or even open conflict occurred. Jokes occurred in an all-male kiln emptiers work group in which I participated over a three month period. The group engaged in a round of jocular insults from the start of work at an early hour each morning. It marked the boundary between home and work - the passage for each man from his particular family obligations to the demands of working interdependently in a group of equals, almost entirely free of supervision. Family obligations would have had to be treated seriously, but were never discussed. Had there been hierarchical divisions in the group, there might have been open conflict or avoidance. However, the men developed an habitual joking relationship similar to the one Radcliffe-Brown (1952) posited between grandparents and their grandchildren, who lacked both the strong mutual obligations of nuclear family members and the hierarchical division between parent and child, yet were interdependent.

Where there were lines dividing groups who worked on the shop floor, open conflict and avoidance behaviour were sometimes to be seen. Conflict occasionally arose between middle managers and workers, especially when interests clashed - as over entitlement to bonuses or the allocation of tiresome work. It was quite common for middle managers to try to break the ice with subordinates by making a joke. This was rarely returned. In one group - of young women - there were sporadic bouts of subversive joking in which men, including managers, were teased about their sexual prowess as they walked past the women's work station on the way to the lavatories. Men could often be seen taking a long way round under cover of machines to avoid an encounter they found it difficult to win.

Like Sykes (1966), Sidaway and I found evidence of joking relationships at the line dividing men's and women's work, in which again sex was the theme. These were almost invariably between men and women who were not likely to be sexually available to each other. They dealt with an incongruity. Sexual innuendo was usually avoided in the more congruent relations between younger men and women who might be available to each other, and, when a young man started such a joke once, it was greeted with genuine shock by the young woman who was the target and did not get a laugh from the audience. However, this marking of gender difference happened only where spatial lines were crossed, not, for example, in the canteen, where cross-gender encounters were routine.

Figure 3.3 represents the *boundary* and principal *line* within the pottery factory. The boundary is the circumference of the circle and within it is a margin represented by light shading. The line is the outer edge of the bull's eye and it too has a margin that is shaded more densely. Finally, there is an in-between space which is unshaded. The horizontal pointer suggests the direction in which the product flows, from nature to the market, both outside the boundary. Half way across the circle it traverses a broken vertical, which divides one in-between zone, the clay-end, where pots are made before firing, from the other, after firing, the glost-end, where pots are selected and packed and may be decorated.

Figure 3.3 Symbolic meanings of space in the pottery factory

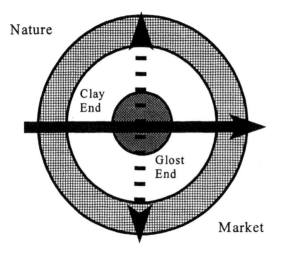

Each of the three units that made up the factory had its own *boundary*. For the management, this was at once physical: the outer walls of buildings; and symbolic: between manufacture and the natural raw materials, stockpiled outside, and between production and the markets for which it was intended. From the employee's point of view, the pottery factory had additional meanings: firstly, as a built not a natural environment. Its walls and roof separated workers from the open air. In this respect, they were depicted alternatively as a shelter from hostile elements - whether efficient (warm and dry) or permeable (leaky and draughty); and as a barrier (stunting and stifling) to the enjoyment of nature. There were emotions as well as physical sensations associated with these boundaries between factory and open air.

Secondly, attendance at work divided workers from the other built environment of major significance in which they spent considerable time - the home. Men and women had similar maps but tended to interpret them differently, especially with respect to the home/factory boundary, where women were more likely than men to value the company of others and relief from isolation at home that the factory offered. At the same time women were less likely to feel 'at home' in the factory than men.

In 'post-modernity', Soja suggests (1996), journeys often involve great distances and people cross boundaries with relative indifference, and Augé (1995) goes so far as to suggest that these journeys are in 'non-space'. However, each factory unit had a definite boundary and principal line, and, between the factory unit and the open air and the kilns and what went before and after them in the production process, there were *margins*. The product often and persons rarely made journeys across the boundary and the line in the course of a working day. When persons approached margins, they attached particular health and safety significance to them.

The sliphouse was at one margin, adjoining the boundary at which the solid raw materials were stored. Here the pot made its first step from nature to culture. The sliphouse margin was typically cold and wet (in all weathers). Only men worked there, and the jobs involved heavy lifting. They and other workers considered the sliphouse to be where men were pitted against the elements, but where women and even some men other than sliphouse workers, especially managers, ventured at some risk. In the other margin was the despatch warehouse. The despatch warehouse took on the characteristics of the outside weather - cold, wet and also windy on some days, but not constantly so. It was considered to have some of the benefits of an outside job, and men worked there.

Within each factory unit of Masspro, value was added to the product in discontinuous steps, while the intermediate product was kept for varying periods (depending on its shelf-life) until needed in the next stage. The passage of the product inside the boundary crossed a *line* which divided the kilns in which pots were fired from the rest of the production process, before and after. Until the modernization of pottery manufacture (much of it after the Second World War), kilns had been coal-fired and separated from the buildings in which other operations were carried on by a bricked or stone-flagged yard. At Masspro, they were no longer separated from the main body of the factory. However, they continued to be set apart within the factory. Tunnel kilns were the means of firing most ware. Ware was stacked on trucks that were pushed in and out of the tunnel kiln on rails. Operation was continuous, round the clock, seven days a week, the only element of the process to be so. The kilns themselves were very large and the sidings required to store trucks awaiting firing or cooling after firing took up a still larger area. They can reasonably be described as the core of the pottery factory and were certainly a separate domain.

Work close to the kiln itself, much like work in the sliphouse, was seen as exposed to the elements, but the kilns had the opposite climate to that of the sliphouse: they were hot and dry, not cold and wet. There was a distinction of status between the production side that preceded the kiln and the warehouse work that followed the kiln. Workers on the so-called clay end had dirtier and noisier jobs than those who selected and packed. While pots could be spoiled at any stage in the process, they were particularly vulnerable in the green condition, and quality control staff attributed most faults in the finished product to the clay end, starting with the slip or body, continuing with ware that had been put out of shape and handles that had sprung off cups and mugs, and finishing with finger marks on glaze.

Both the spaces between core and margins had their own symbolic meanings. They can be characterized as *in-between* (liminal), a concept made familiar in social anthropology by van Gennep earlier this century (1960) and Victor Turner nearer to our own time (1970, 1982). Following Victor Turner's example, 'antistructure' may be expected in-between, where individuals lack definite identity and are in process. Indeed, for workers, such spaces contained conflicting properties. For instance, workers within them might be exposed to draughts, as selecting and packing were, because carried on in the inner zone of the warehouse with its open doors; or they might be hot and dry at face level and cold and wet to the feet, as making, decorating and glazing were, when carried out on an assembly line, with dryers overhead and slip or glaze dripping onto one's feet.

In-between spaces must be compared with two other kinds of space. First spaces with temperate conditions such as offices. Here there was central heating when it was cold outside and, when it was hot, the prospect of reducing the ambient temperature with open windows or fans. Noise levels were low. There were no dust and fumes. Office workers could move at will, go to the lavatory or prepare drinks more or less as they chose. No one on the shop floor enjoyed all these advantages, and many had none. On the other hand, the meanings attached to in-between spaces must also be contrasted with those attached to the extremes - to the margins of sliphouse and despatch and to the kilns at the core. At the three extremes, workers were exposed to the elements, but in a non-contradictory way. They were either hot and dry or cold and wet, habitually one or the other as were sliphouse and kiln workers, or - because partly out in the open air - from time to time in one condition or the other, as were workers in despatch. The men in the despatch warehouse were distinctively on the move, not from a sitting position only, but on their legs. When it was too cold or wet outside and too hot or dry inside for manual work, they could temper the exposure by moving to where it was more comfortable. By contrast, workers in in-between spaces typically sat or stood at their work stations and had no means of moving to temper the contradictory climates to which they were exposed.

Body and Space - Where People Live

The supply of labour to the pottery factory came from those who needed income to live on. These are essentially households, not individuals. Households have certain socially defined needs, which the overwhelming majority can only meet if one or more of the members is in employment and earning an adequate wage or salary. These needs are not the same at all stages of the household's history: for instance, when there are no children rather than when children are young and physically dependent.

Households are located in space, no less than workers. The social status of households depends largely on the life style their economic activity allows them to sustain. In suburbs, inner city areas - gentrified and poor, and even commuter villages, households of similar status live near to each other in neighbourhoods that are too expensive or too unrespectable for others to venture into. Thus status combines with position in the market and power relations in the workplace to form what is generally understood by 'class'.

The workforce at Masspro was drawn largely from within a three mile radius of the site. Seventy eight percent of the male and 76 percent of the female manual workers lived this close to the workplace. About one in fourteen only travelled in from surrounding villages in the countryside, and one in six from north of the then recently opened inner ring road.

On the whole, management had a different pattern of residence and travel to work. The seventeen supervisors who were interviewed were promoted from the shop floor, and their homes were in the same districts as those of workers. However, 65 percent of those 37 interviewed who were of departmental manager to director standing lived outside a three miles radius of the workplace, very nearly the reciprocal figure to that of the workforce. Within that limit, most housing was rented, usually from the local authority, or had been so originally, and many adults of working age worked nearby - in a large colliery, an electrical assembly plant or Masspro. Beyond it on three sides lay countryside and dormitory villages for Stoke-on-Trent commuters. Older residents of Stoke-on-Trent associated it with smoke- and dust-filled air, and the surrounding villages, even the adjacent borough of Newcastle which was on the other side a hill, with salubrious living. From the mid nineteenth century, the rich had responded by moving their homes out of Stoke-on-Trent.

The contrast between where management and workforce lived at Masspro was writ large for the Potteries as a whole. In 1981, more than half of those working within Stoke-on-Trent, but living outside it, were in Social Classes I, II and III Non-manual, as defined by the Registrar-General; while less than a third of those who both lived and worked in the city were in these categories. Further, the higher the social class the less likely was someone working in the city to live there, so much so that a mere two fifths of Class I (higher professional and managerial and large employers) lived in the city, but nearly nine tenths of Class V (unskilled workers).

Conclusion

This chapter has explored in close up in one work setting how workers are disciplined so that self, mind and body accommodate to rather than resist the demands that their jobs make upon them on a day to day basis. Because the 'docile body' is normalized and ill-health and injury occur when the normal is breached, it is essential to understand how the normal was produced historically and is accomplished daily. The larger picture is filled with the contradictory relation between capital and labour, institutions which regulate markets and   the shaping of actors who respond to economic incentives. In the foreground are culture and social relations in the workplace, and the accommodations workers learn from and reinforce in each other. These are to do with the 'lived space' in which work takes place and a contest to control time between managers and workers.

Whether inside or outside the workplace, managers and workers at Masspro acted in spaces that were socially produced and were laden with meaning. The most immediate of such spaces was their own embodiment. Depending on the more remote space occupied - the neighbourhood, the type of work station - embodiment was a different experience. Managers and workers had also learned ways of coping with the temporal pattern of demands that their work made - rhythm as the antidote to repetition, and stress management as the antidote to having to meet deadlines.

Part II will suggest that the body becomes vulnerable when the spatial and temporal patterns that secure a docile body break down. Then one feels discomfort, fatigue, even pain. Whether or not that condition is made social and results in sickness absence, depends on the *moral* context and on how much latitude workers and managers have in the control of time, both internal and external to the workplace.

PART II
ILL AT WORK
AND OFF SICK

4 Vulnerable Bodies: Illness in the Workplace

You must not fancy that I am sick, only over-driven and under the weather.
R.L.Stevenson, 1850-1894, *The Wrecker* (1892, Chapter 4.).

To be ill is to *experience* ill-health individually. This may well reflect a known or underlying disease, or it may not. It represents *vulnerability* - being under threat and not able to cope.

There is a range of experience covered by 'illness'. Short or long term is but one dimension. Another arises from the fact that health itself is conceived either negatively or positively - as an absence of ill-health or as a presence of well-being. When the negative concept applies, people might speak of 'having an *illness*', which is feeling incapacitated for normal activity. When they fall just below a positive standard, they might speak of 'being under the weather' (as Stevenson does), an experience sometimes called *illth*, which is feeling less than well but not incapacitated.

The devil lies in what is 'normal'. There is no single standard that applies to all. Thus, the threshold at which illth becomes illness tends to differ with culture. For instance, the Japanese tend to take everyday ailments more seriously than the British do. Careful attention may be paid to daily stools, and they are likely to be discussed with other members of the family and in a manner that is routine, rather than, as when the matter is raised at all in Britain, in grudging response to spouse or parent or as a joke. Furthermore, the Japanese tend to take recurrent minor illness as a sign of a sensitive constitution that is to be admired, and colleagues and the employer are expected to sympathise (Ohnuki-Tierney, 1984). The British are likely to congratulate themselves on being free from illness and certainly for treating minor illness lightly - for instance 'working it off' rather than 'making a song and dance of it'. As the comparison with Japan makes clear, however, attitudes to illness are not to be confused with the work ethic.

Within any culture, the threshold between illth and illness will differ according to age and disability. When the distribution of disability with age (based on the OPCS Surveys of Disability) is compared with that of reports of limiting long term illness with age (based on the OPCS General Household

Surveys), disability appears less prevalent than limiting long term illness at all ages, but the excess of limiting long term illness is far higher among younger than older people. The Surveys of Disability did not assume that disability increased as one aged, whereas older people reporting limiting long term illness must have assumed this and so discounted their age or disability (Martin, Meltzer and Elliot, 1988, Table 3.5).

The demands of employment contribute to setting norms for health. Thus, being an able-bodied person of working age is considered inconsistent with having illness (though not necessarily illth) most of the time: instead, one must sustain capacity for the effort employment requires and renew it if it breaks down. There are incentives for employees to *contain* illness (Alonzo, 1980), and, perhaps even more so for them to *mask* it from employers (Steward 1998).

Even so, illness can be functional. When individuals feel ill, they have unpleasant sensations and emotions and are often tired. They not only feel, they also reason about their feelings and seek a label for them from among those in common use where they live and work: if only, 'there is a virus going about'. If they seek advice from a doctor, nurse or pharmacist, the label they are given then is likely to be the one they assume for their illness, because it is authoritative. Having a label crucially provides legitimation for leave from normal responsibilities. Defining tiredness and misery as 'illness', and even more so giving illness a specific title, has psychological as well as social functions. It often relieves anxiety: 'what is the matter?' is dissonant, whereas 'I have such-and-such' restores assonance.

Forms of Illness

In this section, I consider how different forms of illness are socially distributed in the workforce. They are limiting long term illness, temporarily restricted activity and injuries *as reported* in the course of work.

Limiting Long Term Illness

Even among those who are of working age, reports of limiting long term illness are more common as age increases. They also reflect occupation. Figure 4.1 presents published results from a recent wave of the General Household Survey - a regular representative sample survey of households in Britain, in order to show how sharply the percentage of reports of limiting long term illness reflect socio-economic group, especially among older workers who are men. However, in the GHS, women were assigned to the occupation of their 'head of household', not their own occupation. This practice reflects a situation that may be changing in which women are either non-earners or secondary earners in households, and an assumption that - perhaps even for men - occupation influences health through the living standards it finances rather than the working conditions it involves.

Figure 4.1 Limiting long term illness and socio-economic group: Britain in 1996

Source: *Living in Britain: Results from the 1996 General Household Survey*, London: HMSO, 1998, Table 8.3

The same assignment of women applies in Figure 4.2 (below), which singles out rates per 1,000 for the three major conditions that contribute to limiting long term illness - musculo-skeletal (of which back strains are a major part), cardiovascular diseases (among them heart disease and strokes) and respiratory diseases (including asthma, bronchitis and emphysema, but not lung cancer). Here socio-economic group is pared down to a dichotomy of manual (including personal service) and non-manual groups, but men and women of 65 and over are included with those of working age. It will be noted that, on the whole, the risk increases with age, but that respiratory diseases are a partial exception - asthma bulks large in the 16-44 age group. It will also be noted that, on the whole, manual workers are at greater risk than non-manual workers, regardless of age and sex. This is particularly true of musculo-skeletal conditions among men aged 45-64, which are much more common in that age group than any other condition.

Figure 4.2 Selected longstanding conditions and non-manual/manual occupations: Britain in 1996

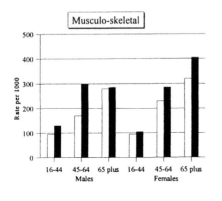

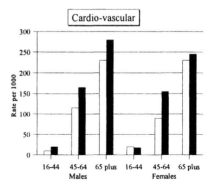

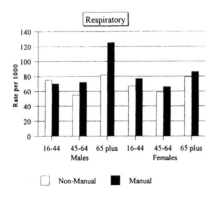

Source: *Living in Britain: Results from the 1996 General Household Survey,* London: HMSO, 1998, Table 8.13

At Masspro, in analysing the sample of 187 manual shop floor workers that we interviewed, women were classed by their own occupations, not those of the heads of their households. When asked the same question as in the GHS, men were slightly more likely to report long term illness than women, and there was a sharp tendency in both sexes for reports to increase in frequency with age. The apparent advantage of women over men is among those of child-bearing age. This could reflect health selection for the dual role of worker and child-rearer among women of this age - to cope with both these roles they need to be fitter than their male counterparts who only do paid work.

It was found that musculo-skeletal disorders were the largest single category of long term illnesses for both sexes. However, while 11 of the 15 men reporting musculo-skeletal disorders referred to the continuing effects of past injuries, all but 1 of the 11 women in the same category mentioned degenerative conditions, notably arthritis. Males are more prone to accidental injury from early childhood and this sex difference is eliminated only in extreme old age. It reflects both masculine self-identity and the circumstances to which males are exposed, including the type of work they do. Only one woman referred to a gynaecological problem. Other trends were similar for men and women..

The prevalence and type of limiting long term illness among the 48 managerial and supervisory staff whom we interviewed confirmed the view that occupation is implicated in injury proneness. Injury-induced illness was rarely reported by male managers and supervisors.

Temporarily Restricted Activity

A distinct form of illness is the 'episode' of restricted activity. This may be an acute flare-up of a long term illness or a new condition altogether - this year's 'flu, for instance. On the (safe) assumption that people find it difficult to recall with any accuracy when they last had an illness episode, especially a minor one, it is customary to ask about episodes in the two weeks preceding interview. The GHS (again for 1996) shows that episodes of restricted activity are more common as one grows older, but that this age gradient is much less sharp than for limiting long term illness. It also shows that, with advancing age, females report being progressively more prone to such episodes than males - though they are not more prone as children. Among people of working age, only those of 45-64 are more likely to have illness episodes if they are manual or personal service workers rather than non-manual workers.

In the Masspro interviews, the same questions were used as in the GHS, but in addition there was a question on the cause of restricted activity. Of shop-floor respondents, again all manual, and classed by their own occupations, 53 (28%) said they had been ill in the previous two weeks. Almost a third were attributed to recurrence of long term illness and a similar proportion to new illness.

Injuries, Diseases and Dangerous Occurrences

On the face of it, injuries arising from work which are reported to authorities are quasi-natural events and belong in the same category as 'disease' not 'illness'.[5]

---

5   I am grateful to Kevin Maguire - who is studying how social organization and culture impinge on accidents in the construction industry - for discussion of this material.

However, there is a case for including them in the present chapter - as matters of variable individual experience. If this case held, the experience of injuries might have a pattern, but it would derive not so much from events 'out there' as from culture and social relations. The case begins with reason to say that the statistics on accidental injuries at work are *unreliable* and continues with the suggestion that accidents are not defined in a consistent way - the basic data are not *valid*.

Reliability Since the publication of the Health and Safety at Work Act in 1974 and, in particular, the tighter enforcement of some of its provisions by the Reporting of Injuries, Diseases and Dangerous Occurrences Regulations in 1985, employers and the self-employed must notify the Health and Safety Executive when certain defined major injuries or any injury resulting in more than three days of absence occur. This puts accidents at work onto a similar footing as diseases which medical practitioners must notify, except that, in the case of accidents, the onus to report rests on the employer.

The HSE has long had doubts about the reliability of reports of accidents at work. It included a trailer in the Labour Force Survey of 1990 (repeated in 1993/4 and subsequently) that was designed to test the reliability of RIDDOR reports by establishing the actual frequency of work-related injuries and diseases and the absences that they sometimes lead to, and how they are distributed in the workforce of England and Wales (Stevens, 1992, Nichols, 1997, p.201). A representative sample of 40,000 households was surveyed and 77,000 of their employed members were reported on. The interview asked about injuries sustained in the year before, singled out injuries arising from accidents which involved consultation with a doctor or absence from work, and separated those 'at work, or in the course of work' from others, including those that occurred travelling to and from work. While this showed that almost twice as many workers had accidents outside work as had accidents in the course of work or at their workplace, the rate for work-related injuries requiring medical attention or an absence was 6% - around 1 in 16 of the workforce.

To avoid understating the risk and reach this figure, adjustments had to be made to respondents' reports. The adjustments made by HSE were conservative. They singled out two kinds of under-reporting: one arising from the fact that 38% of respondents were proxies - other household members answering for an absent worker at risk and thus out of relative ignorance; the other stemming from the impression that actual workers' recall became less reliable the more distant the event in time.

The issue for HSE was how closely their conservatively adjusted survey results conformed to RIDDOR reports. They concluded that only a third of reportable accidents were actually reported by employers, and only one in twenty by the self-employed. The official statistics proved considerably more reliable from some sources than others - the official rate was only 7% of the survey rate in business services, but the corresponding figure in coalmining was 80%.

It seems that a minority of employers and even fewer self-employed reported what really happened and many failed to report much, if anything. Smaller establishments (under 25 employees) were less likely to report than larger ones - 24% as opposed to 38% of the rate of accidents revealed by the survey, and (unsurprisingly) establishments that kept records (an accident book) were more likely to report than those who did not. Where, as in coalmining, there was a positive health and safety culture, deputies to enforce regulations on behalf of employers and union representatives to check employers' practices on behalf of workers, reports to the HSE tended to be reliable. Elsewhere, there might be pockets of good practice in reporting accidents, but quite widespread indifference.

If the survey is taken as the true picture, this implies that the official statistics overstate the risk of coalmining and understate that of business services. The survey does not suggest that business services (900 reportable non-fatal injuries per 100,000 employees) are more dangerous than coalmining, but it does lead us to conclude that in 1990 construction (4,150) was more dangerous than energy (3,610), that agriculture (3,560) was just as dangerous as energy, and that manufacturing (3,330) and transport (3,260) were not nearly so far behind as official statistics suggested (Stevens, 1992, Table 13).

Validity Accidents at work are rarely fatal (between 1986/7 and 1991/2, the average was 456 a year, a rate of just under 2 per 100,000 workers - Cooper, 1995, Table 11.1). Of all accidents, those leading to death are the most reliably reported. The reports are also likely to be more valid, because they are examined before coroner's courts, an autopsy is usual and so is investigation of the circumstances.

When fatalities are the focus, it appears that (aggregating figures from 1986/7 to 1991/2) construction, closely followed by agriculture and energy, are the most hazardous by far, with manufacturing, then services, making up the rear (Cooper, 1995, Figure 11.8). Is there an equivalent source of independent validation for non-fatal accidents? Does it seem as if the RIDDOR categories are consistently applied by those who actually make returns to the HSE?

Instructively, the HSE found that the distribution of injuries by type in the survey results was similar to those in the RIDDOR statistics (Stevens, 1992, Table 11). If there were no common practice in interpreting the RIDDOR categories, this similarity would be puzzling.

Fatalities, which are comparatively rare, are clearly the most likely to be reported and the best documented of injuries at work. It may be concluded, from the evidence just reviewed, that categories of non-fatal accident reportable under RIDDOR come in a poor second to fatalities. They are greatly under-reported, but such reports as do appear are probably valid.

However, field work in the pottery factory suggested that culture affects what constitutes an accident, in deciding whether a particular type of injury is a routine part of the job - something to be relegated to the background and not made a fuss about - or an event that should be drawn to management's attention, warrants absence from work and requires medical attention. In the pottery factory, managers and official procedures were not usually involved when accidents occurred. In the three months that I worked with the emptiers I witnessed several injuries - cuts to hands from broken ware, shoulder or back strains - but when I came to examine the official incident books over ten years, I found mention of a couple of incapacitating back injuries, but none of cuts.

However, when women evening shift workers occasionally emptied a few trucks if their line was down and production the day or two before firing had been exceptional, their cut hands appeared frequently in the records. This suggests a rule: unless an injury caused incapacity and so palpably affected earnings, an accident at your own work was not volunteered for the records. An apparent exception to the rule was an injury recorded for *Pamela*:

> When I (J S) returned from breakfast and went to the machine, Pamela did not appear as usual. The machine started. I switched on the belt, and Anne leapt over to help me. She said that Pamela had fallen down and hurt herself. Pamela appeared. She quickly resumed her work. She explained that she had taken a short cut across the floor and tripped over the corner of a truck. Pamela then told everyone what had happened and showed her wounds. Later she told everyone in the toilet. She made quite a song and dance about it all. Some time later [a supervisor who had helped her when she fell - not her own] came over to ask how she was and Pamela was very grateful for her sympathy. Neither of the supervisors on our line had come to see how she was: 'Even if you were dying, they'd prop you up and make you work.' Next day [the quality control assistant - not her supervisor] arranged for an account of the episode to be written up in the accident book.

But this exemplifies the same rule: Pamela's injury took place away from her work. It was also reported by a supervisor not her own.

Figlio (1985) shows that in nineteenth century contract law, hazards that any reasonable person would associate with taking a particular employment were seldom construed as the employer's liability. It has a counterpart in workers' behaviour in the potbank. To admit frequent injury at your own work was to invite doubts about your competence.

Reasons for Vulnerability to Illness

From what has gone before in Part I, it can be deduced that vulnerability in employment appears where one or two underlying factors are present and a third immediate condition is absent. The underlying factors are present where qualities of body and mind accentuated by selection for jobs can no longer be produced by the individual or are no longer relevant to the job and/or where qualities depreciated by the same process can no longer be successfully suppressed. The immediate condition is absent where the ways of coping with sustained work in employment that are learned in the course of being made docile break down.

Illness Associated with Qualities Accentuated by the Job

Occupations are elements in a division of labour and, within organizations of some size, in a hierarchy of command as well. Selection for them accentuates some qualities of body and mind over others: say, for heavy lifting or dexterity, tidy administration or creative thinking, energising others or maintaining equanimity. Survival in the job demands sustained performance of the necessary qualities.

Many shop floor jobs at Masspro, especially those of women, required dexterity and capacity to repeat manual operations in short cycles. 'RSI' (repetitive strain injury) was becoming an issue in pottery work that occupied personnel managers, union officials and lawyers representing both sides. The term itself was rarely used in our hearing, but 'tenosynovitis' was. An orthopaedic surgeon for the district spoke of it. Of course, he knew that this was inflammation of tendons and not generalizable to all injuries, far less all discomfort in the wrists, arms and shoulders, but tenosynovitis was already a recognized industrial disease and RSI had not been recognized. Medical opinion was divided and, especially after the so-called 'epidemic' of RSI in Australia in the early 1980s (Reilly, 1995, Nichols, 1997, pp.85-7). A substantial body concluded that RSI was a malaise associated with unrewarding and monotonous work. Even before matters reached a head in Australia, our informants in the Potteries, unionists and employers alike, were treating 'teno' as a bandwagon which was likely to be joined by people who could not cope with their jobs and sought industrial injuries compensation before they were due to retire. The people they had in mind were preponderantly women.

Another class of emergent illnesses was associated with 'stress', especially 'executive stress'. Managers were selected for their capacity to 'cope', but this was sometimes stretched to the limit. The illnesses involved had various primary labels - from anxiety and frozen shoulder, through Crohn's disease of the small intestine to cardiovascular diseases. There was a certain prestige attached to stress-related conditions. A trade union official claimed in a report on the industry that it was no less typical of shop floor workers' illnesses than those of executives. Contentious and stigmatising labels, like 'RSI' tended to be applied to the illnesses of people who are not considered entirely trustworthy, that is those of relatively low status. It was women, the young and feckless and manual workers who tended to attract such labels. 'Executive stress' played a role in Masspro (as elsewhere in the West today) somewhat like that of tuberculosis in the nineteenth century, which, Sontag (1991) suggests, was seen as a sign of a refined disposition, until it was later acknowledged to belong with poverty and overcrowding (Bryder, 1988).

Qualities Depreciated by the Job

Just as jobs accentuate certain qualities of mind and body, so they depreciate others. In the hierarchical element of the division of labour, mental qualities are given primacy over physical. Thus, a physically disabled person, Stephen Hawking, the theoretical physicist who performs outstandingly in a mental job, is celebrated in obvious contrast to the many who are able-bodied but mentally impaired. The same values make *Mary* hesitant to say what she admits to JS:

> Mary became a bit more talkative as the morning wore on - she was watching me for a bit and then she said to me, 'You've switched off. haven't you?' I asked her what she meant, and she said, 'It's this job - it's bad for you - you just go right into yourself and shut yourself in your personal worries.' She said that after a bit you don't even notice what is happening around you - you are so cut off. This is indeed exactly what had been happening to me. Mary explained that in the long term this is a very bad thing: when you come to work you see nothing but cups all day. Stuck up there you hardly talk to anyone. You have no idea what is happening around you - and you lose touch with what is happening in the world. After a while, it gets so that you have no conversation, and when you go out socially you do not know what to say - eventually you lose all your self-confidence. She felt that going to work ought to be about meeting people and taking part in things. Pamela agreed very strongly with all of this. Mary said to me, 'I know all about this - and I'll go along to [the university] any time to tell them all about it - all I'll need is my soap-box!' She added that at the factory, they didn't care about any of this - all they wanted out of you was 'more, more, more!'

Jobs that depreciated the mental abilities and social skills of those employed to do them might give rise to 'neurasthenia' or 'malaise', terms sometimes given on medical certificates, especially to women.

When Coping Breaks Down[6]

The making of the worker (as a 'docile body') lays the ground for coping with work, but, by the same token, when coping breaks down the worker becomes vulnerable to illness. In what follows, I consider this from two points of view: first, the control of effort and its breakdown, and how that differs for manual workers and managers; then, how places within the factory that have different symbolic meanings come to be associated with vulnerability to illness.

At Masspro, managers and workers had rather different routines for occupying the time at work. Zerubavel (1981) has suggested that organizations typically give higher grade personnel more flexibility in use of time and space than their subordinates. The manager can vary his or her activity, pause in the middle of an operation, and escape from surveillance into an office. Some workers - for example, craft workers and warehouse labourers - have some of these facilities, legitimately or not, but most - especially machine attendants and assembly line operatives - have their work-pace and spells of activity determined for them, and work in full view of managers and other workers.

Another factor is whether time is of predominantly linear (progressive) or cyclical (repetitive) character: this too differs for managers and workers. For semi-skilled workers, especially on machine- or line-paced work, the cyclical aspect dominates the linear. Linear time is typically broken down into units of different length: spells between breaks, the shift, the five day week, intervals between holidays, and ultimately the working life itself. Within each of these categories, units are of the same length. Thus, linear time takes on a largely cyclical aspect: one day is much like another, week succeeds week; and the cycles are of varying length, the longer overarching the shorter.

Managers too have quite regular work schedules, more so than academics but less so by far than those they manage. Indeed, the schedules become the less regular the higher the manager is on the career ladder on which he or she started. The Vice-Chairman of Masspro said he felt entitled to a round of golf on a working day every now and then, because he frequently worked late at the office or took work home. Not only is this cyclical aspect of work blurred in the case of managers, the linear aspect is accentuated. Time tends to be divided into unequal lengths which correspond to assignments - batches to be produced, new products to be brought on stream, a marketing campaign to be brought to fruition and evaluated. Instead of these lengths being laid end to end (one day after another, and so on), they often overlap, such that one is beginning while another

---

6   This issue is discussed at more length in Bellaby (1992).

ends and a third continues. Moreover, managers have 'careers': they usually aspire to be at certain points on a ladder by specific ages. In that sense, their working life itself is linear, not only part of a life cycle shared with peers and family and kin.

As was pointed out above (p.9), when drawing an analogy between time in employment and on a long rail journey, a distinction must be drawn between internal time, which is occupied during work, and external time, which elapses while at work, so eating into time available for other purposes. External time can be altered only by ceasing to be present, by not boarding the train, by absenting oneself from work. Both managers and workers have to present a front of sustained effort to superiors and peers and, if managers, to subordinates. As will be seen below (Chapter 6), absence arises to some extent from insuperable difficulty in controlling effort in time internal to work.

Employees' control of effort and its breakdown: broken rhythm After participant observation of work in mass production, Roy laid stress on the pastimes that individuals and work groups devised to while away the hours and counter the monotony (Roy, 1952). What makes it possible to turn work into a game, to day-dream while working or to soldier on grimly - whatever one's personal adaptation, is rhythm:

> The line ran more smoothly than yesterday and I (PB) tried hard to feed the ware through with the right gaps. By mid morning I was feeding more or less automatically and was able to attend to things around me a little. I felt far less fatigued at the end of the day, in spite of the pressure of work. [Field notes taken when learning to feed a moving line that sprayed glaze on tableware.]

In the course of its development, industry must periodically have disrupted rhythms: at first, those of darkness and light and the seasons that the life and work of peasants has to obey; and, later, rhythmic patterns which had been steadily remade by industrial workers after each wave of technological and organizational change. There is synergy between workers' rhythm and the disciplines that work and its organization have imposed, but maintaining rhythm is also in conflict with capital's drive for economy of labour-time.

Potters, notably Josiah Wedgwood, are credited with early innovation in the division of labour and production management (McKendrick, 1961). However, most forms of work, here as elsewhere in British industry, remained manual, rather then becoming mechanized, until well into this century (Samuel, 1977). Direct employment and management were also slow to develop, as may be judged from Shaw's (1969) autobiographical account of pottery work (above p55, see also Pollard, 1968, Littler, 1982). Since the major reorganizations following the Second World War (Gay and Smith, 1974), the pottery industry has been rather rapidly converted to near-flow production and mechanization, and has already ventured into automation (Till, 1987). By itself, change breaks rhythms in manual work. But making the potter's body an adjunct to a machine and moving line, presents further possibilities of disruption of rhythm due both to mechanical failures and to the non-variable pace of moving lines.

There has been much attention to biological rhythms in the literature on work: in particular, to the relation between the circadian (daily) inbuilt clock and patterns of shift work (Reinberg *et al.*, 1984, Waterhouse *et al.*, 1987). In the present context, circadian rhythms have little relevance. To sustain repetitive manual labour, it is plain that each individual must find his/her own rhythm, and that biology constrains or enables - but no more. An established rhythm for a given job is a property of the workplace and often of generations who have worked there. It is taught to novices by experienced workers. For instance, when I began lifting loads of around 15 kilos off a roller-conveyor repeatedly through the day, I was told by my experienced mate not to 'maul', that is to pull loads towards me, but to allow them to fall gently onto my outstretched arms, which, of course, saved considerable muscular wear and tear. Similarly those who printed patterns onto mugs by machine had learned to move their whole bodies to reach mugs from pallets to their right, apply the print and then place them on pallets to their left, in a pendulum like motion. This minimized back strain. In general, workers may use pop music on the tannoy or singing to help sustain rhythm.

As Laban and his followers understood, dance is a useful analogy for the way manual work is performed to rhythm (Laban and Lawrence, 1947, Maletic, 1987). Each job has its unwritten choreography. This has two components of particular interest: beat and phrasing. Machinery, while it operates smoothly, has a beat, but workers on machines have to develop their own beat, which cannot be slower or faster than the machine if the job is to be comfortable. Breakdowns will be welcome if the worker is out of synchrony with the machine, but disrupt rhythm if his or her beat coincides with that of the machine. The beat of the body is variable not constant: it takes time to get up pace, and fatigue slows normal pace. Any organization in which each worker's pace is dependent on that of others or a machine, is likely to cause individuals discomfort whenever their pace is quicker or slower than the one set externally. Phrasing is the equivalent of a sequence of steps or a completed routine. The scheduling of work between breaks, by day, by week and between holidays, provides for the development of phrasing. However the worker's own phrasing does not necessarily coincide with work scheduling, as was obvious to Muslim workers in the potbank, for British working hours cut across Islamic religious festivals, Friday prayers and daily times of prayer. This is one of many instances of the usually unremarked ethnic patterning of work in employment. Working hours are also gendered. In Masspro, women with relatively dependent children of school age had to make special arrangements to cope with working hours during school holidays.

Work groups sometimes take control of their members' effort by imposing collective rhythm. The kiln emptiers imposed the discipline of an almost autonomous work group (Trist *et al.*, 1963) upon the beat and phrasing of members. They had to empty a quota of kiln trucks each day and could start and finish at whatever times they chose. Most members of the team had worked together for at least 15 years, and they spoke of how, in the face of many threats of disruption by management, they had steadily evolved a fast beat, and a phrasing that permitted an early finish with only one break during the shift. So finely tuned were individuals to the collective rhythm that one complained of muscular pains and a headache when a supply failure carried work well over the usual finish time, and another showed how he had lacerated his hands on the rough structure of a kiln truck by having to set himself fractionally out of position as he began work.

Workers who, unlike these men, had lost a traditional rhythm, experienced it as loss of control. An instance was casters (usually male) and spongers (usually female), who had been recruited recently from a company that closed down. In one Masspro workshop, they had been obliged to work set hours regardless of whether they completed what they saw to be their quota for the day, and found even the enforced breakfast and lunch breaks disruptive.

Employees' control of effort and its breakdown: unmet deadlines On the whole, managers' performance was less visible than that of shop floor workers. Crucially, it was made visible to superiors by the imposition of deadlines by which certain tasks had to be completed. Managers were made to account for their achievement, which as often as not depended on that of their subordinates. Sometimes deadlines were frequent and specific. The lowest level of departmental manager in the potbank had production targets to meet each week, which included levels of waste and of quality control. The next level of management was responsible for budgeting for consumables on a monthly basis. In Jaques' (1982) terms, each had his or her own 'time-span of discretion'. Different types of deadline occur at regular but infrequent intervals throughout managers' careers and are the points at which they are judged ripe for promotion, or unlikely to be able to carry greater responsibility.

A corollary of control by deadlines is that what at first appears to be managers' greater freedom to use time at work, turns out to be the right of superiors to invade their informal time - in the canteen, the washroom and the corridor, often also at home. In Masspro the kiln manager was permanently on call, because tunnel kilns were only shut down during the Potters' Holidays. Managers also took work home. The right of the firm to call for this commitment was symbolized by the fact that over-time payment was usually denied to staff above the lowest levels. It was of course paid routinely to shop floor workers. Middle managers, who were in a grey area from this point of view, were made aware that to press for overtime payment was to risk being defined as one who lacked the 'right attitude' for management.

Managers were encouraged to view their future with the company in individual terms. Rather than adopt the (steady) rhythm of the experienced managers, new recruits should seek to outpace their peers. In spite of a public grade system, salary levels and fringe benefits varied widely on the same grade. Managers who were interviewed could not guess the earnings of their peers in the same company. Each, it seemed, was the beneficiary of patronage by a superior, or else victim of its withdrawal. Managerial structure was not so much a bureaucracy: rather it was 'patrimonial' (Weber, 1968: pp.217-237).

Senior managers had a clear view of what they required of their subordinates. The latitude that managers were given was expected to be used 'responsibly'. They were not instructed in so many words on how to use it, yet they must organize the time and the material resources put at their disposal so as to deliver what was required at the time it was called for. The latitude given to production managers coincided with what for senior managers was an area of uncertainty: how to induce shop floor workers to produce the effort and how to coordinate that effort. A senior manager who had been through the ranks might know how to set about this task, but, if he or she took it on, the span of control would be too great. Thus the task had to broken down into smaller units and delegated. Those to whom it was delegated would be judged by how far they met the targets set for them. They might fail because the means they needed to succeed were outside their control, but such an excuse was unlikely to be accepted by superiors, because the principle of good management from above was delegation, and at middle management level was organizing time so as to deliver on target.

These organizations can be illustrated by a case study of the power relations between four managers (all, as was typical, male), who were in direct line of command: Charles the managing director, Nigel the production director, Bob the second tier manager, and Jack the departmental manager.

The MD had a private income and did not have a great deal to lose by retiring and giving up his salary, though it allowed him to support his sons' private education and gave him the satisfaction of not being a 'parasite', as he put it. The other men were career managers, Nigel and Bob having reached managerial status before they joined the firm, but Jack having been promoted first to supervisor, then to departmental manager from the shop floor at Masspro. They worked in a unit which was beleaguered by poor sales performance.

'Stress' was on the lips, or at least the tip-of-the-tongue of Nigel, Bob and Jack in discussing their work and their health:

> *Nigel* In the last two weeks I have felt more tired than usual. The pressure of the business has changed so much. I am under pressure to turn the business round, and under fierce attack from Charles. Charles has acted on a customer's complaint by turning the aggro on individuals. I was never consulted.....The down side to this job is the way the human relations aspect is handled. There should be more forward planning. Mistakes are bound to be made. Then individuals are blamed. People are got down by it. (On being asked whether he was given sufficient control to do his job properly, laughing) I decided a long time ago, it is easier to become a yes man. So yes, I am given the authority. I carry the responsibility. But make a mistake and you are dealt with severely.

> *Bob* Over the year, my health has deteriorated because of my job. I suffer from chronic muscular tension. The doctor puts it down to stress. Fifteen months ago it reached its peak. I was not delegating: I was prepared to take all the stress on my own shoulders.....I find it frustrating that the established work force do not accept that we mean to make things better - there is mistrust, they suspect any change as a management tool. It is also frustrating seeing things not going right, and that you could jump in and solve it. But I have to leave subordinates to do the job.

> *Jack* (All four men said they enjoyed responsibility) I admit I enjoy responsibility. In management as opposed to the shop floor I bring in the word 'involvement'. I enjoy seeing something coming together, fulfilling a plan on a daily, a weekly basis: good counts and quality. (On being asked about the bad side of the job) How long have you got? Pressure - an awful lot. Can be a tremendous mental strain. A manager, unlike an operative, is always on trial, always got to be 100% committed. You take the knocks for other people's lack of interest. We get the rough side of (superiors') tongues, a dogmatic approach. Sometimes I wonder if the financial rewards are worth it. Other people come in and change things I have set up. You're the bad guy, you get the backlash from the (shop floor) people and from senior managers and the director.

The three men in the beleaguered unit all personalized their stress: both its source, which in more or less veiled manner was seen to be each person's immediate superior and a mistrustful work force; and their responsibility to cope - Bob said he had learned to delegate, and Nigel to be a 'yes-man'. The managing director was, of course, the immediate (though not the sole) source of the pressure upon the production director, a pressure which was transferred, as in Newton's cradle, down the line of command to the point at which Bob and to a greater extent Jack experienced the cross-pressures of men in the middle, between top management and shop floor.

Toughening and weakening spaces in the workplace When people were exposed regularly in their work to the elemental extremes of earth/water or fire/air, they believed that they were toughened by them. Work in the sliphouse and on the kilns was heavy. Inert kiln trucks, weighing more than a ton, must be put in motion by pushing or levering with back and legs. Slabs of clay weighing around 250 pounds must be dropped from filters and then lifted onto conveyors to feed the pug mills. There were, needless to say, periodic back injuries. However, the jobs were supposed to inure people to disease and injury: for one sliphouse worker, a 'slipped disc' was a source of pride, because he overcame it by lifting on his good side, and lying flat on his back when the injury became aggravated; a kiln worker said that his job kept him fit and that coping with its physical demands was a matter of 'attitude.'

That it was not heavy lifting *per se* that was supposed to toughen, but rather the extremes in which it was done, will be seen from the fact that heavy lifting was said to weaken women and to cause back strains for male screen printers who were in intermediate spaces. The 'tough men' of the sliphouse and kilns had a life style at sharp variance with *Health of the Nation* advice. They disparaged diet, temperance, sport and jogging. A man would show himself to be fit by turning in for a full day's work after a night of hard drinking. Almost all women were in intermediate spaces; fortunately for our purpose in showing that spaces, not only gender, carried health properties, so were many men. These men and women generally were unable to move, except for short breaks, whether, like handle-makers, packers, glazing line workers, some decorators and making machine emptiers and feeders, they stood, or, like most screen printers, selectors and those who put handles onto ware, they sat.

Depressions and anxiety states were not uncommon, though rarely admitted to in company. A screen printer said in a confidential interview that he had been treated over some years for anxiety states. Another, also male, said he was concerned that working in a sedentary position might be bad for the heart. When a report was being drawn up for senior management about the subjective responses of workers to our various experiments in changing work organization on production lines, a group of women wanted to ensure that it was made clear that, while a couple of changes at least had made it easier to cope with the pains of the job, the pains had not disappeared and coming to work in the morning was no more acceptable than it had been before.

Such feelings were as foreign to labourers in the warehouse as to sliphouse and kiln workers. Labourers were on the move, sometimes between the extremes of cold/wet and hot/dry, sometimes across the boundary between the inside and outside of the factory. They were not penned in by machines and work-benches. At the same time, they were not hardened by consistent exposure to the 'elements'. As a result, they complained of some of the ill-effects the culture attributed to exposure to contradictory extremes - to getting cold by going outside after the warmth of the factory in winter, for instance. It also has to be said that men at the extremes believed that ageing would reduce their immunity to the ill-effects of work. Their concepts of what the ill-effects would be were based on humoral aetiology. Kilnmen, confronted with hot and dry conditions, expected to develop catarrh and sinusitis, while slipmen, working in the cold and wet, feared rheumatism.

Gender and Vulnerability

Men seemed (on the whole) more reluctant than women (on the whole) to say that their jobs left them vulnerable. The random sample of 187 Masspro shop-floor workers were asked, among other questions, one that sought to explore the relation between health and work as workers themselves saw it. To avoid biasing the response by specifying that health and work was a concern, all that was asked was the 'good and bad points of your job'. There is no doubt that these patterns are stereotypical, but they are not stereotypes of the researchers' making, rather of the setting.

Especially once they had responsibilities, whether domestic or managerial, men and women alike were expected to show stoicism if they were in pain or under stress at work. But there were important differences in their approach to the expectation. Men saw physical work as a sign of manliness: it was good for you. Women tended to see it as a risk to their health. Men in physical jobs had contempt for managers and office staff who did not roll up their sleeves and get stuck in. Women who did physical jobs tended to cast envious eyes on well-dressed and made-up women when they walked through the factory. Men said they liked to be their own bosses, and, when asked to think of what was bad about their jobs, often mentioned management that was on your back all the time. This did not usually spring to women's minds. They tended to think first of the working environment, and often the health and safety aspect: heat and cold, draughts, dust and dirt were mentioned. Women were as often bothered as men about the lack of freedom in their jobs: in fact more often so, and with good cause. In compensation, they looked for ways of making their place on the shop floor their own. It was not uncommon to see women coming in early to clean up their machines or bench before they started work. Space to keep outdoor clothes and belongings was important to women for similar reasons. Men identified with the job often enough, but they were not so concerned about a patch of the shop floor or a bench as women tended to be. Men were also less bothered about getting dirty. Of course, women on the potbank put up with this, but they disliked the effects that hot air and dust had on hair and complexion, and rough or broken ware had on hands and nails.

In short, men appeared to believe that they must master their bodies with their minds, in order to sustain attendance at and performance in work, and that in so doing they would grow fitter and more resistant to invasion of their bodies by the work-environment and by germs. Women, similarly stoic on the whole, sought rather to fend off the dangers with which a hostile work environment confronted them, warding off or complaining to management about draughts, broken ware, spillages of clay dust or glaze.

Conclusion

Illness is what we *experience* in ill-health, whether a disease is present or absent. This chapter has focused on the conditions workers report, whether to management, to doctors, in social surveys like the General Household Survey, or in the course of everyday conversation on the shop floor. The more public the report, the more likely it is to represent illness causing incapacity, not mere malaise or illth. However, as the review of injuries arising from work showed, reporting is highly conditional on industry and occupation - on factors such as the presence or absence of trade union representation, and, at Masspro at least, on the circumstances in which the injury arose.

I have also argued that what stitches the docile body together and what attaches it to employment and a specific form of work are the very seams which become strained and make workers vulnerable to the experience of ill-health. Qualities which are accentuated by selection and induction for jobs become a source of weakness, as dexterity does in repetitive work when RSI develops. Qualities which are suppressed, such as social skills and reasoning in many line-paced jobs, cause the worker's body or mind to become recalcitrant, should the conditions break down which normally make it docile.

Employees learn to accommodate to day to day requirements by acquiring a rhythm and/or coping with the pressures of meeting deadlines. However, rhythm, which sustains repetitive work, may be broken; coping with the pressure of meeting deadlines may fail: both usually because of factors outside the individual's control. Finally, the spaces to which working bodies are exposed vary in how strengthening or weakening they seem to their occupants. Yet what seemed a system immune to injury and ill-health because of hardening in extreme conditions may turn on itself as the worker ages. These are the immediate circumstances in which illth and illness emerge.

To this point, illness has yet to be made social. It has been understood in a cultural context, to be sure, but now attention must turn to how social relations bear upon health, in particular the moral ambiguities surrounding what counts as a 'genuine' reason for taking time off from work.

5 Bodies Off Sick:
Moral Ambiguities and
how they are Resolved

Les absents ont toujours tort. [The absent are always in the wrong]
'Destouches' (Phillipe Néricault), 1680-1754, *L'obstacle imprévu*, I, iv.

As distinct from *disease*, which is a biological or psycho-biological process, and *illness*, which is individually experienced, *sickness* is the representation of ill-health in social relations. Sickness is involved when people are granted leave from normal obligations on condition that they take appropriate steps to get well. In Parsons' original formulation of this idea (for mid century North America), the medical practitioner is the key regulator of access to the sick role (Parsons, 1951, 1958). Not only is leave conditional, it is rarely given as a matter of course. In work, leave often involves taking time off or being absent when one is otherwise expected to attend, though it may entail no more than the individual having a break in the usual pattern of the day's work.

Sickness is inherently to do with conduct in social relations (Dodier, 1985, Bellaby, 1990a). Some events, including diseases, are ambiguous as matters of fact. Did they happen or not? Human conduct is often morally ambiguous. Did it happen for the reasons that the actor or others publicly attribute to it?

Absences from work, military duty or school are social not natural, yet unambiguous factually and easy to count, so long as there is a rule about attending at such a place at certain hours. One is either present or not at a roll call or when work stations are manned. This helps explain the frequent use of absences as 'hard data' in studies of organizational behaviour (e.g. Edwards and Scullion, 1982). Of course, when there is no rule or the rule does not require a particular employee's, soldier's or student's attendance at a given time in a given place, their absence has no more meaning than that of anyone unconnected with the institution.

Sickness absence combines the unambiguous and countable absence with the qualitative and often ambiguous reason given for it. The sick absent differ from those who are absent without leave. They not only make an excuse (which

93

AWOLs neglect to do, at least at the time) but also lay claim to the leave from normal obligations that others are expected to give to the sick. Without denying that 'genuine sickness' often does underlie absence from work, it is clear that there are perils in using absence as an index of morbidity (disease) as some have (e.g. North *et al.*, 1993. Marmot *et al.*, 1995, Stansfeld *et al.*, 1995).

The moral ambiguity of sickness absence is constitutive, that is, it defines the nature of the thing to be studied. Having established this, I go on to ask how managers, workers and General Practitioners involved with the absence resolve its moral ambiguity for the practical purposes of preserving trust and getting work done. The chapter ends by considering the vocabularies and implicit meanings that are employed in accomplishing this.

The Ambiguous Relation between Sickness and Absence in the Pottery

We begin by asking what sickness involves before it becomes absence, and only then how absence on grounds of sickness may be understood.

Sickness in the Workplace

The granting of leave from normal obligations is a situated activity - it occurs in a given time and place, with a cast of social actors. As Frankenberg (1986, 1992) suggests, it is a 'cultural performance'. This is corroborated by situations observed in the course of fieldwork in the pottery factory:

> *Jackie's illness* I (JS) started out sitting next to Jackie, who had been away yesterday. She said she had had a wisdom tooth removed and was feeling awful. In fact she had not felt like coming in at all. I don't think we had been working for half an hour when she suddenly announced that she felt sick. The others stopped the belt and shouted at her to run, which she did. A couple of minutes later someone from the dipping end arrived to take her place. About 20 minutes later Betty arrived to collect Jackie's bag and said that she was going. This was the extent of my conversation about Jackie. Nobody commented further.

> *Alan's seizure* Events of the day were overshadowed by Alan having an epileptic fit. It was not allowed to interfere with the pace of work to any great extent. He had a premonitory tremor before breakfast (several it seems last week). Then, after breakfast, I (PB) noted that he was sitting on the rollers with Sam by him. (The manager) was passing through and was told to come quickly. Alan was now standing, held on either side, and convulsing, his eyes closed. (The manager) seized his false teeth and (as he described dramatically afterwards) removed them with

Off Sick: Ambiguities 95

difficulty. (The safety representative) and (the first aid woman) were called on. A blanket and a pillow were brought and Alan was carried from the line and laid out on the spur, covered over. (The first aid woman) was left by him. Sam told me he was trying to get his leg over. (The first aid woman) was much amused. Sam said Alan was in trance.

(Next day, the usual replacement, a young man) was drafted in early. I thought it was to cover for Alan. He said (surprised), Alan was on. The young man was there to cover for someone else. My mate told me Alan was perfectly alright when he got home.

Jackie could only act the martyr, but she eschewed the role. Alan was an anomaly, for he was an involuntary participant 'in a trance', and the performance was enacted around him by fellow workers, the manager and the first aid person. The case of Pamela referred to above (p.81) completes a set, because there was a 'song and dance' about her suffering, but, apart from the researcher and a supervisor who was not her own, no one seemed to offer sympathy, and so the performance fell flat.

We learn from this that expressions of suffering were seen to be voluntary in the normal case and to be rarely appropriate at work. At work one did not dramatize feeling ill, but showed fortitude in the face of suffering, or else left the stage quickly as did Jackie. The appropriate thing to do was to 'work off' a cold, menstrual pains, anxieties, a hangover.

The parts played by peers in these episodes suggest the felt urgency of keeping up production: thus a fellow process worker stepped over the moving line to take Pamela's vacated position; someone quickly stepped in to take Alan's place, and most of the others continued work. But the team also organized itself in Alan's case to deal with his seizure and call in help: what made their prompt sympathy appropriate was that Alan could not have intended his suffering (the 'leg over' interpretation attended humorously to this otherwise unthinkable possibility).

Each of these was a temporary and acute disruption of a sustained performance of work. However, Alan's was beginning to be turned into a degenerative case. One of his colleagues whispered to me, so that others in the team did not hear, that Alan should begin to think about doing work that was less of a risk to an epileptic, because his wife worked too and he no longer had dependent children. Others said more openly that Alan was not supposed to drink when taking medication to control his condition, but he did so. Steadily, Alan was being 'disabled' both physically and morally for the job he had been tuned to perform.

A Genuine Reason for Absence?[7]

In the commonsense view, a sickness absence is either genuine or fraudulent (malingering). On interviewing people about absences in the previous two weeks, they were sometimes frank about taking time off without being sick or for any other reason that would excuse it in management's terms. However, these were confidential interviews with investigators, who, at this stage of acquaintance at least, were virtual strangers. There was nothing to lose by being frank. The more that was invested in an ongoing relationship with managers or fellow workers, the more there was to lose by revelations like these. In any case, if one was not trusted, it was difficult to be convincingly genuine when one told the truth. As a result, the reasons for absences were frequently obscure and often not addressed. This is exemplified by the case of *Jim*:

> Overnight there was a snowfall. When I (PB) got in at about 7am, Jim was absent. When Mike arrived for his noon shift he came in wellies. He said that Jim had not failed to come in because of the snow, since they lived very near to each other.
> Much earlier, at about 8.30am, I asked Tom whether he expected Jim to come in. Laughing, he called on Harry to confirm that Jim would be taking the first day of snow off to go sledging with his kids, and giving them a day off school too. He used to take several days off to build a bonfire for Bonfire Night. He was only stopped by the council which refused to let him build so high a fire. He was as compulsive as a child in other ways too. He once had a day off then turned up on Saturday morning for overtime. He got in an hour before the others and had done a third of the work before anyone else arrived. Harry said, 'Jim had children so that he could have an excuse for carrying on being a child.'
> The next day, I got in half an hour early to find Dai there already. He told me he did not expect Jim, and later in the morning, when Jim had failed to turn in, Dai told me that Jim had caught the 'flu: he had been out watching a football game on Sunday with only his pullover on. Though Dai was a mate of Jim's, he had never been able to understand his behaviour.

Jim's absence on this occasion lasted all week and when he returned the following Monday he had catarrh and a wheezing chest. On an earlier occasion, Jim had another week off:

> On the Wednesday, Geoff, the manager, told me that Jim was the only one in the work group who often had days off [the next day Jim began a week's absence].

---

7   The issues under this and the following two main headings are dealt with at greater length in Bellaby 1990a.

Geoff said that Tom, as the union man, would not accept that Jim should have a formal warning, because his uncertified absences were below the agreed minimum to issue a formal warning. Jim was unpredictable. He did the opposite of what you told him if he had a mind to. For instance, when told not to send broken ware down to the women, when they complained of cut hands, he had merely sent down more pitchers, though eventually he mended his ways. Later in the morning, Bert independently underlined the manager's complaint against the union man, saying that it was Tom's fault that Jim was still troubling them with his days off. I kidded Johnnie (the temporary replacement for Jim) that he must have used voodoo to get rid of Jim. Tom said that Johnnie would not need voodoo because Jim would get rid of himself if he kept taking days off.

The following day, when Jim was absent again, Tom said he thought Jim was deliberately taking off a second day because he had taken six uncertified single days out of the last forty, and this cast suspicion on him and made him liable to a warning. He expected Jim to try to get a medical certificate. I asked whether he thought a doctor might give certificates even if he considered someone was not ill. He sidestepped this and suggested that confidentiality between employee and General Practitioner was a major problem. Some days later Tom said he knew nothing of why Jim had been absent on this occasion. He believed he had brought in a medical certificate.

About a month after the second of these episodes, Jim was given a formal warning for absenteeism. He had worked on the same job, and mostly with the same men, for twenty seven years and, according to his fellow workers, had always taken odd days off unpredictably.

To be sure, medical examination might determine whether Jim had the 'flu. But the 'flu might not be seen as a genuine reason for Jim to take time off. Medical certificates *per se* might not resolve doubts, as is plain from Tom's cynical analysis of how Jim might seek them to cover for his absences in case the level of his recent absences might put his job in jeopardy. Furthermore, as Dai's response suggests, there are good and bad reasons for having 'flu: he felt Jim had been negligent, and that his not wearing more than a pullover at the football match was typical of his unreliability.

Whether Jim was truthful on each of these occasions is not the question of prime interest to an outside observer. That is rather how managers and fellow workers resolved the moral ambiguity they found in his actions for practical purposes, such as sickness payment and discipline, and yet left a lingering doubt which was carried forward to the next occasion when he was absent.

An alternative analysis would be that there was no truth or falsehood to speak of here. The label 'odd day off man' was arbitrary. Once applied to Jim, it became his *raison d'être*, an identity to be lived up to. Such a 'labelling' account usually has people with power (such as managers) imposing the arbitrary label. Its meaning is precarious when the label is applied by peers, who were less reticent about it than the manager, much less so than the union official, and when the person who is labelled wants, like Jim, to justify himself and be accepted, not be regarded as a deviant.

Indeed there is little in this case (or in others Sidaway and I observed) to justify the typical labelling account that might be applied to sickness absence. The moral ambiguity of sickness absence - the question of truth or falsehood - was far from negligible. Rather it was the defining characteristic of sickness absence for those engaged in this set of social relations. It is also the case that ill-health or injury was a necessary part of the case for *genuine* sickness, even if not always sufficient. Moreover, there were ways of corroborating the claimant's own word on his health. A doctor's certificate might not remove doubts, but it had to be accepted. The means of resolving whether a particular sickness absence was genuine thus resembled a judicial process.

Resolving the Ambiguities of Sickness Absence for Practical Purposes

As Garfinkel argues (1967, 1986), social order is not pre-given, but continuously accomplished. Often it is accomplished only by allowing ambiguities to pass.

Negotiating the Genuineness of Absence: Management and Workers

Fellow workers, acting on expectations that are widely shared, are an important social control over the transition to the sick role. As the case of Jim makes plain, they do not necessarily align with the absentee against management. However, management relations with an absentee worker are on a different dimension from those of fellow workers. Managers, as agents of the employer who are accountable for the performance of the workers they manage, must exert and conserve authority.

Shop floor workers must clock on and off. Staff, however, were trusted to come and go as was deemed necessary to do their jobs. The personnel manager accepted that controls over shop floor attendance betrayed mistrust of rank and file workers, but argued that this was justified by the conduct of a minority who, perhaps because of upbringing, could not be trusted and would take advantage of any harmonization in conditions of employment by turning in late and taking unnecessary or longer absences.

Jim was proof of the mistrust shown towards a minority by line managers, not only those in personnel. However, line managers were directly involved with workers and depended on trust to ensure that their targets were met, especially when they could not rely on fear or financial incentives. Line managers found it both congenial and effective to use the peer group as their agency of control over deviants, such as Jim. If they did not do so, there might be a partial breakdown of control. This happened in another work group. The manager was considered by workers to have favourites, some of whom were people who should be disciplined, and to use discipline unfairly against people whose absences were felt to be genuine by peers. There was a vicious circle of mistrust between him and his subordinates, except for a loyal but apprehensive band of lieutenants. This man was in turn subjected to an intensity of pressure bordering on mistrust by his boss, and so on up the line to the managing director.

Clearly any perceived miscarriage of justice can generate mistrust. Those involving sickness seem to have a particular force:

Margaret Margaret was off yesterday because her husband went down with pleurisy. She said she wondered whether she ought to have come in today.
[Several days later] Margaret is feeling aggrieved because of Don's (the manager's) attitude over absences: sickness is not taken as a valid reason she says. She was told when she was off with glandular fever some time ago, that anyone can get a doctor's note. In the course of her bed rest, she was asked by phone to come down to the factory, which she did. However, when she took a day off recently to nurse her husband, Don told someone else that Margaret would get no overtime on Saturday as a result.

Helen Helen said she was not feeling like work. She said she had a green card,[8] which excused her from lifting, since her neck was bad and she had to have a collar sometimes. But Don often put her onto heavy work, in spite of her protests: 'We are all used here, like so many numbers,' she said.
[The next day] Helen felt she was used because she was relatively easy going. She had been put onto heavy work before the holidays to cover for someone else's absence, and not paid the rate for the job. After the holiday, she refused that job, and was called to the office. She went there clutching her green card. Don said, 'Won't you do the job, as a favour.' She said no, because she had to follow her doctor's advice, and she looked Don in the face and said, 'You use me, you use everybody.' His reply was, 'Is that really what you think? You have been storing that up all holiday haven't you.'

The force of these feelings arises from the fact that the sick expect sympathy.

---

8   The green card is the certificate that is carried in employment or when seeking employment by those who are registered as disabled (see above, p.44).

Work Discipline and Medical Practice

Medicine, as an institutional complex, sits uneasily between employer and employee. It is not an unequivocal ally of the employer in the social control of workers, but neither is it necessarily the workers' friend, whatever the attitudes of individual medical practitioners may be.

Managers, especially those in personnel, tended to mistrust certain medical diagnoses. Another ceramics firm in the area challenged the Family Practitioner Committee by refusing to accept 'debility' as a valid reason for sick leave, while a bakery complained of an excessive number of certificates issued for diarrhoea and vomiting. In Masspro, suspect diagnoses included 'lower back pain', repeated notes for nervous disorders and a long absence for which managers considered there was a string of unrelated causes.

In each case immediately to hand, the issue was whether or not to sanction sick pay. A medical certificate was a more or less guaranteed claim on sick pay, and proved so for the firm who challenged the FPC: it lost its case. However, in the long term, management interpretation of medical certificates (and of course self-certificates too) adds to the biographical knowledge on employees accumulated by supervisors and in personnel files. A reflection of this is that Masspro's employers' liability insurance had been used more frequently to finance severance payments for employees considered unfit for work, than to meet claims made by employees on grounds of industrial injury or disease.

The mistrust surrounding medical certificates also led to occasional attempts by management to gain inside knowledge to crack the codes in which doctors wrote causes of sickness. The personnel director told me without a hint of embarrassment that he was able to telephone many local GPs for amplification of their notes. In one instance only (out of the 1200 medical certificates examined) did the GP clearly signal to the employer that the employee's claim to leave was unjustified: he or she wrote 'LOM', which the personnel manager decoded as 'loss of momentum'. Even so the doctor gave the patient sick leave.

On the other side of the coin, medical practitioners sometimes used coded expressions on certificates that helped the employee, and not only by protecting confidentiality. In the industry-wide agreement on company sick pay, which considerably supplemented the minimum then required by statute, pregnancy was specifically excluded as an acceptable pretext. One device for enabling women to claim was for GPs to write 'hyperemesis' as cause of absence (in this context, morning sickness). Sick pay was also precluded for absences to care for others who were sick, but there were cases in which doctors gave the employee a note for (say) 'anxiety state' in such circumstances. Conversely, three industrial physicians with whom I separately discussed these data expressed outrage that any general practitioner could write 'debility', 'neurasthenia' or 'malaise' on medical certificates, on the grounds that these terms had no medical meaning or had lost it. That these were quite common diagnoses suggests that many GPs met their patients half way when asked for a sick note.

However much they may prefer to do so, medical practitioners cannot avoid being caught up in the ongoing conflict between employer and employee about effort, the conditions under which it can be relaxed, and even the rewards of effort (of which sick pay is after all one aspect).

The doctor/patient relation of 'healing' is the centre-piece of Parsons' model of the sick role (Parsons, 1951, 1958, but see, among many critiques, Alexander, 1982 and Turner and Sampson, 1996). Here sickness is treated as a transitional status. The doctor is the specialist who sanctions separation from normal roles, guides in the period of exclusion and pronounces fitness for return. However, any analogy with rites of passage in traditional societies (van Gennep, 1960) is superficial. For Parsons, the patient enters the sick role individually, voluntarily and with self-interest in taking advice and recovering. The patient is not propelled by custom. It is not appropriate for the community or even close kin to play a part in the process, least of all in the clinical encounter (compare Johns and Xie, 1998, on China). So it is that, in Parsons' thinking, the sick role both resembles the contract of employment and complements it, by regulating temporary deviations in performance at work.

The evidence from the pottery factory lends some support to Parsons' view. Employers were obliged to accept medical rulings. On the other hand, workmates and managers mediated the path to a clinical consultation, and their reaction after sickness was certified did not necessarily endorse the doctor's interpretation, even if that ruling had to be accepted for sickness payment purposes. The pattern was also less uniform for men and women and for people of different ages than Parsons' model of the modern Western sick role suggests.

Accomplishing a Sense of Order

Where there is moral ambiguity, a sense of order has to be accomplished, but if it is to be so, there must be a code that gives individuals some confidence in recognising when a sickness is genuine. The same code can be used deceitfully by a skilled performer to pass malingering as genuine sickness. The code is largely implicit. It consists of a range of types, a vocabulary of the motives of absence as these apply to people with differing social characteristics - men and women, people of different age, managers and workers - who work in different places or types of conditions in the factory.

Gender, Age and Absences - Qualitative Observations

In the pottery factory, both men and women who had the responsibilities that marriage and children imposed were expected to encounter work and its occasional pains stoically, while young people before marriage, especially if male, had certain licence to take time off for pleasure.

> The week before the Potter's holiday, so Bill told me, Steve had 'just upped and offed' to London. To everyone's surprise and the disappointment of Terry, the temp, who thought he had laid claim to Steve's job, Steve reappeared two days after the holiday ended. He told me and the lads over breakfast that his absence before the holiday was due to taking too much beer on three consecutive days, and was spent in bed for the most part, sleeping it off. He was asked what he had told 'them'. He muttered, half apologetically, that he had told them just that (a claim that everyone treated with a show of incredulity). After three days on the beer, he had gone to France, hitch-hiking, and stayed on a farm in Brittany. He spoke with relish of the cheap wine.

> Of a similar good-time lad, a married women in her early forties said, with an indulgent laugh, referring to the young man's complaint that he had a back neck through weightlifting at the weekend and would need to go 'on the club': 'All these young 'uns think about is getting out of work'.

According to the folk-model of the life cycle prevailing in the potbank (Bellaby, 1987b), when a young man started going steady, his responsibility to his 'lady' should restrain his hedonism. The expenses of a new household and the restriction on a wife's earnings expected with the birth of a child, should straiten his conduct further still. Thus a supervisor, promoted from the shop floor in his twenties, reflected on how, with courting, marriage and a family, he had ceased to be a good-time lad. And the weightlifter, referred to in field notes above, told me four years later that he too had settled down, expecting my approval as an elder, as he had earlier wanted me to indulge his tales of sexual exploits, drinking bouts and fights in the street, and sometimes his time-off as a result of these.

Young women prior to marriage had some but far from all of the same licence as young single men. Youthful hedonism was interpreted as proof of incipient manhood - a necessary stage for one who would in due course be ready to 'settle down'. However, the same drinking and sexual freedom in a young woman, carried the risk of being seen as a 'slag' - one who might never settle down herself, and with whom no man might ever want to settle down. 'Slag' was an epithet used more often by women of other women, than by men of women. Thus a young woman of seventeen made an aside to me, when another woman, a little older, had just invited a young man to her party: she was 'no better than she should be'. The discontinuous liminal phase that characterized the passage of young men into the status of responsible adult was much less pronounced for young women. Young women were being prepared day by day to assume the exacting dual roles at work and in the home of what might be called the 'matron'.

The matron was normally sober and chaste. Yet she could have a laugh, swear, make obscene jokes, get drunk at hen parties, flirt with men. What lay beyond bounds, was for a matron to carry on an affair at work. It was forbidden even to flirt if it was to curry favour with management, for managers were considered susceptible to a pretty face and unjust to older women. Deviants made themselves conspicuous and the subject of both female and male gossip. A supervisor, herself married, who was believed to be having an affair with a married manager, was thought to be doing so in order to get a job in management. A young married process worker who gained a much sought after work station was considered to have got her way because the manager fancied her. Thus, being faithful to one's partner went along with being a loyal member of the sisterhood at work. The sisterhood also enforced domestic obligations. Should a member of the matron's family fall ill, die or get married, she was left in no doubt, and rarely felt any, that she must take time off or even give up work to cope with the domestic obligation.

The volume and complexity of relations with family and kin that fell on women, especially married women with children, was readily apparent from the accounts that many fellow workers gave us in diary form for a fortnight after we had ceased to work with them. Men rarely had much to tell about their life outside work except for the odd unusual event, but women had a great deal to tell, most of it routine, not extraordinary. At work, men rarely spoke of their family or kin, and sport was a more significant topic of their conversation, but the difficulties with family and kin that a matron (and even a matron-in-training) might encounter were a major topic of conversation. Whatever the conflicts, a good matron handled the demands upon her competently. One of her competencies was in caring for others in illness and containing her own illness.

So far as a man was concerned, to give in to illness unnecessarily or to take time off without being ill, was to 'skive off'. This was indulged in the young and single man, but seen as a mark of unreliability in others, such as Jim, the odd day off man, who acted in ways that his colleagues considered 'childish'.

So far as a woman was concerned, it was (for example) inappropriate to suffer with 'nerves', unless you were of an age when the change of life might be taken as the cause. A young married women with children had no cause to be depressed, to suffer inwardly, though - like all matrons - she could reasonably have external troubles with her children and partner and share them with work-mates:

> Mary stomped up and down in front of Diana and waved her brush: if Diana had any more time off work, she would smack her with the brush. At lunch, Mary reported that she had asked Diana what was wrong with her, and Diana had replied, 'The same as you.' Mary has been depressed, but says that it is just the change of life. She said to Diana, 'But you are twenty not sixty.' Mary said that she herself had been feeling down, and had cried for most of the holiday, but that she would not take time off work: 'You've got to get out of yourself,' she said, 'you've got to work it off.' Most fellow workers expressed disapproval of Diana's depression. Jean said, 'I'm depressed every time I walk down that gangway, but I've still got to come to work.' She also felt that twenty was too young an age to be depressed, especially when you have just got married.

Diana's depression was as inappropriate to her age as Mary's and Jean's were appropriate to theirs. It is also clear that a good matron was expected to *act* her age, and, depressed or not, bear her suffering stoically. This applied to men with responsibilities too. However, in their case, having an emotional illness might be socially problematic at any age. A man who suffered recurrently from what his medical certificates gave as an 'anxiety state' and had once had two months off for this reason, told me the nature of his illness in confidence, saying that none of his colleagues knew about it and would not understand. What Mary and Jean were prepared to accept as an aging woman's condition was for a man a sign of unmanliness - of being, though a man, a sort of 'old woman'.

Diana's deviance in being ill and also absent because of depression had another counterpart among men in being unable to cope with alcohol and/or taking time-off as a result of it. If men with responsibilities acted as Steve did, they ran the risk of being defined as having a 'drink problem', a fate that was overtaking a middle-aged man with whom I worked, for sightings of him in the pubs were whispered about behind his back, and, though he usually turned in for work afterwards, he was considered to be 'the worse for wear' when he did so. Not being able to hold drink and perform as if it had no effect was judged a sign of either immaturity or being 'over the hill', in either case not *manly*.

Not all men were hard workers/hard drinkers. In the group of nine kilnmen with whom I worked, two shunned the daily ritual of a few pints together at lunch time. One was a quiet and serious man who hastened home to DIY tasks, and sat apart in the canteen in the morning break, reading a conservative broadsheet newspaper, the *Daily Telegraph*, not the usual tabloids. The other did eat with colleagues. However, he made the tea for everyone else and was the butt of humour about how tight he was with money, how subject he was to his wife's instructions, and how much of an over-achiever he was at work. Jim - the odd-day-off man - sought acceptance by contrasting this man's puritanism with his own readiness to down a pint.

Non-drinking or merely occasional drinking was relatively common among women and alcohol was not part of womanhood as it was of manhood. Two marked minorities of men approached drinking in this way. The first was largely white and included managers and workers. These were amateur athletes in training to run the marathon, which was quite a significant feature in the Potteries calendar. The second was Muslim men of South Asian background who abstained from drink throughout the year and fasted in daylight hours during the festival of Ramadan. Women, athletes, Muslims and hard workers/hard drinkers shared the stoicism that made it preferable not to be absent from work in the event of illness, and marked out the frequent absentee as either immature or over the hill.

Gender, Age and Absence - Quantitative Observations

The effect of these conventions on absence in the event of illness can be seen from interviews with representative samples of shop floor workers and managers and supervisors. They were asked about disability days and absences in the fortnight before the interview. These were confidential interviews in private and occurred with shop floor workers after the investigators had made themselves known, but before they were allocated to the work groups with whom they did participant observation. Interviews with managers and supervisors occurred after the investigation of work groups (Figure 5.1 below).

Many days were reported on which people were absent but not sick, and many on which they were sick but worked rather than took time off. Sickness absence - that is, being sick and absent - accounted for rather less than half the disability days and half the absences overall. However, young men and women (under 30) reported many more absences than days of disability. Older men and women reported many more disability days than absences. The male managers did the same,[9] but most of them were 30 or over - it was not a mark of managerial status, as many of them thought it was. Indeed, the rate of being sick and absent was lowest among shop floor workers of 30-44, and highest among managers and supervisors, though this may have been an effect of the different fortnight in which managers and supervisors reported. Absences reported on interview by

---

9   I have singled out men because there were too few women managers and supervisors (16 were interviewed) to form a comparison group.

Figure 5.1 Sickness and absence reported over two weeks by shop floor workers and managers

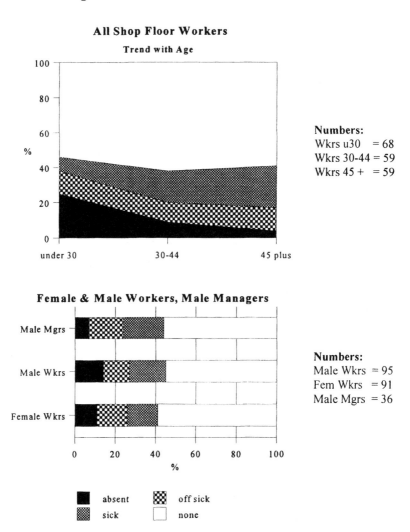

shop floor workers were corroborated from absence registers. However, most absences were accompanied by self or medical certificates and most of the reasons were personal sickness (80% for men, 73% for women), even when respondents had said on interview that sickness was not the cause.

We traced absence records from department registers for each member of the initial sample of 107 men and 104 women on the shop floor for up to three years - 1981-3. This enabled us to collect more reliable data on absence and to offset the possible bias inherent in asking for reports from the 89% we could find and persuade to be interviewed over a one month period when some of those not interviewed may have been absent throughout. Most of the initial sample had been employed for this length of time in the company. The men had a total of 619 episodes in the period or just under two (1.93) per head per year; while the women had a total of 1,283 episodes or just over four (4.11) per head per annum. Men in the sample lost 3.1 percent of working days per annum and women nearly 5.5 percent (based on a 230 day working year).

In April 1983, before our fieldwork began at Masspro, Employers' Statutory Sickness Payment (ESSP) was introduced. The effect was that employers now paid benefit directly for up to two months. Previously employees had to apply to the state social security department. Employers continued to deduct contributions for National Insurance from employees' wages and to make their own contributions as required in law. However, now they could reclaim the statutory element of the sickness payment from the state.

Until the introduction of ESSP, there was a three day waiting period before an absentee could apply for sickness benefit from social security. For one year beforehand, medical certificates were required only for absences of more than seven consecutive days (including the weekend). Previously they had been required for absences of more than three days. BCMF and CATU agreed at this point to require people to certify their own absences of more than three but fewer than eight consecutive days. They had earlier agreed an industry-wide scheme for sickness payment. It was to exceed statutory sickness benefit and guaranteed four fifths of the basic wage.

Both before and after self-certification was introduced in April 1982, short absences (of one to three days) were 'unexcused' and were marked as such on the registers. Throughout the period that included these changes, men took a marginally smaller proportion of their absences in the 'unexcused' or short form than women, but the more marked variation was with age. Men under 30 took 1.24 short for every longer absence, and women under 30 0.91 short for every longer absence. There was a sharp change among men of 30-44, among whom the ratio fell to 0.44, only to rise to almost 1:1 among the oldest groups of men. Women's tendency to take short absences rather than long fell consistently with age. This pattern is consistent with the argument that as people acquire the responsibilities of a family so they are less likely to be absent if they do not have to be. One person gave the lie to what 'responsibility' meant when he said that he was not like other men of his age: he preferred to have no car and to rent a house than own it and have to repay a mortgage, because then he was free to take time off when he felt like it. This construction bears much more on the absence of men in parenting years than of women, because child care puts women under equal and opposite pressure to take time off for child care.

For comparative purposes, probably the most comprehensive source of information on sickness absence in Britain is the Labour Force Survey. Clarke, Elliott and Osman (1995) have reanalysed its results for 1987-91. Though they are principally concerned with occupational differences, their findings overlap with those from the pottery factory on age and gender. Thus, higher sickness absence was found among women in all occupational groups except farming, fishing and related. Our estimates for the sample from Masspro's registers are only slightly lower than the 3.8 percent of days lost per annum for men and 6.0 percent for women, that are derived from the 1987-91 LFS sample for the occupational group within which potters appear (XI, see Clarke *et al.*, 1995, Table 13.2). In similar vein, in the LFS shorter absences are found to be more common among younger than older workers. However, managers were not less likely to be absent than shop floor workers, whereas the LFS has a rate around half that of Occupational Group XI for managerial staff of all kinds (that is, Occupational Group V). Our figures were based on small numbers at interview at a single point in the year and we did not have access to the same run of years of absence for managerial as for hourly paid employees.

The Vocabulary of Reasons for Absence

We examined certificates for absence supplied by the sample of hourly paid, shop floor workers throughout Masspro over a three year period - 1981 to 1983. These were kept in personnel records. We classified the causes for absences recorded on both self-certificates and medical certificates, using the Royal College of General Practitioners' classification for diseases and injuries, and developing our own for other causes. Sometimes individuals had more than one certificate for the same cause. Sometimes a single certificate gave more than one cause. I have adjusted the number of self-certificates to the equivalent over three years, so that it is comparable with the number of medical certificates. Figure 5.2 separates the absences of men and women and focuses on personal sickness as a cause. The greater volume of personal sickness among women than men (almost exactly 2:1) is conveyed by the area of the pie-charts, and the divisions in each represent the percentage of causes of different kinds.

The two main causes for both men and women are respiratory (mainly upper respiratory tract) and gastro-enterological diseases, and they account for almost half the certified causes for both sexes. They are largely common infectious diseases. The next largest group for both is musculo-skeletal. When trauma (injury) is taken out, the percentages of all personal sickness attributable to other

Figure 5.2 Certified reasons for absence 1981-3

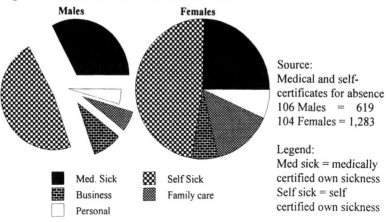

Males   Females

Source:
Medical and self-
certificates for absence
106 Males   =   619
104 Females = 1,283

Legend:
Med sick = medically
certified own sickness
Self sick = self
certified own sickness

Med. Sick   Self Sick
Business   Family care
Personal

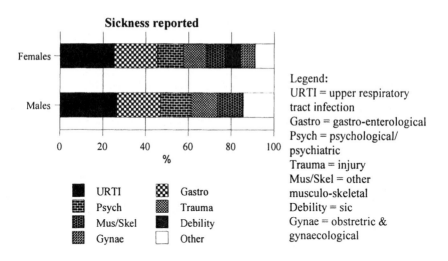

Sickness reported

Females

Males

0   20   40   60   80   100
%

Legend:
URTI = upper respiratory
tract infection
Gastro = gastro-enterological
Psych = psychological/
psychiatric
Trauma = injury
Mus/Skel = other
musculo-skeletal
Debility = sic
Gynae = obstretric &
gynaecological

URTI   Gastro
Psych   Trauma
Mus/Skel Debility
Gynae   Other

musculo-skeletal diseases, such as arthritis, are similar for men and women. However, a much higher proportion of men's sickness is attributed to injury, and their incidence of injury is almost twice as high as that of women (162 per 1000 per annum as against 92). Psychological conditions account for almost as large a slice of personal sickness for men as injuries and more than they do for women, but women have a slightly higher incidence of psychological conditions (209 per 1000 per annum, as against 156 for men). Debility is a much more common condition among women than men, though slight in the overall pattern of their personal sickness. It should probably be added to obstetric and gynaecological factors, for it is a euphemism used by some GPs for period problems. Conditions specifically mentioned under that heading account for 1 in 11 of women's absences, and their unique presence among women accounts for only a small part (about 20%) of the excess of women's absences over those of men. Finally, 'other conditions' can be divided into specific and unspecific. Unspecific ones account for similar proportions of men's and women's causes of absence, but specific causes (such as gall stones) account for more of women's than of men's.

Also of interest is that women are rather more likely than men to certify their own condition, with the result that the ratio of medically certified causes of absence for women to those of men is 1.7:1, but of self-certified causes is 2.4:1. Both men and women show a substantially more than average tendency to certify their own debility, gastro-enterological and unspecific other conditions, rather than refer them to a doctor, which is a function of the fact that self-certificates cover either short absences or the early part of long absences. Both are more than usually likely to have injuries and *specific* other conditions mentioned on a medical certificate than on their self certificate. The same applies to obstetric and gynaecological and psychological conditions for women, and to non-injury related musculo-skeletal conditions for men (many of them unspecific back pain).

Finally, women are more likely than men to give reasons other than personal sickness for their absences. While 19.9% of men's causes of absence were in this category, 27.5% of women's were so, and of course the disparity is much larger when given in terms of incidence: men had 305 such reasons for absence per 1000 per annum, but women 973. For women, just over half the incidence of non-personal sickness absences were attributed to care for family or kin, and just under a quarter were called 'personal'. For men, just under half were put down to 'domestic' causes, and just under a third to care of family and kin, which was excluded from 'domestic'. Women were almost as likely to take time off to look after someone else as they were to be absent because of their own gastro-intestinal upset (509 per 100 per annum, as against 548).

In summary, men and women share around half of their reasons for absence in equal measure: the common infectious diseases. Yet, the ratio of women's to men's causes for absence is about 2:1. Conditions unique to women account for no more than 20% of the difference, suggesting that it has more to do with gender roles, inside and outside the workplace, than biological sex. Men are more likely to be off because of injury than women, and women more likely to be off than men because of 'other specific' diseases. Some of these differences between men and women seem to reflect their respective occupations, some their respective lifestyles. Women are much more likely than men to take time off to care for family and kin, or at least much more likely to report that they have done so to management.

Given the fact that men are more likely to be absent through injury than women, it is of interest to estimate days of absence attributable to injury. The Labour Force Survey of 1990 carried a Health and Safety Executive trailer questionnaire on injuries in the course of work (see Chapter 4). That provides an estimate of 21.1mn days lost to a total workforce of 23.5mn through injuries arising in the course of work, i.e. 0.9 per head per annum (Stevens, 1992).

Clarke, Elliott & Osman (in Drever, 1995) estimate that nationally men lose 2.7% and women 3.4% of days in absence, using LFS surveys for the run of years 1987-91. Taking account of the balance of men and women in the labour force and the proportion of women who work part time, a base can be derived for calculating that around 15% of all days lost in sickness are attributable to injuries received in the course of work.

Embodiment, Spatiality and Absence - Implicit Meanings

In Chapter 3, it was shown that space at the extremes of hot and dry and cold and wet had different significance to those who worked in them than did those in-between, and in Chapter 4 it was shown how the first kind were associated with toughening and the second with weakening the constitution. Again, if the job allowed movement between extremes and through in-between spaces, this was seen as offering protection that being seated or standing permanently in the contradictory climates of the in-between spaces did not afford.

I have stressed that one should not expect a one-to-one correspondence between illness, however generated, and sickness absence. However, there were relationships between days off for sickness and the type of space in which people worked.

We drew on departmental registers of absence over a three year period for the three separate units that comprised the Masspro production strength. The statistical base was large. Each individual had some 1,440 half-day work spells from any of which he or she could be could absent. Departments varied in size from around 10 to 50 people, but there was one of each kind for each of the three units that comprised Masspro. Our participant observation in the four different work groups reported above enabled us to check all absences recorded in our diaries with absences in the registers over three months for each group. There was no misreporting, for hourly paid staff had to clock in.

The results correspond to those for illth and illness. Men at the 'toughening' extremes - in the sliphouse and kilns - lost an average of 7.4 working days per head per annum over the three years that they were monitored, and their counterparts on the move in despatch lost 6.5 days. In contrast women (all in spaces in-between) lost 13.8 days. Men working in similar in-between spaces lost as many as 10.6 days on average, more than their counterparts either at the extremes or on the move.

Both men and women in spaces in-between had an average of one episode per annum of at least eleven days long (more than two working weeks) per four persons; men in the sliphouse and kilns had one such episode every seven persons, and those in despatch had one for every twelve persons. The men in despatch had fewer relatively long absences than the men in the sliphouse and kilns, but they made up in the comparison by taking considerably more one-day absences - 2.3 per head as opposed to 0.8.

We also examined the pretexts for absence cited on sick notes by the random sample. The distribution of pretexts for absence on the sick notes reflected the symbolic meanings ascribed to the various work spaces. Kiln and sliphouse workers reported injuries on sick notes about twice as often as the average. They typically saw industrial injuries as *accidents*, akin to acts of God or even campaign wounds (Green, 1997). Nevertheless, they had only a third as many reports of unspecific lower back pain as the screen printers (one of the major groups of men working in spaces in-between).

In sum the records of absence and sickness notes provide quantitative support for the qualitative analysis of the relation between embodiment and spatiality that our field notes generated.

Conclusion

In this chapter, I have considered how ill-health and injury at work is made social, becoming, in a specific sense of the term, 'sickness'. Sickness is public representation rather than private experience. Other things being equal, when known to be sick, an individual should be indulged and granted leave from normal obligations. However, this is a zone of moral ambiguity. Leave is not freely given. It is conditional on seeking to recover and return to the normal pattern, and on more, being seen as a 'genuine' case. One who *takes* leave frequently - in the sense of being absent - risks being seen as in the wrong, and thus undermining their credit for the future. It is not surprising, then, that negotiating sickness absence entails recourse to a vocabulary of acceptable reasons, which depend on gender, age, management or worker status and the area in which one works.

People who are ill do not necessarily take time off. 'Soldiering on' or being stoical is a cultural performance with strong resonance, especially in the Protestant tradition. Not all traditions require stoicism, but the regulatory function of the sick role may well be universal. Lewis (1975) has shown, in the Gnau, a

Sepik people of New Guinea, a society in which the sick role operates even without specialist healers, so profoundly modifying Parsons' original model. In the late modern West, professional health workers *are* invoked, but not in most cases, and, where sickness at work is concerned, only after the performance is well advanced before an audience of lay people.

In Chapter 1, I speculated about the differing circumstances in which sickness absence would appear often and rarely, and identified the contest for control of time at work between managers and workers as a likely area to search. This search is the subject of the next chapter.

6 Bodies Off Sick: The Control of Time

But thought's the slave of life, and life time's fool;
And time, that takes survey of all the world,
Must have a stop.
William Shakespeare, 1564-1616, *Henry IV Part 1*, Act iv.

Employment is a relation of power, not merely a contract. The employer has a clear interest in getting the employee to put effort into the job, and gaining that compliance involves rewards and punishments. Employees have an equally clear interest in conserving their capacity for labour, because, without it, they cannot continue to make a living. At its most basic, these divergent interests entail a struggle to control *time*. Time at work (or in any other activity) has both internal and external aspects. 'Internal' time includes the deadlines for the completion of tasks and the tempo and beat of the process, while 'external' time is time which elapses while work is going on - time lost for alternative activities and, by the same token, time that is recovered by absence from work.

Control of time internal to work - being able to take breaks electively or pace one's own work - enables people to accommodate many otherwise disabling symptoms, physical or mental. If that control is lacking, for instance because the pace of the job is controlled by a machine, even trivial suffering (boredom included) can come to seem intolerable. Other things being equal, the sufferers will take time off.

What is not always equal is the penalty that may have to be paid for absence. For instance, in a weak labour market, where jobs are few and applicants many, employers are likely to have greater control of absences - that is, of use of time external to work. Employers will tend to oversee absence and penalize 'malingering' as best they can. They may make the penalties of absence, especially repeated absence, prohibitive to those who need to earn at a consistent level to pay a mortgage or must hold onto the job they have for lack of others.

In a relatively strong labour market, such as that of the 1960s, Baldamus (1961) proposes that taking time off can be understood as an element in the unwritten 'effort bargain' between employer and employee. Employment contracts may state explicitly the number of hours an employee must work and

114

the holiday entitlements and payment he or she is entitled to. They rarely, if ever, specify the effort an employer can demand within the hours laid down. Where employees individually, and even more so trade unions, are able to counter the employer's power, relatively high levels of absenteeism may be written into the baseline calculations of employers for the labour they require and individuals who are frequently absent or absent for long periods may be protected from dismissal without consultation.

Control of Time and Absence[10]

In the pottery, control over time in their work was restricted both for kiln-emptiers and for workers on the production lines (most makers, handlers and glazers). But it was more restricted for the latter. On the lines, toilet relief was an habitual focus of discontent for workers and supervisors alike. Any unusual need for relief was unlikely to be satisfied. Even a cold could be incapacitating, because the worker could not wipe a dripping nose and keep up with the line. Furthermore, the pace of the line was pre-set. Breakdowns might provide temporary relief, and were sometimes contrived with that in view. More often, they occurred accidentally and caused frustration because the workers' rhythm was disrupted, and the habitual dissociation of mind from work was broken, like arousal from deep sleep.

Kiln-emptying was repetitive and fast, but it did offer more control of time both to individuals and to the work group as a whole. The emptiers were, as they called it, 'on contract' to clear nearly 100 trucks each shift for a fixed payment (which is equal for all members), and then leave work when they finished, not (like the women) when the clock reached a set time. They were proud of having forced this arrangement on management, who had now come to see it as mutually advantageous (though they were actually direct employees not sub-contractors). The emptiers aimed to leave work in time for dinner or a drink at the pub down the road on a Friday (around 1:00 pm). They worked together to this end. There was a pace-maker. Slower members (like Alan, who had an epileptic seizure at work (pp.94-5 above)) often came to work a little earlier than the others to do their share.

The effects of this variation in control of time by individual and work group upon absences were palpable. Between 1981 and 1983, emptiers lost half the

---

10   Aspects of the argument of this chapter are discussed in presenting a critique of stress and coping discourse and offering a sociological alternative in Bellaby, 1986.

days of process workers, and had fewer episodes, both single days and longer periods (see Figure 6.1).

Workers on the production lines were closely supervised. A department of some 40 people had five supervisors, four managers and two quality control officials. The emptiers, however, shared a single manager with some 30 other kiln workers distributed among three shifts, some of which continued seven days of the week.

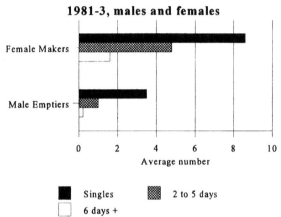

Figure 6.1 Average episodes of absence:

1981-3, males and females

On the initiative of the personnel director, a team identity programme had been introduced throughout the firm. On the shop floor, each team's production performance was recorded on their own notice board in full view of the members, changing from day to day. As an experienced manager noted, the workers on the lines attended closely to the notice board. The emptiers, however, considered theirs an irrelevance. If they needed a manager, as they did for Alan's seizure, they called the manager in. Otherwise they were their own bosses. The team's performance board, which the process workers see as an access to their meagre control over their work, emptiers view as an intrusion on their liberties.

Since process workers are women and kiln-emptiers are men, the difference in absence may be due not to work organization, but to gender roles outside work. In order to control for gender, we investigated a third work group that made up of men and women in roughly equal numbers. They all did similar work - glazing. One section worked on machine paced lines, much like the coffee mug lines, where glaze was sprayed automatically onto ware as it passed through a tunnel along a conveyer belt, though half the workers were men in this case. The other section (again equally divided by sex) involved work either individually or in small teams, where control could be exerted over stops and starts and overall pace. Here glaze was either sprayed onto ware or ware was dipped into glaze. In each section men and women lost similar numbers of days from 1981 to 1983 and had similar numbers of episodes of absence, but the machine-paced workers lost twice as many days as the self-paced workers. Figure 6.2A shows average

Figure 6.2A Average episodes of absence:

1981-3, males

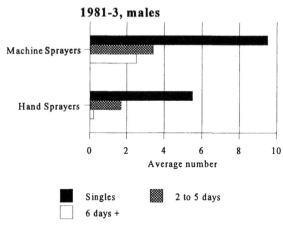

Figure 6.2B Percentage of days lost:

1981-3, males and females

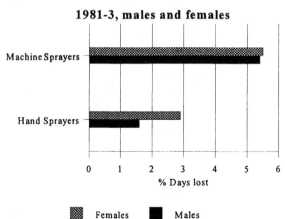

number of episodes of absence and Figure 6.2B the proportion of days lost per worker per annum.

Thus, the third work group confirmed that how far workers controlled time internal to work affected men and women in similar ways, whatever the differences in absence that might be attributed to gender roles (see above, pp.102 -112).

Messing *et al.*, 1996) reached a similar conclusion from a study of 560 men and 790 women in 17 poultry slaughterhouses in France. They found that women were absent with sickness more often than men overall, but largely because they had very different working conditions, not because of gender itself.

Experiments in Changing Work Organization at Masspro

After we had completed the major study of sickness and pottery work (Bellaby, 1987a), Masspro invited us to make experimental changes to the way coffee mug production was organized in two of their production units and to monitor the results (Bellaby, 1985). The general basis on which changes were to be made was the findings of the major study and subsequent examination of the firm's quality control records.

As was shown above, absence appeared to be related, both statistically and in process, to the degree to which employees could control time at work, and thus expenditure of effort. Men rarely did jobs in which they were as restricted as women commonly were. Where men and women did equally restricted jobs their absence levels were both relatively high. A retrospective comparison of quality control data with absence records for making departments revealed that, under some conditions, high levels of absence were associated with reduced quality and increased losses. This was particularly true of processes requiring several consecutive handlings of the ware, for the absence of experienced operatives might have a marked effect there. The two findings together led to the hypothesis that, if operatives had greater control of time in their work, absence would be reduced and quality and losses improved. There was a preliminary investigation to establish how great a change in production indicators the company would require to realize a significant financial advantage.

A further observation from the earlier study was that when the work group had autonomy from management, it often imposed its own discipline on potential absentees. It did so, for instance, when the whole group benefited by everyone being present: in one set of circumstances (the kiln emptiers) this was where the quicker the job was completed the sooner everyone could leave the workplace. We assumed that this solidarity could be harnessed by inviting work-groups to suggest changes that might benefit them, and - as far as possible - putting the groups in control of the day to day running of the experiments.

Accordingly, we set up and monitored experiments in which work was redesigned on the moving line, to enlarge line workers' control over when they came and went to work and when they took breaks in the working day. The three experiments were set up on lines that made and glazed coffee mugs, before sending them for firing in the kilns and selection prior to further decoration and/or packing.

One of the three experiments was agreed upon jointly by management and workers (the change of hours trial). The second was set up to a pattern suggested by the women working in that area, and, indeed, remained substantially in their collective control (the added relief worker trial). The third was initiated by production management (the deseaming trial). We chose small groups only for the experiments. This was partly to minimize the direct costs and the possible consequences of failure for the company. It was also partly to ensure that we could monitor the experiments effectively. Each group worked on a separate production line.

The Designs of Individual Trials

Change of hours trial The women suggested a change in hours of work: from

8.00am-4.45pm on Monday to Thursday, with an hour earlier to finish on Friday, to a 7.30 start Monday to Friday and a much earlier (12.30pm) finish on Friday. The women involved said this early finish on Friday would 'make time' for them. Thus, the focus of the proposed change was time external rather than internal to work. More time on Friday made the domestic side of their dual role more manageable. Some of the women involved had children, but none was completely dependent. If responsible for or contributing to a household, they could shop or do the washing well in advance of the weekend rush. If they did not have pressing domestic responsibilities, they saw the free Friday afternoon as time in which to refresh themselves after work, so as to enjoy a night out or the weekend's leisure. Because of technical constraints, the hours were collective, not individually variable as 'flexi-hours' would be. Keeping to them called for varying sacrifices by individuals in the morning when they were required to turn in half an hour earlier than in the past. In every other respect, the line was unchanged, and the experiment cost the firm nothing. But the change cut across several lift-sharing arrangements among employees.

Added relief worker trial This grew out of the investigations of a quality circle. The members suggested adding a 'relief worker' to the team. Her job would be to take over from others whenever they needed a break, not at pre-set times, as was the case when supervisors relieved line workers. An effect of the relief worker would be to allow the supervisor to supervise all the time, attending to supplies and to quality. Also built into this experiment was the idea that the relief worker should be chosen by and acceptable to the group as a whole, and that this job could be rotated as the group decided. Of course it added the wages of one person (per shift) to the direct costs of the firm. The direct cost (including superannuation and national insurance) was £114 per week for full time workers.

Deseaming trial In this case, women did not have collective control of the original idea or of the conduct of the experiment. On the other hand, for some on the line, at least, the change introduced did increase their control of their effort during time on the job. The change separated two jobs previously done by one person: 'deseaming' by machine the previously moulded handles, and 'handling' - sticking the handles to the mugs with a smear of slip. Deseaming was taken off the line, and handles were stock piled for use by handlers on the line. Deseamers could now work at their own pace, though often more quickly than if they had been both deseaming and handling, as in the past. An incidental though very important effect was that three deseaming machines, instead of the usual four, were kept in use on the line, with the fourth usually standing idle, pending a breakdown in one of the others. This should mean that downtime was reduced significantly. While the added relief worker trial required one extra worker, the deseaming trial required two extra workers and a corresponding cost of £218 per week for full time workers.

Monitoring the effects   The effects of the changes were monitored for three months and in two ways: first, by asking people on the line at regular intervals about the impact the changes had made and whether it was in their interests or against them; second, by collecting data on absence, lateness, the quantity of production and quality and wastage. Quantitative assessments were controlled by comparing the run of data for the three months of each experiment with the corresponding run for the previous year on that line, and with a simultaneous run for a closely similar production line in the same unit. The controls were as close as we could make them, because we knew that numerous changes would be made in raw materials, moulds and decorative effects in the course of three months and might occur in absence figures because of seasonal effects. None of these changes would be within our control, for experiments in a factory are a far cry from the conditions of the laboratory.

A Qualitative Assessment

Change of hours trial   Every worker involved in the experiment thought it had been successful and would have liked to see the early start system made permanent. Several people had initially stated that they were reluctant to get up any earlier, but, in the event, they quickly got used to this and said that the extra half-hour at work each day was now scarcely noticeable. At first, there was an increase in the number of workers who were slightly late each morning, but this problem was foreseen by management and was soon remedied.

This change in working hours seems a relatively minor one, yet the effect on people's lives was marked. As one worker put it, 'We now have a four and a half day week and a two and a half day weekend'. Many people claimed that the atmosphere on the line had improved - it was a happier place to work and people felt more of a team. Some of this was undoubtedly due simply to the fact of being involved in an experiment, but some sense of a lightened load did seem directly attributable to the changed hours themselves. A frequently used phrase was, 'We have something to look forward to'. The feeling of tiredness which often hit workers by Wednesday was seen as less severe because, looking forward, Thursday was pay day and Friday was only half a day. On the glazing line especially, the workers seemed to be setting out to impress with their approval of the scheme and to stress that they had thought it made them feel more of a team. On the line as a whole, two people said they thought it had reduced their absenteeism because they could make arrangements for Friday afternoons which would normally have required time off.

However, no-one claimed that their job was more interesting or enjoyable, or that they felt that they had established a better relationship with management. In terms of an increase in quality and production, only one person saw the experiment as having a beneficial effect; about one third of the line saw the experiment as having no effect in these areas and about another third thought that, over the period of the experiment, counts and quality may have been low and were at pains to point out that this was not the fault of the experiment, but was caused by mechanical difficulties outside their control.

A more positive aspect of the experiment was the line's willingness to cooperate in trying something new and in adjusting personal timetables. In spite of some complaints about transport difficulties and, in one case, some loss of overtime earnings, there was a sense of commitment to the scheme which was regarded as an attempt to improve working conditions and to improve the quality of leisure time.

Added relief worker trial This scheme was adopted with enthusiasm by most people on the line and continued to work very successfully. One or two women had originally not felt that they would benefit much but, as time went by, became enthusiastic about the way their day had been altered by the system (although in the beginning the added worker had to teach them how to use the system by encouraging them to take extra breaks).

The advantages of having an added relief worker were variously seen by the women on the line as: a happier atmosphere on the line; less tiredness; less boredom; less need to take time off work; a greater sense of freedom associated with being taken off the machine at will, rather than at a set time; less dependence on the supervisor; and improvements in the quantity and quality of the ware.

Without underestimating these improvements, it should be pointed out that where people had felt that their job was boring and tiring they still felt this to be intrinsically true. The effect of the relief system was to make it all more easy to cope with. As one worker expressed it, 'It makes a lot of difference to the way you feel at work: you don't feel so penned in. But it doesn't alter the way you feel about coming to work'.

Although no one expressed it in these terms, it was obvious to an outsider that the people on the line became more articulate and confident, willing to talk about their work and offer opinions. They admitted, too, that some differences of opinion had occurred about how the system should operate, but these seem to have been ironed out over time. The personality of the relief worker herself was clearly important. She must be able to get on with the other workers and be capable of performing all the jobs efficiently, as well as ensuring a fair distribution of time off from various machines.

As the system continued it clearly made the women on the line more interdependent and aware of the need to operate as a team. At the same time it gave them more control over their effort in time internal to work, and allowed them to make choices among themselves, rather than having them superimposed by the supervisor's schedule. The supervisor gained greatly from the system. Freed from the need to take everyone off the machine twice daily, she too had more control over her time and could devote greater attention to improving quality.

The experiment had another unexpected advantage, which the line was quick to recognize and make use of. As the position of added worker was rotated and some workers undertook different jobs, it became apparent that they performed better and were happier than the original incumbent. This meant that by exploring the skills and preferences of each worker, improvements could be made in quantity and quality.

Deseaming trial This experiment was set up on a managerial initiative following a long-running trial in another unit which had produced marked improvements in quality and quantity. We were not involved in monitoring this experiment until it had been under way for some time and so were unable to record the initial reaction to its introduction.

In the early weeks some alterations were made to both the speed of the deseaming machines and the way the handlers and deseamers operated. At first, each of the three handlers had as partner a deseamer who had to keep up a handle stock and take the handler off for toilet breaks. When we first interviewed the women, it was obvious that the line was a most unhappy place. The women who were new to the line declared themselves satisfied with the experiment, but the original workers at the clay end were exceedingly upset by it. They felt that it destroyed team identity, worked against a cooperative spirit and physically exhausted them. They all thought that the experiment was successful in terms of production, but that it required more effort from them than they could possibly maintain. The tension on the line produced personality clashes and arguments.

At this point, an attempt was made by the handlers and the deseamers to reorganize themselves on a happier basis. Each handler handled for one hour only and then swapped with the deseamer to deseam for the next hour, whereupon they would swap back again. This turn and turn about approach produced a more settled and cooperative atmosphere among the handlers and deseamers, who now found the system acceptable.

The extra ware produced by the line placed a heavier burden upon the three glazing end workers but none of them complained or said that they found it impossible to cope. The burden on the maker and the emptier appeared to be greater and was deeply felt. They were worried that it would have an adverse effect upon their health. To reduce this problem, where possible other workers provided them with extra breaks.

For a time the line seemed calmer as the experiment settled in, but when the experiment continued after our period of monitoring, further eruptions of dissatisfaction were reported to us. In general the line lacked the buoyancy of the other experimental lines. While this experiment had produced a certain flexibility for the handlers and the deseamers, it had not had similar benefits for the other workers. Nor had it improved the atmosphere on the line, fostered team identity or positively altered attitudes to work. Workers and supervisors on the other lines all acknowledged that the system produced gains in production terms, but criticized the wear and tear on the people involved. All said that they preferred the added relief worker system, which was beneficial to both workers and supervisors as well as to productivity.

Quantitative Assessment of the Trials

The trials were carried out in the two units in which coffee mugs were produced. The results led Masspro to adopt the added relief worker for future production, a pattern continued by new management after the takeover of the company. Productivity, as measured by the number of pieces per week per head that were classed as 'bests', rather than all the product, 'seconds' and rejects included, was marginally higher on the added relief worker line, dissection faults much less common and absenteeism substantially less, than on the deseaming trial line.

A multivariate analysis of all the measurable factors influencing outcomes over time showed that technology - especially breakdowns - determined the variation in numbers of the product, though the human factor - lates and absences - had a definite impact on quality (Bellaby, 1985). Given that the deseaming trial removed a major breakdown bottleneck on production lines of this type, it is not surprising that total weekly output (bests, seconds and rejects) should be higher on the deseaming trial line than on the added relief worker line (15.7 as against 14.9 thousands). In spite of this, quality output per head was slightly higher on the added relief worker line than on the deseaming trial line, implying that an improvement was brought about by the extent to which this trial released workers' time to attend to quality . It should be noted that the changed hours trial was in a unit whose production was of higher value in the market but needed more workers because of the number of decorative effects involved - this accounts for its much lower productivity. Table 6.1 summarises the balance sheet.

Table 6.1 The balance sheet for the trials

	Low Value Units		High Value Unit
	Deseaming trial	Added relief worker	Change of hours
Number of Workers	11	10	21
-added	+2	+1	0
Cost of absenteeism per head/per week	£17.25	£5.93	£3.42
-increase/decrease 1984 to 1985	+£12.81	-£1.25	-£1.03
Productivity during trials per week	1110.4	1122.0	364.0
Dissection faults over target	1.98	1.31	2.12

For each of the three months of the trial and the month after it finished, the added relief worker trial progressively improved the percentage of bests, by 6 percentage points overall. The deseaming trial added conspicuously to the count, but quality remained more or less level, having achieved a plateau in the first month. For the first two months, this line ran level for count and wasted a high volume of clay, but, in the succeeding two months, clay loss was halved, and the count increased by 2,500 a week overall. The turn-around in performance corresponds to the reports of women who worked on the line that were noted above. They reorganized work among themselves to cope better with the relentless flow of production that the removal of the breakdown bottleneck had brought. This adds further to the argument that the human factor played a significant part in quality of product.

The outstanding quantitative advantages of the added relief worker trial lay in reduced absenteeism and a smaller number of dissection faults in the product. Absenteeism increased considerably by comparison with the previous year on the deseaming trial line (from 3.9% days lost to 15.1%), while it fell slightly on the added relief worker line (from 6.3% days lost to 5.2%). The trials lend weight to added relief worker line (from 6.3% days lost to 5.2%). The trials lend weight to the evidence already reported for the proposition that control of effort in time internal to work is one of the keys to low absence, for the deseaming trial reduced that control for all on the line, with the exception of deseamers (whose work was detached from the line), while the added relief worker trial increased it.

A lower number of faults was found on dissection of sample kiln trucks of fired ware on the added relief worker line than on others. This finding appears to be consistent with my explanation of how the human factor may affect production, for increased control of time would enable workers to play closer attention to faults and eliminate waste in the course of production. There was an average of 1.31 faults over target on the added relief worker line, but 1.98 on the deseaming trial line. The two lines monitored as controls in the same unit produced more than two faults above target on average. The added relief worker line also achieved no faults or only one above target on 68 percent of days in the trials, while the three others in the unit managed this on only between 27 percent and 8 percent of days.

Examination of the types of fault found at dissection reveals the specific effects the various experiments had. Thus the deseaming trial improved on the average performance for 'bits' left on the handles of mugs: because handlers no longer had to deseam handles before attaching them, they could attend more closely to the quality of the handles they attached. On the other hand, this trial so far increased the count, and therefore the uninterrupted pace of the line, that 'nipped' faults were above average (a 'nip' is a chip in the beaker part of the mug). The added relief worker allowed both operatives and supervisor to attend more closely to quality: as a result fewer 'finger' marks occurred on the ware and fewer mugs were placed ready for firing with excess glaze that would cause them to be 'stuck' to the kiln placer's cranks on which they stood for firing. It was suggested that the quality-mindedness engendered by this trial may also have caused a reduction in the normal count, as the supervisor stopped the line to remove faulty ware. The change of hours trial may also have had a specific impact on faults. In spite of the greater degree of handling of ware that occurred than on the line's 'control', it had fewer mugs that emerged 'knocked' and fewer with handles that were 'sprung' (or became detached in firing) than average.

In the trial which changed hours it is difficult to assess the effect on productivity, if indeed it had any such effect, for the trial line was quite different from others. There was a small fall in productivity as compared with the same three months in the previous year. This was entirely attributable to a reduction in the count, which, was heavily dependent on the smooth operation of the machinery. Quality actually rose (from 71.4% bests to 75.7%). However, the striking effect of the change of hours trial was on absenteeism. At 3% days lost this was but a fifth of the level on the deseaming trial line during the trial period, and represented a small fall (from 3.9%) as compared with the same period the previous year.

The trials have a family resemblance to the many other 'job redesign' exercises. One might expect exercises in job enrichment that increase productivity to lead to reductions in the workforce, as employers take advantage of increased productivity to cut labour costs. The added relief worker trial at Masspro seems to have squared the circle by adding to the workforce while improving quality enough to produce a return on the employer's extra investment. Even gains in quality, however, may ultimately lead to job cuts, should they enable a smaller volume to be sold for an equivalent profit. The deseaming trial shows that there is also competition for human factor solutions from technology, which can lead to further fragmentation of jobs and restriction of control over time for workers. It would be naive, therefore, to think that benefits for workers can be easily won from changes in work organization.

The trials were imperfect experiments, for other lines could not, in the event, be treated as exact controls, because of unexpected technical and organizational differences between them. Even so, the quantitative results make sense in the light of evidence from the first phase of the potteries study and in relation to the testimony of women involved in the trials. Not least, the results fit well with the theoretical argument that has been developed about sickness absence and its relation to control of time.

Taking Time Off with Impunity[11]

While control of time *internal* to work makes a difference to rates of absence, its impact could be masked if the employee had little control of time *external* to work. Lack of control of external time might cut in either direction. Women with dependent children and kin may have a prior responsibility to take time off to care for them when needed, rather than attend work (pp.102-5 above). Conversely, when younger men and women acquire the responsibilities of a mortgage and other regular outgoings from income, they appear to rein in a tendency to take days off. These patterns vary by age and gender, but are relatively constant within each category.

Another possible variation in control of external time reflects labour market conditions and (perhaps in conjunction with them) management's strategy for

---

11   The following section is an adaptation of material published in Bellaby (1989).

time discipline. In weak labour markets and in face of a determined management, the options for time off may be significantly curtailed.

We shall consider these issues in three contexts: first, the cycle of absence by day of week; second, the cycle of absence by season of year; and, finally, the trend of absence with recession.

Day of Week

Throughout 1981-3, the period for which we collated the attendance and sickness certificate record of a representative sample of shop floor workers, 'unexcused absences' were of one to three days duration. Figure 6.3 shows that average working days per worker per annum lost on each day of the week to unexcused absence peaked at the beginning of the working week in the sample of 107 male and 104 female shop floor workers.

Explanations sometimes given in the workplace for odd days off were drinking to excess for men and period pains for women. However, staying away from work after hard drinking at the weekend was discouraged by peers - it was considered as unmanly as not drinking itself. It was especially shameful for a man with family responsibilities, though, as we saw in Chapter 5, relatively indulged in young single men. In any case, women took more short absences involving Mondays than did men, even than men under 30.

Figure 6.3 Short absences by day of week: 1981-3, males and females

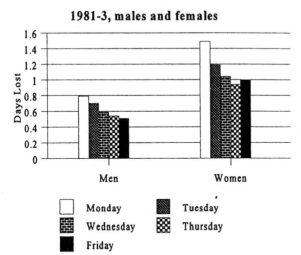

The interviews asked women when they had last had time off because of obstetric or gynaecological reasons. From their answers we concluded that 1 in 200 women's working days were lost in this way. This would be more than enough to account for the Monday excess, but there are two reasons for doubting that it did so. First, obstetric and gynaecological causes were often certified and therefore relate to longer absences. 'Personal' was used - almost entirely on self-certificates - 24 times a year by the 104 women, and obstetric or gynaecological reasons were give in a similar number of cases, making up at least half of the 1 in 200 days lost. Second, it is improbable that sufficient women would have PMS to coincide with Mondays as often as would be necessary to explain the pattern in Figure 6.3.

Thus it seems unlikely that either hard drinking or period pains would account for the regularity of Mondays off. An alternative explanation suggested itself to both field workers from our own six months work in the pottery and we tried it unobtrusively on fellow workers. For example, on returning after a weekend, one of us had dizziness and nausea on taking ware out of a making machine and putting it on a moving conveyor. A woman of similar age who had worked there for many years sympathized and said she often had the same sensation on Monday. The other field worker had pains in the wrist when doing similar repetitive movements and in arm and shoulder joints when lifting, which were echoed by regular workers. Our expressions of pain as novices of similar age to much more experienced workers often allowed them to admit to theirs. They were to do with a break in rhythm and the problem of finding it again. But on closer inspection, other people's problems on restarting on Mondays were less tractable than ours. A recurrent theme in diaries completed for us by fellow workers and again in follow-up interviews during the experiments with changing work organization in the company was boredom, compounded by a sense of being unable to escape the same old round. Sometimes, there was also dislike of a supervisor or manager or some fellow worker or other.

The introduction of Employer's Statutory Sickness Payment with effect from April 1983 was intended to tighten discipline over absenteeism (as Dean and Taylor-Gooby (1990) demonstrate). The employer now lost the value of up to two months statutory sickness payment for every absence of more than 3 days, and, in the pottery industry, more still as a result of the agreement for industry-wide sickness payment of four fifths of the basic wage. For their part, every absentee of one to three days continued to forfeit the wage for that 'waiting' period. In new arrangements of 1983, Masspro began to tie bonuses to weekly production targets and to exclude absentees during the week from a share in the bonus, so adding to the employee's penalty.

Not content that the financial disincentive would deter short absences, Masspro management was determined to monitor them, especially frequent odd days off - as Jim's case illustrated (pp.96-98) - and, to ensure that the worker's side of the case was heard and instant dismissal impossible, the union, CATU, had negotiated a procedure for warnings that could lead to dismissal, but only step by step. The procedure was activated if, within a period of forty days prior to the warning, eight days of absence had occurred without being excused. A union representative was to be present when a warning was given. Thus, April 1983 ushered in a new regime for absence from work.

When comparison is made between single days off in 1981, prior to self-certification and ESSP and the new agreements with the union, and single days off in 1983, after the changes, a test can be made of how effective economic and managerial discipline had been. Figure 6.4 focuses on one of the three units at Masspro and compares for 1981 and 1983, the incidence of single day absences by day of week.

In 1981, 47 percent of single day absences occurred on Mondays, more than twice as many as expected by chance. Indeed, the proportion was highest for men at 57 percent, and, even where lowest - among part time women on evening shifts - still 41 percent. However, in 1983, Monday single days off accounted for only 28 percent of the total. It was no more than would be expected by chance among part time women and only 31 percent among men and 33 percent among full time women. Yet the overall level of single day absences per head fell by only 5 percent between 1981 and 1983. It remained constant for men and fell most for full time women (by 5 percent), some of whom had been redeployed from the full-time day shift in the slimming down that happened that year. Single days off did not fall, so much as take on a new distribution. Friday became a second peak day, especially for women. Thursday was pay day, when hourly paid employees received their earnings for the week in cash. The new penalty of losing the bonus for unexcused non-attendance during the week was a dead letter after that day. Thus the financial incentive had an effect, but not as intended, while the disciplinary procedure for single days off seems to have had little effect of any kind.

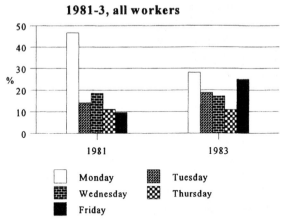

Figure 6.4 Single absences by day of week: 1981-3, all workers

Monday / Tuesday / Wednesday / Thursday / Friday

The results suggest that the interests of employer and employee were not congruent, that employees were calculative in when they took their odd days off and that they could avoid making the pattern as conspicuous as 'Monday blues' without losing control of time external to work. Thus, for management, the campaign had perverse consequences.

Season in Year

Further support for this interpretation may be found in the distribution of men's unexcused - that is, short - absences by month of the year (Figure 6.5). Until national figures on new claims for sickness benefit ceased, with the introduction of ESSP in April 1983, there were regular peaks of claims in February and October. At first, we attributed this to epidemics of infectious disease, especially influenza. However, the distribution of causes of absence given on self and medical certificates did not bear this out. The February peak in the national figures was absent in the 1981-3 series at Masspro, though October did have the highest levels of absence, excused and unexcused for both men and women. Among men, 'bull weeks' and the gaps between them proved to be a more satisfactory explanation than influenza. Bull weeks are a longstanding part of pottery culture. They are the weeks leading up to national holidays, like Easter and Christmas, and to the industry-wide potters' holidays - a fortnight in July and the first week in September - when there is a complete shutdown, except for essential maintenance. During bull weeks, it was said, men sought to maximize their earnings to put money by for the coming holidays. Short absences peak for men in the aftermath of holidays:

Figure 6.5 Days lost in short absences:

per 100 males each month

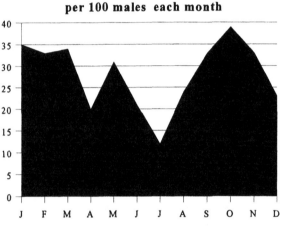

per 100 females each month

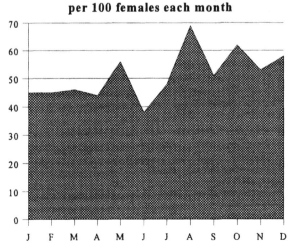

from January to March and from September to November. They are lowest in April (prior to Easter), June and July (prior to the first and longer potter's holiday) and in December (prior to Christmas).They return to a relatively high level in May, between Easter and when preparation begins for the summer holiday. Of equal interest is that women only seem to have few short absences in June, prior to the major holiday. In December, their short absence rate is relatively high. They may take time off to shop, while men are focusing on higher earnings. Women's short absences are very high in August, during school holidays. Figure 6.5 summarizes the distribution by month of working days lost in short absences. It remains to explain the peak in October. It accounts for 11.3 percent of men's days lost in absences, whether short or long, and 11.5 percent of those women. In a private conversation, the only woman shop floor manager said that the period between the second potters' holiday and Christmas was the longest without a break of any kind, even a bank holiday, and that taking time off in the middle of it enabled her to see light at the end of the tunnel. She, like other staff - as opposed to hourly paid employees - had single holidays allotted for length of service, known as 'service days'. It was one or more of these she took around October. In a similar way, women in the change of hours trial said that the prospect of using Friday afternoon to get straight at home before the weekend made the working week seem shorter, even though it was not so in fact. At a meeting of all managers at which we fed back preliminary results (we held such meetings with staff at all levels), production managers helpfully suggested that bull weeks explained the pattern of monthly absences by shop floor workers, but denied that October was a peak month because of the 'long tunnel' effect. This prompted us to examine the use to which service days were put by staff. The results showed that staff as well as shop floor took short absences unusually often in October.

Plainly, while control of time is the common theme running through patterns of absence, the logic often differs for men and women, more precisely for the majorities of men and of women who had family responsibilities and discharged them in the different ways expected of male and female partners. These domestic ties took much of the control of time external to work from the hands of individuals. Might weak labour markets do the same?

The Impact of Recession

The study of Masspro happened between 1983 and 1985 at a time of severe recession in Britain, especially in manufacturing, steel and mining, the staples of Stoke-on-Trent. Jobs continued to be lost throughout the period. However, in pottery, jobs had been lost more rapidly still from as early as 1978, when a downturn occurred in the important American market.

We traced records for Masspro back into the 1970s. The most obvious effects of recession were that both redundancy and dismissal for disciplinary offences increased while voluntary turnover diminished. The options elsewhere declined sharply. Women's jobs were more vulnerable than those of men. A secondary effect was that days lost in absence per worker fell. It is not possible from aggregate data to determine to what extent this was due to a fall in absence for each person who remained in employment or to redundancies and dismissals removing people who were more likely to be absentees, perhaps by health selection.

There is corroboration in Sweden for the effect of what may be broad economic incentives on sickness absence, including those of weak labour markets. In Sweden, quite unlike Britain or the USA, the state controls the economic incentives for attendance at work, by replacing a fixed and substantial proportion of the normal earnings of a worker on sick leave. From the late 1980s, the disincentive effects on attendance at work have attracted increasing attention and prompted reductions in the earnings replacement rate for the first three days of absence (from 90% to 60% in 1990-1). Johansson and Palme (1996) find this when analysing results of the Swedish Level of Living Survey for 1981, and succeed in replicating it for aggregate state sickness insurance records of absences during 1990-1. In a study of insurance records in two counties in the Swedish midlands in 1992, Knutsson and Goine (1998) show that long-term absences (of 30 days or more) are inversely related to local unemployment rates in an occupation, sex and age group, though only for men, not women.

Job prospects wax and wane with the business cycle, but the prospects also diminish for workers as they get older and have done so at an accelerating rate from the late 1950s (see above, pp.32-5). This is reflected in the finding that older workers take a smaller proportion of their more numerous sickness days off work, and instead seek to work off their condition (above, pp.105-7. As they become prone to limiting long term illness, so their few absence episodes are likely to become relatively long ones, a finding that is corroborated for the national sample drawn for the Labour Force Survey (Clarke *et al.*, 1995, p.227).

Vahtera *et al.*, 1997 (see also the same team's Kivimaki *et al.*, 1997) imply from Finnish data that a distinction has to be drawn between a tendency of 'downsizing' to increase long-term absences among workers of 50 and over, and the general tendency for days lost to fall as unemployment rates rise. When organizations downsize, they may either increase disproportionately the stress and risk of related chronic illness experienced by older workers whose redundancy now seems imminent or make their struggle to remain employed seem futile.

Absences of a month or more were surprisingly common in Masspro. We examined all such absences over the three years 1981-3. In 'Stoke' unit alone, they represented under 3% of all absence episodes even in 1981, but they accounted for more than a third of days lost in absence. There were 32 (1 for every 10 workers) in 1981, but this fell to 22 (1 for every 13 workers) for 1983. At first, we were tempted to suppose that the reduction was caused by redundancies among long-term absentees.

In Masspro as a whole, half the 52 women under 30 who had an episode of absence of a month or more in 1981-3 were on leave for obstetric or gynaecological causes. There were 96 long-term absences among women of 30 and over, 11 of which were for such reasons but 27 for psychiatric illness, which became more frequent with age. The approximate equivalent for the 70 men of all ages who had month long absences was musculo-skeletal disorders: 30 men fell into this category, most of them with lower back pain. This became more common among older men.

In the company as a whole, two fifths of people who were absent for more than a month at any stage in 1981-3 had left Masspro by three months into 1984, not to go for work elsewhere but to withdraw from employment on grounds of sickness or to have a child. Given long-term absentees might be a target for redundancies, we were surprised at how *low* this figure was and sought an explanation.

Production managers 'at the sharp end', where large mechanized making lines had to be fully staffed, rarely experienced the long-term absences as a disruption. It was the unpredictable short absences that caused their difficulties. When one or two people failed to turn in, the start of a line had to be delayed, while others were drafted from less urgent work elsewhere. Loss of even half an hour's production was costly.

It was left to the personnel office to monitor long-term absences. In due course a severance offer might be made. However, where the employer's liability for an injury or disease was in dispute, such an offer would be delayed. Once two months had elapsed, there was no further cost to the employer, because shop floor workers exhausted their entitlement to 80 percent of the basic wage and had to resort to social security. Women who were absent because of pregnancy (as opposed to complications arising during pregnancy) were not eligible for industry sickness payment. Thus many long-term absentees were in effect 'off the books'. Indeed, when making the annual return of absence figures to BCMF in 1984, the personnel director decided to treat long-term absentees as if they had cease to be employees, thereby reducing 'days lost' at a stroke, and bringing them into the line with companies who had been following this practice for some years. This combination of management interests helped explain the relatively relaxed view of long-term absences. It was not the case, as might be supposed, that management would cast around for long-term absentees when redundancies were in prospect, because long-term absentees were virtually redundant already.[12]

Implications for Stress Theories

A major theme in the psychological literature is 'autonomy and control' in work (pp.4-6 above), the stress that lack of it engenders (pp.17-19 above) and the alleged benefits of increasing it. A recipe for indifferent attendance at work that stems from this idea is to make workers feel identified with management by putting them on trust to use a quota of days of sick leave 'responsibly'. I have argued that the control that affects absence is specifically about time. If allowing a quota of days of sick leave only increases workers' control of *external* time but leaves control of internal time unaffected, it is likely to lead to higher absence, not the reverse. The recipe supposes, unrealistically, that the conflict of interest over effort that is central to my findings can be eliminated by 'partnership'.

The focus here is upon strategic action in the face of suffering, a position that is approached by Christensen (1991), who argues that sickness absence should be seen not as a pathology, medical or organizational, but as coping behaviour. Peter and Siegrist (1997) have something similar in mind when they speak of 'active' coping and claim that their model is distinctively 'sociological', though they remain within the stress and coping paradigm. However, in my theory, suffering may arise directly from physical and non-work causes, not only stressors within the organization of work (pp.19-21 above).

The control of time proposition lends itself particularly well to sociological elaboration. For instance, the case becomes more complex sociologically if a person has two work-situations, as women do more often than men. Married women typically lack control of time in both paid work and running their households. However, especially if they have children or older dependents, they can offer care for them as a pretext to escape attendance at paid work. This is an individual strategy which is made possible by the belief among managers that women as a whole are less reliable in attendance than men. Further, while married women may take more time off, they are unable to use it as a means of relaxation and recovery from suffering.

---

12   This is of course a cautionary tale for would-be users of industry wide statistics on days lost in absence.

Continuing to elaborate on the core proposition, we note that there are various ways in which workers can develop control of time internal to work. Among these is learning a rhythm. This is something to which short-cycle activities lend themselves, but which machine and work-flow paced production inhibit. Another is managing time when having to meet competing deadlines. This is suited to long-cycle activities, but inhibited when superiors make unexpected demands or subordinates do not deliver what is required of them. Another device sometimes available is completing a quota of work in a shorter lapse of time than the normal shift, then being allowed to leave work, as the kiln emptiers did with whom I worked. This enhances control of internal time, and also permits expansion of external time. Flexi-hours differ. They do not expand external time, but they allow people who have to serve two sets of demands - for instance, those having to take their children to and from school as well as attend paid work - to dovetail one with another. This will make absence less likely.

Conclusion

In this chapter, I have advanced to the limit of the territory in which a sociology of the body in employment seems in its element and virtually indispensable. Clearly, sickness absence cannot be reduced to morbidity on the one hand or deviance on the other. It is lodged in a context of both culture and social relations that is subtle and complex. It is morally regulated, as was shown in Chapter 5, and, as this chapter has demonstrated, is sharply affected by the circumstances and outcome of the contest to control time, both internal and external to work, that goes on between employer and employee, manager and worker

The new territory that has to be entered has to do with 'risk factors' and is peopled with epidemiologists. What has sociology to offer to the study of bodies at risk of disease and injury in employment?

PART III
BODIES AT RISK OF
DISEASE AND
INJURY

7 Bodies at Risk: Explaining Workers' Risk Behaviour

Men make their own history, but they do not make it just as they please; they do not make it under circumstances chosen by themselves, but under circumstances directly encountered, given and transmitted from the past.
Karl Marx, 1818-1883, The Eighteenth Brumaire of Louis Bonaparte, *Die Revolution*, New York (1852).

To risque the certainty of little for the chance of much.
Samuel Johnson, 1709-1784, *The Idler*, No 67 (1759).

In spite of the disruptions that migration and constantly changing lifestyle must have caused in the 300 hundred years since Ramazzini's pioneering work on the health of occupations, the *net* effect has been that life expectancy has increased. Thus, the evidence does not support the gloomy prognosis, made first by Malthus, for a civilization that puts strain on the biological capacity of a species evolved to be hunters and gatherers. Humans have completely transformed the ecological niche to which they were adapted in the stone age, not to speak of the agricultural mode of production that superseded it, and have not endured more than temporary or sporadic damage to their health.

In the UK, life expectancy has improved markedly in the twentieth century, rising by 26 years for males and 28 years for females by 1994-6.[13] Life expectancy is a measure of probable life years at birth, not of the typical span of life. Thus, by the end of the century, at 65 years of age, a woman can be expected to live 6 years longer than her counterpart in 1901, and a man just 4 years longer than his. Life expectancy at birth is so much longer mainly because a far higher proportion of the population live to see 65 than did so in 1901. The main cause has been falling death rates in infancy and childhood, which accounted for half the improved life expectancy of males and 44% of that of females. A further third of the improvement for both sexes was due to reductions in mortality between 15

---

13   Sources: *Social Trends* No.17, Table 7.1, HMSO 1987; *Annual Abstract of Statistics*, No.135, Table 5.22, HMSO, 1999.

and 64 years of age. Since this is the span of a working life, it might seem that better health and safety at work has brought about the reductions. However, the changes affected women as well as men, in spite of the fact that, on average, women's life time exposure to paid employment has been consistently lower than that of men (Hakim, 1994, 1996). It is likely that death rates among women fell in the age group 15-64 for reasons specific to women, such as reductions in pregnancies and improvements in obstetric care. In general, whatever did improve life expectancy in the twentieth century, it did not favour men disproportionately, as conspicuously better working conditions would be expected to do, but affected both males and females and, above all, infants and children.

In this chapter, I begin with the important issue of continuing class inequalities in life expectancy and mortality at different ages, and make a preliminary assessment of the part that occupation plays. Then I turn to one of the two competing explanations of class inequalities and focus on its relevance to the relation between work and health. The competitors are health-related behaviour and material circumstances. In a work context, the issue is whether workers *take* the risks they incur, or have those risks imposed upon them. Here I take a relatively novel tack and suggest that health-related behaviour and risk cultures in the workplace are in turn to be explained by material circumstances, in particular, the relation of employment. I support this view with evidence not only from the pottery factory and behaviour in relation to health and safety risks but also from the NHS and smoking and drinking. If it can be sustained, it implies that the apparent contest between the two ways of accounting for class inequalities is not a real contest at all, and a more complex account than either by itself is required.

Life Expectancy and Class Inequalities

Risk of early death is associated with social class - the life chances of people in manual jobs, especially unskilled, are much worse than the life chances of people in non-manual jobs, especially employers and professionals. Using evidence from death certificates collated by the Registrar General for 1969-73, the Black Report of 1980 (reproduced in Townsend and Davidson, 1988) showed that the class differential applied to both males and females, at all ages and for the major causes of death. Subsequent updates (Whitehead in Townsend and Davidson, 1990, based on 1979-83 mortality, Drever and Whitehead, 1997, based on mortality up to the mid 1990s) have only confirmed that trend, indeed suggested that the gap has widened. In 1970-2 men in Social Class V (unskilled) were twice as likely to die by the age of 65 as men in Social Class I (higher professionals, employers and managers). By 1991-3, this difference had widened to three times (Drever and Bunting, 1997). In short, life chances have continued to improve for most, but people of higher class have benefited more than those of lower class.

The relation between class and risk is far from transparent, however. Support for the hypothesis that occupation causes health cannot simply be read off the statistical association. The association might be spurious and so possible confounding factors have to be examined. Once this is done, the association has to be *explained*, by showing what mechanisms connect risk to class. Among possible mechanisms are: ways of life and behaviour at work distinctive of each class that might put individuals' health and safety at greater or lesser risk; the risks that occupations might impose on individuals; and the risks that employment status and variations in rates of employment in labour markets might induce. The first of these is the main topic of the present chapter, and the others follow in the next two chapters. Before proceeding further, however, the meaning of 'class' and the problems of method that arise in studying 'class inequalities' in health have to be addressed.

Theory and Method in Studying Class Inequalities in Health

'Class' in this context implies the Registrar General's social class scheme (RGSC). It was developed for the 1911 Census and has been modified piecemeal within the civil service departments responsible for it before most Censuses that have followed. It has been roundly criticized by academics - for conflating differences of social status, income, skill and relations of production, even for perpetuating the belief that society is a hierarchy determined by natural abilities (Marshall *et al.*, 1988). Inadequate theory certainly can produce misleading empirical results. However, in this case, other measures of social class seem to confirm those found with the RGSC (as Bartley *et al.*, 1996 found using the Erikson-Goldthorpe scheme). Moreover, far from the RGSC *inventing* class inequalities, investigations based on multiple measures of deprivation suggest that it *understates* them (Davey Smith *et al.*, 1990).

The measures used in the comparisons of class - age-specific death rates and standardized mortality ratios (SMRs) - should be calculated by using deaths in specific occupations as the numerator, and the population at risk as the denominator. The Black Report drew upon Occupational Mortality Tables for 1969-73, which use the 1971 Census as their base. The follow up by Whitehead did the same with 1979-83 deaths and the 1981 Census as their base. In neither case was the population actually at risk used as the base. The population at risk would have been the cohort of people entering the occupation under study at the same point in the past and undergoing similar exposure to it throughout their working lives. If the actual cohort were bigger or smaller than the corresponding occupational group in the Census used as the base - if, for example, the proportion of unskilled workers in the population had diminished or the proportion of professional and managerial workers had risen over the working lives of those now dying - the class gap in mortality might be spurious, a mere artifact of the way the calculation was performed (Bloor *et al.*, 1987).

Matters are complicated further by the healthy worker effect (p.15 and Chapter 2, above; Blane *et al.* 1993). What is actually recorded on the death certificate tends to be current or most recent occupation, if known, not necessarily the occupation in which the person spent most of his or her working life. If, for example, in the course of a working life, the healthy remained in work and the unhealthy made an early exit, the ranks of the unoccupied/occupation unknown would be crowded with people in poor health who were likely to die prematurely (Dahl, 1993). Similarly, if, as their health failed them, people in more demanding occupations were forced into less demanding, lower paid and lower status jobs, this would create the impression that such jobs were more hazardous to health than they actually were.

In 1971, the OPCS launched the Longitudinal Study (LS) of a 1 per cent sample of those enumerated at that Census. This was designed to link subsequent death and cancer registration to data on sex, age and occupation that had not been recorded at the same time as death itself. The linkage came near to simulating the original cohort which people entered at the beginning of their history in their occupation. The LS has helped demonstrate that the class gap in mortality is not a mere artifact - a product of numerator/denominator bias. It also shows that not all the association between class and death can be accounted for by health selection for class, because, after five years of follow-up, class differentials persist and remain relatively unchanged (Fox *et al.*, 1990). The 1981 Census repeated the exercise of 1971 and reached similar conclusions (Harding *et al.*, 1997).

Women, Social Class and Premature Death

Table 7.1 (below) considers the Occupational Mortality tables of 1979-83 for Britain in terms of class, allowing for both sex and age and also (for women)

Table 7.1 Age-specific death rates per 100,000 population and ratios of age-standardized mortality, Great Britain 1979-83

	Social Class	All Britain	West Midlands	East Anglia
Men: **45-54**	I	414	443	377
	IIIM	664	687	487
	V	1155	1136	827
20-64	**Ratio V:I**	2.51	2.51	1.84

	Social Class	Husband's Occupation	Own Occupation
Women: **45-54**	I	262	205
	IIIM	396	179
	V	599	112
20-59	**Ratio V:I**	2.16	0.49

	Social Class	Single	Divorced	Widowed
Other Women: **45-64**	I	497	396	750
	IIIM	686	431	320
	V	655	459	258
20-59	**Ratio V:I**	1.58	1.13	0.34

Source: *Registrar General's Decennial Supplement on Occupational Mortality.* London, HMSO, 1987: microfiches.

marital status. The use of age-specific and age-standardized death rates enables us to compare the risks from one group to the next. The ratio of Social Class V to Social Class I age-standardized death rates shows how great a gap there might be in life expectancy between social classes in each group.

A longstanding puzzle for those who have used the Occupational Mortality Tables has been that women's premature mortality shows a lesser gradient with social class than men's. Moreover, single women, who are assigned their own occupation, show a lesser gradient than do married women when assigned to their husband's social class. This suggests that occupation may play a lesser role in health than health-related behaviour - such as smoking, drinking, exercise and diet - that separates households by social status, and women from men.

Comparisons of the overall levels of mortality of men and women and women in different marital statuses seem to tell *one* story - women have substantially lower death rates than men at all pre-pensionable ages and whatever their class position, and so biological sex and gender roles - either or both - exert a strong influence.

Other data seem to tell a *different* story, notably that occupation might be a major factor in the premature death of both men and women. Thus, single women come close to having the same risk of premature death as men. Married women, when occupied, have lower premature death rates than single women - perhaps because they are less likely to have worked full-time and continuously than single women. Divorced and widowed women, who are classified only by their own occupation, have mortality levels, and perhaps also exposure to employment, that fall between those of single women and married women.

Comparisons of the class differentials in mortality among men and women and between women of differing marital status seem to tell *yet another* story. Married women classified by their husband's occupation show a wider class difference in mortality than do all other women. However, this needs qualification. There is reason to doubt the reliability of all survey, Census and death certificate reports on women's occupations. Women are much less likely than men to work continuously between leaving full time education and retirement. At any given time - when the enumerator or interviewer calls, or indeed they die - fewer are likely to have jobs. Furthermore, when chronically ill and/or disabled, both men and women tend not to survive in employment, but women are more likely to leave or not enter the labour market for reasons other than personal health than are men - notably, to care for children or other family members. As a result data on jobs that women have done in their life times are less likely to be available than they are for men. Moreover, occupations themselves tend to be classified on criteria more applicable to men than women.

Arguably, both health selection for employment and the differential effect of patterns of work are sharper among men than among women, because of men's higher participation in the labour market and individually greater exposure to paid work. This is borne out by three types of evidence. First, the LS (Harding *et al.*, 1997) shows that past occupation produces class differentials in women's life chances, even though to a lesser extent than for men. Second, a longitudinal study in the Netherlands (Stronks *et al.*, 1995), where, as in Britain, women's participation in the labour market is relatively low by European standards, suggests that the lower class differentials of women than of men reflect the smaller number of women than men of low socio-economic group who fall into employment statuses in which many are unhealthy - permanent sickness, unemployment and retirement. Finally, a comparative study of Finland and Britain (Arber and Lahelma, 1993) indicates that, when, as in Finland, a far higher proportion of women are engaged in the labour market, the class differentials in their health resemble those of men. This study also shows that, while British women's health is responsive to family roles and housing quality, in Finland it is occupation alone that counts.

In short, in spite of first appearances, the differences between the risks men and women seem to face support rather than detract from the view that occupational exposure is a powerful determining factor. However, women's health is less likely to reflect the occupation into which they are classified than that of men - notably so where women are employed part-time and discontinuously, and, as a result, women's health is more likely to be a function of way of life outside employment than is that of men. The contribution of biological sex to life chances cannot be discounted either.

Do Workers Take Risks or Have Risks Thrust upon Them?

In common usage, 'a risk' means the probability of an adverse event or a hazard that might be encountered in the future (Adams, 1995, Green, 1997). It may be a natural event, like an earthquake. It may be imposed by other people on those who bear the risk, as unsafe working conditions often are. In recent years, there has been a marked tendency to hold individuals responsible for their own health and safety, even in the workplace but especially outside it. For instance, many of the major causes of death - ischaemic heart disease, stroke, lung cancer - are attributed to individual use of tobacco, rather than to occupation. However, as Marmot and Theorell have suggested (1988), even individual behaviour that has health consequences may have its explanation within occupation. The focus of the remainder of the chapter is what accounts for employees' actions when they incur risks, and whether they can be said to *take* risks.

These are different questions from the issue of which risk factors contribute most to a given hazard. 'Risk factors' are the terms epidemiologists use. Epidemiology abstracts from individuals and the context in which they act and seeks to establish the probability *in the aggregate* of a given outcome. The pursuit of risk factors is entirely compatible with the investigation of how individuals make decisions and the social and cultural context in which they are made, but also quite a different exercise. Epidemiologists, much like actuaries, assess risks on past knowledge. Social actors address risks in prospect - even when they draw on knowledge of the probabilities - and it is how they do so that must seize the sociologist's attention.

A possible model for how risks are encountered in the course of action, much used and debated in economic theory, is 'rational choice'. Risk arises from uncertainty about the future. In the ideal case of perfect knowledge of all possible futures, investments could be entered into without risk. In the real world of imperfect knowledge, the uncertain future makes all present action a risk, even when it is grounded in long experience. Unlike medicine, economics suggests that risk is only one prospect that actors consider. The other is the chance of gain. Since no course of action is without risk, singular focus on averting risks is rational only if the risks appear to outweigh the gains that can be made by taking a chance. Yet the rational choice model has limitations of its own. It assumes actors in calculative mode who act in their own interests. This does not allow for actions which are not independent of others but interdependent: such as when a work group or household members look out for each other. Nor does it include behaviour which is driven by custom and practice, by feelings of loyalty or revenge or by higher values, rather than by gain and loss. Finally, rational choice approaches assume that, when people pursue gain, they act in knowledge of the risks. This cannot be assumed, for one does not have to take a risk to incur one. Many outcomes of actions are unintended.

Indeed, employees encounter risks while working in a context of culture and that culture in turn reflects social relations. Douglas's concepts have been encountered in considering how space is symbolically divided in the workplace (above, pp.64-68). She argues that perceived threats to cultures lie where social classification cannot bring order and anomalies prevail. Douglas (1986) has developed a theory of risk-acceptability around these ideas.

Workplace Cultures and Risk[14]

Figure 7.1 is an adaptation of the way Douglas and Wildavsky developed the 'grid/group' approach to understand the environmental politics of the USA in the 1980s, in order in turn to examine how different groups in the Masspro pottery perceive work-related risks.

Figure 7.1 Grid/group analysis and risk cultures in Masspro pottery

GROUP:

HIGH

Hierarchical	Egalitarian
Complacent	Risk immune
Family	*Slip-house &*
directors	*kiln: at*
Shop stewards	*extremes*

GRID: HIGH   LOW

Fragmented	Individualist
Vulnerable	Risk-taking
Process	*Middle &*
workers:	*junior*
in-between	*managers*

LOW

Douglas and Wildavksy (1982, p.138) offer the following brief summary of grid/group analysis:

> a way of checking characteristics of social organization with features of the beliefs and values of the people who are keeping the form of organization alive. *Group* means the outside boundary that people have erected between themselves and the

---

14   Further discussion of the issues raised in this section may be found in Bellaby (1990b).

outside world. *Grid* means all the other social distinctions and delegations of authority that they use to limit how people behave to one another.

Gouldner (1954) observed in a gypsum mine how prop men were credited with extraordinary powers to protect other miners from roof falls. By entering unsafe tunnels, they took risks that others avoided. In a different context, Willis's bikers (Willis, 1978) were supposed to gain the powers necessary to do the ton in city streets without fatal accident by having had lesser accidents that left scars. In neither case was taking risks valued unconditionally. Only the foolhardy would ride a bike that was poorly maintained, and knowing how to keep a bike in running order was no less the mark of an experienced rider than the scars. Knowing a sound pit prop from a weak one, and knowing where to put it under a roof were as important as bravery. In much the same way, experienced men in the sliphouses and on the kilns considered themselves expert in safe lifting. One man, who routinely handled tons of clay in 2cwt slabs each shift, epitomized all sides of this complex attitude to health and safety by saying that, after a back injury many years previously, he had never had a day off with back trouble, because he 'lifted on the other side' when his back was put out.

The cultural traits that these cases have in common should be distinguished from those of other cultures of risk theorized by Douglas in her application of grid/group analysis to risk-acceptability. The two risk cultures Douglas (1986) identifies as at the centre in American politics are as follows:

Individualism A 'risk-taking' culture is found in societies weak in both group and grid - individualist societies that can readily be identified with the enterprise culture idea. An individualist society has boundaries open to foreign personnel and goods, even other people's waste, for competition is free. On the inside, there is no permanent hierarchy. Each can make or mar their own fortune. On the other hand, there is no economic equality, only equality of opportunity for the rewards that risk-taking may bring.

Hierarchy A 'risk-averse' culture is found in societies strong in both grid and group - hierarchical, bureaucratic and/or aristocratic, societies of the kind that spawned the consensus politics of the pre-Thatcher era in British politics from the Second World War, if not much earlier (Corrigan and Sayer, 1984). A hierarchical society has a strong sense of its boundaries, defining them in terms of kinship among the elite or national language, culture and religion. On the inside, each has a defined place, marked by inequalities of power, rewards and prestige, which are either inherited or made available by those already holding privileges to a select few novices.

There is an incentive to avoid risks that may imperil hierarchical order, and to reach compromises with others rather than to compete.

Douglas and Wildavsky (1982) argue that these two risk cultures-cum-societies coexist in the USA, and jointly dominate politics. They collide but they also need each other. However, these issues are macroscopic. What bearing has the grid/group analysis applied to risk assessment upon the microscopic worlds of everyday work?

The culture of gypsum miners, bikers and sliphouse and kiln workers differed from both individualism and hierarchy. They were neither averse to risks nor risk takers. They valued early exposure to risks because they believed that what they learned in avoiding disaster empowered them to overcome subsequent hazards. Their culture was founded on a society strong in group and weak in grid. The boundaries of that society were sharply defined. Miners and slip and kiln men alike had territories from which managers were virtually excluded, as were workers (above all women) from the surface in mines or from the making and warehouse areas in the pottery. Bikers admitted women but only as camp followers. On the inside there was rough equality. Among slip and kiln men (as among longshoremen, Pilcher, 1972), there was a playful ritual of mutual insults, starting with the shift and continuing well into it, which allowed each to show his mettle, and was at the same time particular to that group. Drinking, smoking and boasts of sexual prowess also defined both membership and equality. Shrugging off small injuries and claiming the skill to overcome major hazards served the same functions.

Douglas singles out the Amish as her example of such a society. The Amish maintain, by rigorous egalitarianism, a way of life cut off from mainstream America and are apprehensive about pollution from outside. The hot/dry and cold/wet extremes in which kiln and slip men worked, and the accident-prone environments of miners and bikers were not seen as 'external', but as the internal source of each group's resistance to pollution of its way of life from without (by femininity and management, among other threats). No doubt the rigours of a farming life without modern tools are a source of inner strength to the Amish communities. The work-groups and bikers share with the Amish an egalitarian society and a culture that is made *risk-immune* to pollution by what is learned in acquiring its battle scars.

There were, however, examples in the pottery factory of both the individualist and the hierarchical societies, writ small. In the making areas at least, supervisors and other middle management tended to be individualist. This was often shown by their attitude to their own health and safety. In pursuit of production targets and bonuses, they sometimes made running repairs to machines, occasionally (two cases in one year) at the cost of serious injury; alternatively, they sped from one job to another and (in their own eyes) endured more stress than was good for them. Such men and women occupied positions that were 'in between' in hierarchical terms. They were often promoted from the shop floor. If men (but far less so, women), they had prospects of further promotion. They felt isolated. Workers blamed them if supplies faltered or machines were out of commission; they were accountable to superiors for maintaining the flow. Thus they were not securely lodged in hierarchy. Nor did they know the boundaries of their group, for they had many competitors for promotion and potential competitors for their existing posts. Risk-taking was both their chance of advancement and their insurance against loss of standing in the eyes of management and workers alike.

The hierarchical society, with its risk-aversion, could be found in two contexts within the pottery: among the company directors, and among shop stewards. Both had a firm sense of the boundaries of their groups - the company directors because this was a family firm, inherited by two brothers from their father and shared in by affines; the union activists because the union was a self-contained world, involvement in which was reinforced by the everyday duties of being a lay official, and attendance at meetings and training courses. The directors were at the apex of the company hierarchy, and part of a local elite of wealthy manufacturers. They showed their aversion to risk, not only in business, but also in health and safety matters. They maintained works safety committees and weekly tours of the shop floor, and quite generously compensated accident victims through company insurance. Much of the risk they avoided was 'trouble'. Trouble was the adverse publicity that court cases or the union might cause. However, the shop stewards and safety representatives were hedged in by the bureaucratic rules and procedures that were the prize of negotiation with management or of employment protection and health and safety legislation, and by the need to maintain their position as reliable and trustworthy negotiators with management and representatives of workers. Stirring up grievances and making trouble for management was itself a risk and on the whole they avoided it in order to keep shop floor organization and their own positions intact.

In applying the grid/group analysis to risk cultures at work, three of the four possible combinations of binary oppositions have been reviewed. This leaves the case of weak group and strong grid. Is it possible to conceive an internally differentiated society that does not also have firm boundaries? The fragmented society that results either from recent waves of immigration from different sources or from recent conquest (for example in Africa after colonization by Europeans), might fit the pigeon hole. Here the ethnic groups or conquerors and conquered would form strata with different wealth and power, but not a cohesive society with a common tradition and sense of boundary: national frontiers would be artificial. There was no precisely similar context in the pottery factory (few immigrants and no conquest), but women and men, of varying experience, who worked alongside each other in making and decorating, between the extremes of hot/dry and cold/wet that were occupied exclusively by experienced men, had much in common with the fragmented society as I have depicted it. Their work lacked the autonomy of the stages of production in which slip and kiln men worked, for, whereas the latter stockpiled their inputs and their products and so had more control of production time at their respective extremes, the makers and decorators were rigidly locked into the flow of production and the quantity and quality of their output was conditioned by stages prior to and following their own over which they had no control. They were not a production unity. Nor were they homogeneous socially. There were differences of gender and age, and between workers and the ubiquitous supervisors, quality controllers and managers. These might have underpinned the division of labour, but sometimes they crosscut it (for example men and women did similar work in some instances) and at other times the division of labour crosscut the latent identities that were brought to the workplace (for example women on moving lines were minutely divided by functions performed noisily by machines). In place of the playful insult rituals of the slip and kiln men and their solidarity against management, there was backbiting and jealousy among workers in the in-between areas and both favouritism and personal dislike as between managers and workers.

What perception of risks would be expected in a fragmented society such as this? What was found in Masspro was something akin to risk-aversion without the protection that the hierarchical societies of risk-averse company directors and shop stewards afforded. For that reason, it is appropriate to call the risk-culture of the fragmented society in the factory *vulnerable*. An example was a man who contrasts with the sliphouse worker with the bad back. His job was to print coloured designs on coffee mugs. This was a matter of operating a machine that had a short cycle. It was a sedentary job. Light lifting was involved, and rhythmic motion of the torso and arms to pick up glazed but not decorated mugs on the right, print them, then place them on the left. Like many other screen printers, this man had chronic back ache. He was vulnerable to it, unlike the sliphouse worker who used it to reaffirm his powers. He had a great deal of time off through back ache. He attributed the problem not to the printing operation itself, but to sitting in a draught. The rhythmic action was considered a way of avoiding the risks of back strain. His perception was shared by the numerous workers in between the extremes of hot/dry and cold/wet who complained about the conditions of their work and what effects they had on health: about draughts from open doors, standing in the wet facing a hot machine, dust, noise, lifting, being rooted to the spot - sitting or standing.

We found theoretical grounds for the risk-immune culture of the egalitarian society among slip and kiln men. Are there theoretical grounds for the perception of being vulnerable in the fragmented society? First, there are absences of qualities found in the other three societies. There is not the internal source of power to resist hazards found in an egalitarian society. Nor is there the prospect of advancement or fear of loss of standing typical of middle management who form the individualist society and who take risks. Finally, while there is hierarchy in the fragmented society, the society is not a unity as in hierarchical form and so there is no sense of 'trouble' that might disturb the equilibrium - in fact there is no balance at all. This leads us to what is uniquely present in a fragmented society - personal troubles (Mills, 1970).

Risk, Culture and the NHS[15]

If there were a stereotype of potters, it would include men and women who were accustomed to a dusty workplace and oblivious to its risks. It would not stand up to scrutiny. Even so, maybe it is time to step outside factory work and examine the risk perceptions and behaviour of those who - again stereo typically - are sharply aware of health and safety risks: health professionals.

The study that is to be reported was of a different order than the one in the pottery factory - almost its antithesis. It was typical of health services research: commissioned by the occupational physician to a district health authority and conducted on a tight budget to a short deadline. It was part of a larger plan to promote healthier lifestyles among employees.

Our commission was to provide base-line information about the health-related behaviour of employees of all grades, from medical staff to hospital porters, from senior managers to ambulance crew, and in all divisions, acute, community, mental health and handicap, the ambulance trust, headquarters staff and students and lecturers in the college of nursing and midwifery. There were 10,000 employees in all. A statistically reliable response was required from each of the major occupational categories and each of the divisions.

We anticipated (and got) a 50 per cent response rate, and took an initial sample of 100 individuals in each occupation in each division (where present). The sampling fraction (that is the proportion of the actual numbers sampled)

---

15   In carrying out the empirical study, the author was assisted by Diana Gilbert. See Bellaby 1999b.

ranged from 100 per cent to 7 per cent. Because of budgetary and time constraints, a postal questionnaire was used. It was sent out with pay slips and returned to the personnel department in anonymous envelopes. This meant there could be no follow up of those who had not returned the questionnaire.

The content of the questionnaire was based upon the national Health and Lifestyle Survey (HALS, Cox *et al.*, 1993, and below Chapter 9). It was a much reduced version of its model, and designed and pretested to ensure that it could be completed by respondents on their own, not in the presence of an interviewer, as was the HALS equivalent. The core was questions on smoking, drinking, exercise and diet, all apparently consumer choices, with no necessary relation to work in the NHS. However, we added questions on work patterns (derived from Swedish surveys - Karasek,1979), ranging from working hours to how repetitious the job was. In the event, 1,275 NHS employees in the district responded to this questionnaire.

Most of the respondents would have been exposed to what 'a healthy lifestyle' meant. Many were under a professional obligation to instruct their patients about it. One should not smoke (at all); one should drink alcohol by all means, but not so as to exceed a 'safe' level of 14 units per week for a woman and 21 units a week for a man (a unit is half a pint of beer or a single whiskey); one should eat a diet low in saturated fats and high in fibre; one should take vigorous exercise, regularly and not to excess.

However, it was not typical for any occupation or any division to have a wholly healthy lifestyle or, indeed, a wholly unhealthy one - findings that corroborate those for the population at large (Blaxter, 1990). In what follows, I shall concentrate on smoking and drinking. They are not equivalents medically, for any smoking but only excessive drinking is considered harmful to health (though the safety implications are another matter). From a sociological point of view, a useful comparison can be drawn between smoking and drinking on the grounds that temperance in drinking is a thing of the past (an old rule), while not smoking is an imperative of the present (a new rule); and what you drink is a mark of social distinction (for instance fine wines and single malt whiskeys), while smoking at all has become a mark of low status.

The historical changes in smoking and drinking rules are well-documented. In the late nineteenth century, alcohol use, especially in public houses and by the working class, was a matter for intensive debate (Barrows and Room, 1991). Temperance or non-drinking became a moral stance, though many men appear to have drunk more heavily then than later - the volume consumed dropped sharply after the First World War (Wilson, 1940). In the ensuing years non-drinking has become exceptional among men, and increasingly uncommon among women. Since 1978, when it was first measured by the General

Household Survey, non-drinking (plus occasional drinking) has been steady at 1 in 6 or 7 men and 1 in 3 women.

Smoking cigarettes has followed virtually the opposite course in the same period. It was relatively uncommon in the late nineteenth century, but from then rose to become the norm for men of all classes during the Second World War (an average of 12 per adult male per day). Liberated women began to smoke in the 1920s, and their consumption also rose to a peak in the Second World War (an average of 7 per adult female per head). From the mid 1970s, however, the numbers smoking began to fall (Wald and Nicolaidis-Bouman, 1991). Prohibition of smoking in public places is now proceeding apace. In many social circles, non-smoking has become the new rule - notably so among doctors, whose smoking and its ill-effects were the subject of a celebrated and seminal study by the epidemiologist, Richard Doll (1976). Doctors, indeed, had become the 'moral entrepreneurs' (Zola, 1972) of the age. The fact that their guiding light was not religion but science should not deflect us from recognising the form of their social practice.

By contrast, people outside the health professions, especially perhaps outside medicine, were to be persuaded that to stop smoking or never to take it up was very much in their interests. Soon after the NHS survey, I undertook a study of health and work in a food processing firm.[16] The firm drew its workforce from within the area served by the health authority that commissioned the NHS survey. The food processing survey asked questions of people in various occupations and divisions in one organization about their health-related behaviour and work patterns, in a similar format to that of the NHS survey, though, like HALS, it used interviews rather than a self-completion questionnaire. The survey was confined to a representative sample of workers and managers on the shop floor, and covered a final figure of 455 people (with a much higher response rate than the NHS survey). In this connection, the major points of interest in the results of this survey are the comparisons in proportions of food processing and NHS employees who smoked and drank.

Far fewer NHS employees than food processing employees were smokers, and, though NHS manual employees and men were somewhat more likely to smoke than NHS non-manual employees and women, there were no such class or gender differences among food processing employees. Drinking was quite a different matter. Whereas, among even male manual workers in the NHS 70 per cent were non-smokers, only 1 in 5 of even female non-manual workers in the

---

16   This, like the NHS study, was commissioned by management. I was assisted by Ray George and Diana Gilbert.

NHS were non-drinkers or only occasional drinkers. Again, while only 1 in 2 male non-manual workers in food-processing were non-smokers, almost 3 in every 5 female manual workers there were non-drinkers or only occasional drinkers. Yet those who did drink in food processing were more likely to drink above 'safe' levels than their counterparts in the NHS.

These differences between NHS and food processing employees are not to be explained by workplace bans, because alcohol and smoking were both forbidden while working in food processing, and, if anything there were more places that gave opportunities for smoking in working time in the NHS than in food processing (among the college students, in psychiatric wards and in the offices of headquarters, for example). To be sure, there was strong moral pressure in the NHS not to smoke anywhere, which was lacking in food processing. This might have caused NHS respondents not to fill in the questionnaire or to conceal their actual smoking when they completed it (Sacker, 1990). We could take steps against the latter. There were several questions on smoking, all on a single sheet. Before we asked whether respondents smoked currently, we first asked whether they had ever smoked, and then whether they had stopped or reduced their. Given the merit in a sinner saved, we hoped that this stratagem would counter the tendency to conceal the habit completely. Finally, even if NHS employees did dissemble about smoking, they were obviously indifferent to the impression that regular drinking might create on others.

In short, in the NHS there appeared to be a particular risk culture of non-smoking that was lacking in the food processing firm. Since both fell within the same locality, this difference could not be ascribed to circumstances outside work. When the NHS data are examined in more detail, it is clear that factors like age and gender, occupation, salary level and work patterns, such as total hours and shifts, make for differences in either smoking or drinking within the sample. Multivariate analysis was carried out to enable the independent contribution of each variable to be isolated and weighted.

The variables were also assigned to 'blocks', each one characterized by the the similarity of its contents and its difference from other blocks. The blocks were 'latent roles', 'occupations', 'extrinsic factors' and 'work problems'. Latent roles are not meant to play a formative part in modern organizations - hence 'latent' rather than 'manifest'. They include gender and age. 'Occupation' implies the classification of health professionals within the NHS into bands of broadly equivalent status and similar function, for example, maintenance workers, professional and scientific staff. 'Extrinsic' simply denotes a factor which has major consequences outside the workplace, yet is manifestly connected with employment, like income. Finally, work problems are potentially adverse elements in work, for example length and pattern of working hours.

In Figure 7.2 each element in capital letters represents a block of variables and the statistically significant ones in each block are given in lower case. The further to the left, the more 'prior' to the outcome the block is (in theory). The emboldened lines indicate an independent relation between that block and either drinking or smoking that is statistically significant at the 1 per cent level, that is to say, would occur by chance in 1 in a 100 random samples and so is likely (though not certain) to be 'real'. Thin lines indicate the lower, 5 per cent significance level.

Latent roles have a bearing on the salary that people earn in the NHS, as does occupation. Indeed, latent roles influence salary even when, for instance, the preponderance of women in the relatively less well paid nursing occupation as opposed to the preponderance of men in the relatively well paid medical and senior management jobs is allowed for.

The relation between latent roles, occupation, extrinsic factors and drinking alcohol is depicted in the top half of the figure. The only extrinsic factor which produces a significant effect on drinking is salary. The greater the salary the more NHS employees tend to drink. Occupation has no significant effect on drinking

Figure 7.2   Social determinants of smoking and drinking in the NHS

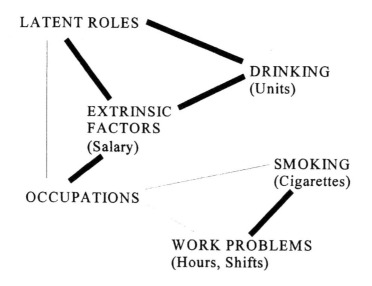

habits independently of salary, but latent roles do have an independent effect. Regardless of salary, very young men and men nearing the end of their careers are more likely to drink than women and men in mid career.

As the lower half of the figure shows, smoking cigarettes is quite differently determined than drinking alcohol. First, salary has no statistically significant independent impact on smoking; nor do gender and age. The largest independent contribution to smoking is that of 'work patterns', and the two variables within that block that are significantly related to smoking are the number of hours worked and whether the employee works 'unsocial' hours. More shift workers smoke than non-shift workers, and the longer the hours the more likely is an NHS employee to smoke, other things being equal, except that very long hours may restrict the opportunity to smoke. Clearly pattern of work is linked with occupation. Nevertheless, with work patterns allowed for, occupation also makes an independent contribution to smoking. In particular, ambulance officers are significantly more likely to smoke than other workers, though mental nurses and student nurses follow closely, while medical staff and scientific and professional staff are at the opposite pole.

In summary, it seems that non-smoking is a feature of the NHS in general, and among groups of NHS employees, it is variations *internal* to the workplace that determine whether a person is likely to be a non-smoker. Foremost among these is length and incidence of working hours, but occupation also has an effect, suggesting that cultural variations matter between jobs as well as between this employing organization and factories. However, drinking relates to factors *external* to the workplace. It relates to the purchasing power of the salary that an NHS employee takes out of their job and to their gender and age. It does not relate to factors internal to the workplace, including occupation.

These results have some curious implications for conventional approaches to how risks are incurred in the workplace. First, the bulk of epidemiological studies control for smoking when examining the impact of industrial processes, working conditions and stressful organization on, say, respiratory disease, cardiovascular disease and cancers of the lung, trachea and bronchus. This makes sense within the restricted framework of an attempt to isolate the specific causes of these conditions, but it is very misleading if it is assumed that smoking is an external factor, rather than behaviour which is determined within the workplace, even if practised outside it. Sterling (1978) asks whether smoking kills workers or working kills smokers. He has in mind the extent to which exposure to dust and fumes in the workplace might have an effect independent of or indeed synergistic with smoking. The NHS findings - which focus of course on why people smoke, not the health outcomes of smoking - suggest that working (in certain jobs and in certain temporal patterns) causes people to smoke and so by this means kills people.

Second, it is clearly important not to conflate the adverse effects of alcohol on performance at work, and the risks it poses for safety, both to the drinker and fellow workers, with how drinking is determined. It seems that it is not determined by what goes on within the workplace, but by how much income employment provides to spend outside and whether one is male and young (single is another factor, though it just fails to reach significance in this study). In addition, the NHS study shows that what one drinks (as opposed to how much of it) is connected with gender, age and social class.

Finally, perhaps the chief way in which these NHS results challenge conventional approaches to how risks are incurred in the workplace is that they imply that smoking and drinking alike must be put into a social and cultural context, not treated as if they were simple matters of individual preference. The much richer sociological understanding of 'life style' demands that drinking alcohol - indeed particular types of alcoholic drink - be seen as integral to a range of behaviours which are expected of people in a given economic and social position, at a certain stage of life, and are embedded in symbolic meanings. Remove what someone drinks from this system and many adjustments have to be made.

To turn back to the analysis of risk cultures summarized in Figure 7.1, it is possible to sketch a grid/group explanation for non-smoking and smoking alike in the NHS. Into the strong group and grid or hierarchical cell, may be placed senior medical staff. The common boundary of the NHS has come under greater threat in recent years from pressure of numbers on what are seen to be inadequate resources and a rising tendency for the public to initiate negligence suits. Senior doctors are also having to defend their line within the NHS from a management that sees an opportunity to raise its position by responding positively to external pressure, and thus increasingly favours accountability through audit, formal rationing, and open complaints procedure. At the boundary and the line, the medical profession's defence rests on its claim to be uniquely able to resolve indeterminate questions of diagnosis and treatment. This leads doctors to try and keep collegial control of audits of practice and disciplinary actions, a mode of action that may make them appear complacent about the risks they expose patients to. One way of reinforcing their position is to deflect the external threat by going on the offensive against what they see as body abuse by the population (self-inflicted illness). What has been called the medicalization of society is, from this point of view, a sign of weakening of strong group and grid, not of medical dominance as is often assumed. Smoking is for several reasons the appropriate focus. The outcome seems unequivocally adverse. There is a 'famous discovery' (Doll, 1976) to serve as its sanction. Doctors have themselves made an 'heroic response' to that discovery, by remedying what used to be a widespread smoking habit among themselves, and the crusade can be renewed by popular assaults on tobacco advertising, sales to children, secondary smoking effects and so on.

There is also an identifiable low grid/high group category in the form of ambulance crews and staff. They operate almost outside the NHS, in non-institutionalized sites, at road traffic accidents, call-outs to homes and workplaces, in shopping malls and streets. The crews have to look out for each other, and must have the scope and ability to innovate without supervision. Crews and headquarters staff are interdependent. There is an egalitarian ethos among them which is unusual in the NHS. The relative autonomy of this solidary group is exemplified in their distance from the moral authority of medicine: they smoke to handle stress and may think themselves risk-immune. There is a case for putting psychiatric nurses in the same grid/group cell.

Ambulance crews and perhaps psychiatric nurses, like the sliphouse workers of the pottery, incur risks, but they cannot be said to take them, because they appear to consider themselves immune to the adverse consequences. Who, if anyone does take risks in the NHS, and thus can be expected to fall into the low group, low grid cell? Perhaps, junior doctors find themselves in this position. They must make many decisions on their own, are expected to show initiative, and yet at the same time are dependent on seniors for references that will carry them further on the career ladder. They are in competition with peers for preferment. It is a condition that juniors find themselves in until they reach the relatively safe haven of a consultant's post, or else step off the ladder prematurely and take up general practice training. The situation favours risk-taking, though not imprudence. It may well be that smoking is too imprudent a course in the present moral climate of medicine, but binge drinking has a long pedigree and is tolerated by seniors. It accompanies more sober forms of enterprise on the job that are considered essential to learn clinical skills

Categories which are low in group and high in grid or vulnerable may include general nurses. After the destruction of the separate hierarchy of nurses headed by matron from the 1970s, acute hospital nursing tended to fragment according to the specialism in which it assisted and by the extent to which nurses were rank and file or caught up in the managerial hierarchy of the service (Bellaby and Oribabor, 1980). However, in this area, as others, the study of the NHS is weak where that of the pottery industry is strong - it lacks an ethnographic study.

Conclusion

Clearly employees *incur* risks in the course of their work, both by engaging in the production process itself and from health-related behaviours such as smoking and drinking alcohol. This is the common ground of studies by the medically trained, psychologists and sociologists into the factors that contribute to ill-health and injury arising from employment. But do employees typically *take* risks with their health and safety? If so, there is *a prima facie* case for holding employees responsible, at least in part. If an employee takes risks knowingly, there might be grounds to dismiss him or her, especially if there are consequences for others or for the employer's property. If employees habitually take risks that endanger them without knowing that they are doing so, there is a case for health and safety education. These are the implications for social action of what may appear a mere nuance of interpretation and is often deemed irrelevant in studies of health and work that apply natural science method to the study of human affairs.

There has also been a tendency in the literature to isolate behaviour that incurs risk from the complex strategic action of which it usually forms part. Even when, as among economists, it is second nature to think of risk as part of strategy, what is often neglected is the social and cultural context which constitutes the threat to be averted and the gain to be made, how individuals perceive these and the actions open to them. I have focused on these neglected aspects of behaviour that incurs risk.

Finally, class inequalities in health have typically been accounted for - if the ideas that they are an artifact or the outcome of health selection are set aside - by either health-related behaviour embedded in culture or by material circumstances. The evidence from both the pottery factory and the quite different employment setting of the NHS suggests that relations of production - 'material circumstances' - go far to explain health (and safety) related behaviour at work. Perceptions of the hazards of pottery work relate to how work groups are organized and their power within the factory. Non-smoking in the NHS is virtually a condition of employment, but, more specifically, a feature of the relation of each occupation to patients and the pattern of work in which its members are engaged. Nevertheless, the explanation of how people encounter risks to health and to safety is enhanced by including *cultures* in the equation. Health-related behaviour is not reducible to material circumstances in a simple way.

It remains to examine for its own sake the other side of incurring risk in employment: the extent to which risks may be imposed, whether by work itself or by the operation of labour markets. These are the subjects of the next two chapters.

8 Bodies at Risk: Can Jobs Still Kill?

The first and most potent [cause] is the harmful character of the materials that they handle, for these emit noxious vapours and very fine particles inimical to human beings and induce particular diseases; the second cause I ascribe to certain violent and irregular motions and unnatural postures of the body, by reason of which the vital structure of the machine is so impaired that serious diseases gradually develop therefrom.
Bernardino Ramazzini, 1633-1714 (1940, Chapter 1).

There are .. unhealthy influences at work in the pottery district quite irrespectively of the particular industrial occupation.
E.H.Greenhow, 1814-1888 (1858, p.72).

When occupations were based in small workshops, as in early eighteenth century Italy, Ramazzini thought he *knew* that they caused disease and injury and killed and that medicine could help remedy this. One hundred and fifty years later, when more than half the population of Britain lived in urban areas, and in many such areas, especially north of a line from the Severn to the Humber, the majority worked in factories and mines, Greenhow puzzled about how much occupation and how much factors extrinsic to work, such as the urban-industrial environment and its way of life, affected health. A further one hundred and fifty years on, the sociologist Beck (1992) speculates rather about how far risks to our health and safety are any longer local and within our control or, on the contrary, like global warming, remote from where people live and work and out of control. But is there still a case for Ramazzini's belief?

In this chapter, the initial focus is physical explanations for deaths in which occupation might play a part. Physical explanations include injuries sustained at work, as well as diseases that might develop from work in the long term. I start with national patterns. Here, it is often difficult to be specific about the effects of occupation, as opposed to alternatives, such as biological sex and gender roles and the environment in which people live. A more focused study of deaths in pottery jobs, which involve many women as well as men and are heavily concentrated in a single area in the UK, enables me to use what I learned in field

161

work to interpret official statistics and help resolve some of their ambiguities. Apart from physical explanations, there are psycho-social explanations on offer, which attribute injury and disease to work organization. I have begun to develop a sociological complement or even alternative to psycho-social explanations. Since the Whitehall studies of the British civil service have made use of psycho-social as well as physical explanations, there is an opportunity to compare their results with those of the pottery study, and ask whether any differences are to be attributed to a divide between manual and non-manual work, or the product of a different approach to explanation.

From Class Inequalities to Differences of Occupation and Industry

Chapter 7 began with large inequalities between the premature mortality rates of classes, and suggested that occupation had a major part in these. There are even greater differences in mortality involving specific occupations and industries. For instance, in 1979-83, men who worked on board ship as deck hands, engine room hands, bargemen and the like were almost three times more likely to die before pensionable age than the average semi-skilled worker. Similarly among unskilled workers, labourers in coal mining were almost three times as likely to die prematurely as labourers in chemical and allied trades.

Physical Conditions

In search of an explanation by physical conditions, I shall examine fatal accidents 'at work'; then, longitudinal evidence of the effect of occupations on death rates; finally, general and specific cause mortality by occupation in the pottery industry.

Fatal accidents at work Perhaps the most vivid illustration of the adage that jobs can still kill comes from fatal injuries at work (see Nichols, 1997 for much fuller discussion). The first thing to be said is that, though fatal accidents at work are much more reliably recorded than non-fatal accidents, the records represent a rather arbitrary segment of the entire picture and understate work-related fatalities by a considerable margin.

'At work' implies a zone for which employers and the self-employed are responsible under the Health and Safety at Work Act 1973. This includes not only the health and safety of workers directly employed on the employer's own premises, but also that of any visitor to the premises, and that of work by direct employees in any other location. Work-related injuries and diseases that involve the self-employed are recorded in the same official statistics, because each self-employed person is held responsible for these in law. However, in Britain, 'at work' does *not* cover road traffic accidents, even if they occur in the course of work, far less so when the worker is commuting to and from work.

The omissions have significant effects on the number of fatalities attributed to work. In the first half of the 1980s, there were around 500 fatal injuries 'at work' per annum, and in the second half (to 1991/2) around 350 per annum. Road traffic accident deaths outnumbered these by 10 to 1 over the 1980s as a whole. However, it has been suggested recently (Royal Society for the Prevention of Accidents: reported in *Independent* 19.11.98) that some 1000 deaths on the roads each year involve commercial drivers in the course of their work. I know of no comparable estimate for deaths while commuting, but it is hard to believe that it is a lower figure than for commercial drivers in the course of their work. It could be that deaths directly attributable to work are understated by a factor of 4, and deaths directly and indirectly attributable to work by a factor of 7 or more.

Fatal injuries in the home also outnumbered the official statistics on accidental deaths at work by 10 to 1 in the 1980s. The age-groups most at risk are children and older people, rather than people of working age. Therefore, among those of working age, injuries leading to death that are attributable to work, directly and indirectly, are likely to constitute the majority of accidental deaths.

Nevertheless, the official statistics on fatal injuries 'at work' allow the differing risks of most industries to be examined with some precision. This is subject to a qualification on numbers of deaths and size of the population at risk. Because deaths are not numerous, they must often be aggregated for a period of years for substantial individual industries in order to avoid making statistically unreliable claims about the rates at which they occur. Thus occupation falls somewhat out of focus and is replaced by larger groupings. Deaths are almost invariably reported, which is far from the case even with major non-fatal injuries (pp.77-79 above). The kind of accident involved is reported without attribution of blame - for example, it is 'fall from height' or 'contact with electricity', and there is a separate record of the nature of the injury.

On this evidence, there has been a decline in fatal accident rates at work in the last twenty years. This is matched by a decline in 'major injuries'. Cooper (1995), for the Health and Safety Executive, on whose report the rest of this section depends, attributes the latter not to improvements in safety, but to changes in the occupational structure - the more hazardous jobs are being replaced by less hazardous ones, as the service sector grows and the industrial sector shrinks.

Among the shrinking industries are agriculture and forestry. For fatal accidents at least, agriculture and forestry are some five times more hazardous than all employment, and deaths by electrocution and contact with moving machinery are proportionately more common here than elsewhere. Agriculture has many self-employed workers, as does construction. Construction is not shrinking in the long term, though its numbers fluctuate markedly. It has an even higher fatality rate than agriculture (8.8 per 100,000 workers in 1991/2, as compared with under 8), indeed the highest of all industries. On average five workers are killed on building sites every fortnight. Nearly half the fatal injuries are due to falls from height. Energy is the other industry group that has high fatality (around 6 per 100,000, if the Piper-Alpha oil-rig disaster of 1988/9 - in which 167 people died - is not allowed to exert disproportionate influence on the average). It is a shrinking industry, but also one of great internal diversity that is undergoing change. As coalmining - hitherto the most hazardous of occupations - thins to vanishing point, energy production - much less often fatal - declines only slowly, and oil and gas extraction - seemingly hazardous - grows, but without involving large numbers.

Manufacturing industry and, still more, services fall well behind agriculture, construction and energy in rate of fatal accidents. In manufacturing as a whole the fatality rate was under 2 per 100,000 from 1986/7 to 1991/2, but this figure conceals considerable differences within the class. The most hazardous part of it involves the 'extraction of minerals and ores other than fuels, manufacture of metals, mineral products and chemicals' (SIC division 2), and includes the pottery industry. Here the fatality rate for the period was just under 5 per 100,000, not far behind that of energy. In the still smaller division within which the pottery industry falls, the rate was higher still, nearing 6 per 100,000, but nowhere near as high as in 'the extraction and preparation of metalliferous ores'. Manufacturing has long been a larger employer in Britain than agriculture, construction and energy combined, but from the early 1980s to 1998 the proportion of the British labour force employed there fell from 24% to 18%. This was merely an acceleration in a long term decline. In 1961 it had represented 36% of all employment.

The place of manufacturing was taken by services. Even in 1939, there were more employed here than in manufacturing. The Second World War temporarily reversed this, but afterwards services took an increasing share of employment, largely at the expense of manufacturing, with 47% in 1961, 58% in 1981 and 69% in 1998.[17] Here the rate of fatal injuries is low by comparison with those for other sectors (around 0.6 to 0.7 per 100,000 employees). However, services is an

---

17   Sources are: *Annual Abstract of Statistics* Nos. 88 (1938-50), Table 127, HMSO, 1952, and 99 (1961), Table 132, HMSO, 1962; *Labour Force Survey* 1981, Table 4.7, HMSO, 1982, and Feb 1999, Table 15, HMSO, 1999.

even more diverse sector than manufacturing. It includes transport and communication at one extreme, where fatalities 'at work' tend to be high, especially in railways. At the other extreme lies office work, which has virtually no fatal injuries recorded. The omission of road traffic deaths would affect people both within the transport and communications division, and outside it, such as commercial travellers, who tend to be classed with office workers. Indeed it is in the comparison of the services sector with others that the omission of road traffic accidents in the course of work gives a particularly misleading picture of fatal injuries at work.

Occupation and premature mortality in the Longitudinal Study The official British study of subsequent deaths from all causes among a one percent sample of those enumerated at the 1971 and 1981 Censuses was introduced in the last chapter. A key objective of this Longitudinal Study (LS) has been to establish what the relative effects of the whole range of occupations might be on mortality, and to do this more reliably than the Black and Whitehead reports and others can manage using the Occupational Mortality Tables. The LS has collated all deaths from all causes. However, the statistical base is too small to pay detailed attention to individual occupations.

The follow-up to the 1971 Census has been reported down to the end of 1989 (Bethune *et al.*, 1995). In almost 19 years, 40,000 died in the initial sample of 188,000 men, and 41,000 in the sample of 203,000 women. In the 1971 Census, only the employed, those seeking work, the temporarily sick and the retired were classified to an occupation. Everyone else - home-makers, those in full-time education and the permanently sick - were defined as 'unoccupied' and combined with those who gave inadequate information about their occupation. A proportion of those assigned to the unoccupied/inadequate data category would have failed to gain or keep a job because of ill-health or disability. In the first five years of the follow-up (1971-6), the differential between their death rate and that of people assigned an occupation was at first high and then steadily declined. Thereafter new cases showed a steady, much smaller differential between the occupied and the unoccupied. It will be noted that their occupations and employment statuses were recorded at successively younger ages as the follow-up continued. Fox *et al.* (1990) concluded that the first five years of the follow-up displayed the effects of health selection into and out of employment among older workers, and that subsequent years were relatively free of this. Accordingly the Longitudinal Study research team decided to omit the first five years in order to focus on what could be said more reliably to be evidence of the effects of occupation (and social class) on subsequent health and eventual death.

It is indeed older workers who tend to become permanently sick. However, these are overwhelmingly men. Women's economic activity is much more likely to be assigned to home-making. Home-making among women has two peaks - one in child-bearing years, the other at pensionable age. The combination of these led to the fact that only 45% of women were assigned an occupation in the 1971 Census, for though women who said they were retired were pressed for their previous occupation, just as men were, relatively few said they were retired, and, of course, women who said they were home-makers were not asked for their previous occupation. More women have no occupation earlier in adult life than men. This implies that the control that the LS team introduced for the healthy worker effect is less efficient for women than men, and, to obscure the picture further, there are relatively few women in occupations, so that statistically significant results are less likely.

Unsurprisingly, then, the findings on occupation and mortality from all causes for men are much clearer than for women. Broadly speaking, non-manual jobs display lower mortality than the average and manual jobs higher. Thus, the unskilled - labourers - have the largest excess of 20% of deaths from all causes. The excess applies in all age-groups - 20-64, 65-74 and 75 and over. As one would expect, it is smallest at 75 and over, for everyone must die eventually and so the disadvantages of being a labourer will have run their course. But the design of the LS is such that disadvantaged occupations, who reach death at 75 and over at an earlier age than others, will appear to have an excess of mortality even in this age group for some years to come in the follow-up. The other occupational orders to have statistically significant excess mortality from all causes are manual workers, with the partial exception of the last one listed here, many of whom are personal service workers:

   textile workers
   miners and quarrymen
   furnace, forge, foundry workers and rolling mill workers
   warehousemen, storekeepers, packers, bottlers
   painters and decorators
   drivers of stationary engines, cranes
   service, sport and recreation workers.

Glass and ceramic workers (the order that includes potters) have excess mortality at a higher level than the last two in this list (at 12% above the average), but it just fails to reach statistical significance.

At the other extreme, with the largest statistically significant deficit in mortality from all causes, are professional and technical workers, who fall 28% below the average. Others with significant deficits are also non-manual, but there are some in manual jobs:

administrators and managers
clothing workers
electrical and electronic workers
sales workers
clerical workers
farmers, foresters and fishermen.

All-cause mortality is a less convincing indicator of a link between occupation and ill-health than is death from specific causes - such as accidents. Thus, farmers, foresters and fishermen have a significant excess of deaths from accidents, poisoning and violence (including suicide), even though they have below average mortality from all causes. Of course, this further breakdown of the sample to examine specific causes tends to produce fewer statistically significant results. Clerical workers have a small, non-significant excess of deaths from circulatory or cardiovascular diseases, which becomes significant for one sub-category - ischaemic heart disease - at the age of 20-64. In other words, clerical workers are more likely to die of a heart attack than the average when of working age.

The highest risk group for all causes of mortality - labourers - is a diffuse category, including people who work in varied conditions: it is to be expected, and, indeed, was shown above (p.163), that the mortality of labourers differs from setting to setting. Factors following from employment but extrinsic to work itself, such as low income, may play a part, for all the main causes of death are in excess for labourers at most ages. On the other hand, deaths from circulatory diseases cease to be significantly different from average at 75 and over, suggesting that the heavy lifting that labourers often have to do may lead to early deaths from this cause. A more specific occupational link can be seen for miners and quarrymen who show excess mortality for respiratory diseases, including bronchitis, emphysema and asthma, all likely outcomes of exposure to dust, whether coal or silica.

The similar follow-up based on a one percent sample of the 1981 Census included some changes, both in the questions asked about employment status and occupation in the Census and in the way occupations were classified (Bethune *et al.*, 1995). Thus, this time, the permanently sick and disabled were asked about their previous occupation, if any, so too was anyone else not in a job in the previous week, including home-makers. This may have reduced the impact of health selection on the results for men, and may have improved the chances of assigning women to occupations, but not by much (48% could now be assigned to an occupation, as against 45% in 1971), because it was their most recent *full-time* job that the Census sought, and women are far more likely than men to work part-time. In analysing the results for occupations, the LS team used a reordering of occupations designed to focus on common hazards (the Southampton job-groups), which promises sharper findings for the future, but also renders them slightly less comparable with those for 1971.

By the end of 1989, 25,000 of the 197,000 men in the one percent sample from the 1981 Census had died, and 26,000 of the 214,000 women. Again the results for men are firmer than those for women. Significant excesses of mortality are found in much the same occupations as in the 1971 follow-up, though 'labourers' have, quite rightly, ceased to be treated as a category to themselves. The following men in Southampton job-groups have significant excesses in descending order:

> other textile workers (who appear to be the less skilled)
> other coal miners (that is, surface workers)
> plastics workers
> other occupations - glass and ceramics (other than ceramics casters, glass formers and decorators and glass and ceramic furnace workers)
> plastic goods makers
> packers and sorters
> face-trained coal miners.

They are all manual occupations. There are overlaps with the 1971 data for textiles (all groups, including the more skilled, had excesses in 1981), coal mining and packers and sorters. Crane drivers and painters and decorators, which were occupations significantly in excess mortality in the 1971 follow-up, just fail to attain significance in 1981. Glass and ceramic makers also had a large excess in 1971, but this was not quite statistically significant. For the 1981 follow-up it is significant, but only for a sub-category, which constitutes the less skilled. Just as one non-manual category with excess mortality appeared in the 1971 follow-up - service, sport and recreation workers - so another appears in the 1981 follow-up - nurses. Male nurses had a statistically significant 19% excess mortality. There is a convincing degree of consistency for excess mortality among men between the results of the 1971 and 1981 follow-ups. The results which do not appear in both might well be so by chance - significance tests do not *eliminate* such a possibility, they only suggest how probable it is.

No fewer than 23 of the Southampton job groups display significantly below average mortality, and of these 20 are non-manual, most of them professional, and another is farmers. The two manual categories that have mortality deficits are carpenters and precision instrument makers, though neither of these appeared in the 1971 study.

Relatively few women were assigned occupations in the 1971 and 1981 Censuses - the proportion was as low as 21% for women over 75 in 1971 - and, consequently, numbers of deaths are often too small to break the data down by occupation, age and cause of death. Women are, in any event, more concentrated in the less skilled manual and service jobs and the more junior non-manual jobs than are men. Moreover, the omission of data for 1971-6 from the 1971 follow-up is not so efficient in eliminating health selection as in the case of men. The net result is that in 1971 only two occupational groups showed overall excess mortality at a statistically significant level. They were in areas that overlapped those of men: textiles and the diffuse category of labourers. In addition a sub-category within service, sports and recreation, that of barmaids, had a significant excess. There were several occupational groups which had significantly *lower* mortality than the average for women, and again they overlapped with those of men: farmers, clerical workers, sales workers and the varied groups of professional and technical workers, among whom primary and secondary school teachers and (unlike their male counterparts) nurses were large enough to produce significant below average results. Only one manual occupation fell below average mortality: clothing workers. The 1981 follow-up confirmed the below average mortality of teachers, nurses and office workers, adding to them retailers, caterers and welfare workers. Textiles appeared again, as with men, among the excess mortality occupations, but specifically among spinners and winders. Launderers and dry cleaners also had significantly high mortality.

The Longitudinal Studies are so designed that they provide relatively reliable evidence to assess the impact that occupations might have on health and subsequent death. A solid case can be made for men, and that of women so far corroborates the pattern for men, that its less solid underpinnings need not concern us. However, these studies are based on only one percent of the population. They cover far fewer deaths, even in a run of years, than are detailed in the Occupational Mortality Tables. If anything more focused is to be said about a particular industry and its occupations, the data have to come from the Occupational Mortality Tables or from original studies of that setting.

Pottery occupations, gender and premature death The Occupational Mortality Tables do not group all pottery occupations together. Rather, quite usefully, most of the various occupations appear with an industry suffix under separate heads (e.g. caster, labourer). In Table 8.2 (and Table 8.4) five groups of occupations on the shop floor are represented:-

casters, makers and decorators
foremen casters, makers and decorators
kilnmen
other makers and repairers
labourers.

Some workers in the pottery industry are placed in such diffuse occupational groups (including many others besides potters) that I have had to exclude them. They include packers, warehouse workers and inspectors and selectors of ware. Since many of these tend to be women, women are more under-represented in the table than are men.

The figures represent death rates per 100,000 for those aged 16-74, for men and women, women of different marital status and each occupational group, which are highly comparable because standardized for age (that is, for between category variations in the size of 10 year age-groups within that range).

Table 8.1   **Age-standardized death rates per 100,000 for the age range 16-74, by gender, women's marital status and occupation within pottery manufacture, 1979-83**

	Men	Women	
Own occupation:		SWD	Married
Casters, makers, decorators	1417	1471	689
Other makers and repairers	1880	2188	727
Man's/husband's occupation:			
Casters, makers, decorators	1417	-	634
Other makers and repairers	1880	-	827
Kilnmen	1167	-	737
Labourers	980	-	455

Source: Registrar General's Decennial Supplement for Great Britain, *Occupational Mortality Tables, 1979-80, 1982-3*, microfiche tables, HMSO, 1986

Among women and also men - who fall into a wider range of occupational categories - 'other makers' have the top risk of premature mortality. The men in the 'other makers' category include sliphouse workers. Another group, largely male, would be sanitary ware formers, none of whom featured at Masspro.

There is support here for the earlier conclusions about how death rates vary for women by marital status, for it is possible to compare men and women doing similar work. The rank order of risks attached to the occupations is consistent for men, single women (including widowed and divorced) and married women, whether classed by their own occupations or classed by those of their husbands. Single women have similar risk as men doing similar jobs, in spite of women's average lower death rates before 75. Married women who work in pottery, on the other hand, have much lower risks than single women and men, presumably a reflection of being less likely to work continuously and full time, so having shorter exposure to the hazards of the job.

When married women are classified by their husband's occupations in pottery manufacture, they also show much lower death rates than the men to whom they might be married, but mirror the rank order of risks associated with their husbands' jobs. Fletcher (1991) argues that this kind of result demonstrates a 'spill over' from stress derived from hierarchy in the workplace to health in the family. However, his claim that this is the typical mechanism by which male as well as female health is influenced by work hangs on the finding from death certificates (Table 7.1, p.143 above) that single women show less similarity to men in class difference than do married women classified by their husband's occupation. This finding is not corroborated by the more reliable data of the Longitudinal Study (Harding *et al.*, 1997), which were not available to Fletcher. Moreover, the stress element in Fletcher's argument does not fit well with the pottery data. The male group most at risk of premature death also proved in fieldwork to be among the most autonomous - sliphouse workers.

If spill over of stress from workplace hierarchy to family is not a general explanation, what does explain the fact that the class differences in married women's premature mortality mirror those of their husbands? One possibility is the relative income of occupations and the lifestyles these support, but this does not fit the potters' evidence either, because labourers and their wives, who are the least at risk of the shop floor workers, are among the least well paid. Another possibility is that the cultures of risk that developed around occupations influenced potters' behaviour towards their wives, and perhaps also how wives led their lives. For lack of independent data on the domestic life of workers in Masspro, I have no means of saying whether this is true.

Deaths by cause: the Ramazzini and the Greenhow effects One hundred and forty years ago, Greenhow claimed that pulmonary tuberculosis was endemic in the district called 'The Potteries' and not specific to the occupations that predominated there. This raises the general issue of the extent to which area rather than occupation accounts for ill-health. This may be called the 'Greenhow effect' to distinguish it from the 'Ramazzini effect'.

In Britain, mortality tables are available for area as well as occupation. Area and occupation are not cross-tabulated. Even if they were so, the numbers of deaths in each cell would in most cases be too small to make statistically reliable inferences from them. However, the pottery industry has long been one of the few in Britain to be concentrated in one district - Stoke-on-Trent - and thus to appear almost as one entity in the are mortality tables.

When male mortality after school but before pensionable age is examined in some detail by cause (the ICD classification), there is a pattern to be seen. All the causes listed in Table 8.2 relate to an incidence of at least 100 deaths for men at all ages. They are listed in order of Standard Mortality Ratio (SMR), which displays the ratio between the age-standardized death rate for that area and that of the population throughout Britain, where 1:1 is expressed as 100. The table is divided into those causes of death more than twice as frequent in Stoke-on-Trent as in Britain as a whole, those at least one and a half times as frequent, those at least one and a quarter times as frequent, and those less frequent.

Table 8.2 Cause of death in Stoke-on-Trent 1979-83 among males aged 15-64: standardized mortality ratios

Bronchopneumonia	268
Bronchitis, emphysema, asthma	
Other heart disease	196
Malignant neoplasm of the stomach	179
Malignant neoplasm of trachea, bronchus and lung	156
Ischaemic heart disease	136
Malignant neoplasm of the colon	134
Malignant neoplasm of the prostate	131
Cardiovascular disease, excluding subarachnoid haemorrhage	130
Diseases of the digestive system	127
Malignant neoplasm of the pancreas	96
Diseases of the arteries	87
Diseases of the nervous system	71

Source: Registrar General's Decennial Supplement for Great Britain, *Mortality Statistics: Area, 1979-80, 1982-3*, microfiche tables, HMSO, 1986

At the top of the list are deaths from respiratory diseases. It is worth remarking that this is not the 'old man's friend' but diseases that carried people off in the prime of life. Older men in Stoke-on-Trent were still dying of pneumoconiosis at more than five times the national rate, but the overall numbers were too small to include this cause in the table. The same applied to deaths from pulmonary tuberculosis (older men died from it at two and half times the national level). These two notifiable diseases had declined markedly here as in the rest of Britain during the life-times of those then pensioners. However, for older men and younger, other respiratory diseases not only accounted for an excess of mortality by national standards but also for a large absolute number of deaths.

In addition, circulatory diseases and some cancers had elevated mortality rates in Stoke-on-Trent among men aged 15-64. Among the excess cancers deaths, lung cancer and stomach cancer are the most notable. The prevalence of stomach cancer in the Potteries has been attributed to dust exposures at work (Coggon *et al.*, 1990).

The table shows lower than national rates for some diseases that accounted for at least a 100 deaths at all ages. In addition to these, deaths from diabetes mellitus, malignant melanoma of the skin, malignant neoplasms of the lymphatic and haemopoietic tissues, pulmonary embolism, chronic pulmonary heart disease and cirrhosis of the liver are comparatively rare. Some of these are acknowledged diseases of life style (diet, sun tans, alcohol abuse). In this class, only lung cancer (largely, though not only smoking related) shows an excess of deaths in Stoke-on-Trent men under 65.

Superficially the Stoke-on-Trent area data suggests a case for making occupation a prime factor in premature deaths, but, on this evidence alone, the Ramazzini effect cannot be substituted for the Greenhow effect, because the area had a long history of air pollution and particle fall out from industrial processes which, though improving after the second war, was only decisively tackled in the decades following the 1959 Clean Air Act. Moreover, even if occupation were the prime factor, it would not be clear that pottery jobs were the main culprits. In spite of the soubriquet 'The Potteries', potters were just a large minority of the workforce of the area and tyre-making and coal-mining accounted then for large minorities too, as coal-mining had done to a larger extent still in the life-times of those dying in 1979-83.

There are insufficient deaths in the pottery industry to permit treatment of both sexes by specific causes. However, if major causes of premature death in Stoke-on-Trent are divided into three broad classes - respiratory diseases, circulatory diseases and malignant neoplasms - and attention is confined to males, the problem of small numbers can be overcome. To enlarge the pool of deaths further, I have included death rates at 65-74, which can be justifiably included as 'premature'. These are cited separately from death rates at 20-64.

My interest is to achieve - as far as possible - a measure of the specific contribution of potters' work to premature mortality, that is, how far potters diverged from the average death rate for their age, sex, area and social class. Thus in Table 8.3 are cited SMRs for men aged 20-64 in which both area and social class are taken as the bearers of the norm. In Table 7.1, by contrast, the norm was Britain as a whole, regardless of social class. In normalising the death rate at 65-74, I have used area, but not social class, for lack of numbers.

Table 8.3   Major causes of death among male potters in various occupations at 20-64 and 65-74

	SMRs at 20-64 relative to area & class	SMRs at 65-74 relative to area
Respiratory Diseases		
Casters, makers, decorators	95	94
Other makers & repairers	170	184
Foremen casters	(57)	63
Kilnmen	176	94
Labourers	69	76
Circulatory Diseases		
Casters, makers, decorators	104	102
Other makers & repairers	125	156
Foremen casters	74	54
Kilnmen	90	83
Labourers	53	56
Malignant Neoplasms		
Casters, makers, decorators	117	119
Other makers & repairers	102	146
Foremen casters	70	48
Kilnmen	103	75
Labourers	67	71

Figure in brackets is based on fewer than 5 deaths

Source: Registrar General's Decennial Supplement for Great Britain, *Occupational Mortality Tables, 1979-80, 1982-3*, microfiche tables, HMSO, 1986

Table 8.3 has to be read while bearing in mind that the norm from which potters' occupations were varying was already much higher than that for the population of Britain as a whole: more than twice as high in the case of respiratory diseases. The outstanding results are:

- that respiratory diseases, followed by circulatory diseases, show greater variation of potters from the area and class norm than do malignant neoplasms;
- that 'other makers' were well above the area and class norm, at both ages and for all three types of cause of death, and that foremen in casting, making and decorating, and labourers in general, were well below that norm at both ages and for all three types of causes of death, indeed close to the national average.

Both types of result suggest that occupation plays a large part in premature death. Pottery work is distinctively dusty, though some parts of the workplace and some jobs are much dustier than others. Some work involves heavy lifting, which is a major contributor to heart disease. There are still some toxic hazards, notably some glazes and additives to clay slip, though the notorious effect of the intensive use of lead glazes has receded into the distant past, beyond the lifetimes of most potters in the 1980s. However, airborne fine silica (that is, ground quartz, SiO_2) is a major ingredient of the clay used in making pots. Possible causes of early death arising from or aggravated by free silica include silicosis, bronchitis and emphysema, cancer of the trachea, bronchus and lung, stomach cancer and pulmonary tuberculosis.

Among men, 'other makers and repairers' - the occupation most at risk - were engaged in the preparation of the materials for pottery making. 'Other makers' thus handled the dry ingredients of clay slip and body, including chemical additives, preparatory to mixing them with water, and engaged in the heavy lifting work of blunging, pugging and pressing of the clay. The others who worked 'at the clay end', that is who made pots and worked with them in an unfired or 'green' condition, when the clay was relatively friable and prone to dust, included casters and makers, but, since 'fettling' by hand (to remove seams left by moulds) had ceased to be common practice and all work in these areas took place under dust extractor systems, they were less at risk than sliphouse workers. Far less at risk were those who worked only with the ware in a glazed and fired condition - that is, at the glost end - who included most labourers and all selectors and packers. Those less at risk included workers who placed ware for firing in the kilns, though they once placed ware on fine sand (silica) rather than the dust-free porcelain cranks now widely used.

A study of lung cancer risk, in the Dutch ceramics industry of the Maastricht district, used assessments by specialist occupational physicians to grade parts of the process by this risk. It confirms my impressions of dust exposure risks (Meijers *et al.*, 1990, p.22). The authors conducted a case-control study, where the cases were 382 men with primary lung cancer and the controls their matches in age. Only a fifth of the cases were ceramics workers. The study did not yield conclusive results, but the trend pointed in the same direction that my use of the Occupational Mortality Tables for England and Wales suggest, and was independent of smoking behaviour, an obvious confounding factor.

It will be recalled from Chapters 4 and 7 that men in the high risk occupation tended to consider themselves immune to risk, hardened by the extremes of cold and wet and the heavy lifting involved in their part of the pottery. By contrast, the casters, makers and decorators, men as well as women, considered themselves vulnerable, partly because they were located in draughty space between the extremes of cold and wet (in the sliphouse) and hot and dry (in the kilns) and usually stood or sat on one spot, with hot dry air in their faces and their feet in cold and wet clay on concrete. However, their risk of death by 64 and even 74 was around the average for the area, except for a somewhat elevated risk of cancer.

It will also be recalled that sliphouse workers were considered something of a law to themselves. Indeed, they were little supervised and used rule of thumb methods (e.g. a stick with a nail in it to judge the consistency of slip), which was a sharp contrast to casters, makers and decorators, for whom technology dictated pace and pattern of work, there were many managers, supervisors and quality control inspectors, and often boards and posters displaying production targets.

The paradox, then, is that the risks of premature death from all the major causes lurked where there was an egalitarian peer-group operating free of managerial control, not where workers felt their health was vulnerable and management considered the product itself to be so much at risk that they must monitor the process closely. The initial stage of production was among the least rationalized and most labour intensive.

To turn to the potters that fell so well below the area and class norm that their risks of premature death resembled the national average, it is no surprise that these include foremen in casting, making and decorating, but may be a surprise that they include labourers, that is workers considered unskilled. However, as was noted above, labourers are a diverse group and have widely varying risks of premature death depending on industry. In pottery manufacture, as in chemical and allied trades, their risk is not exceptional. Much like foremen, labourers in the pottery moved around the plant. They used hydraulic trucks to move clay, ware or packed goods on pallets, and did little lifting. Much of their work was in relatively dust free warehouses and sometimes in the open air.

In summary, the evidence for men's risks of premature death in pottery work appears to confirm the Ramazzini effect, at least when the Greenhow effect is allowed for.

Organizational Effects: Stress Explanations and an Alternative

Culture and power relations are essential to any general explanation because they address how workers come to be exposed to hazards. The hazards themselves may be organizational rather than physical. To investigate the effects of organizational patterns on mortality, I turn now from a segment of employment that is predominantly manual to another that is predominantly non-manual: central state administration.

One should not jump to the conclusion that in manual work the hazards are exclusively physical and in non-manual exclusively organizational. Indeed, probably the most influential psycho-social theory of organizational effects, that of Karasek (1979), purports to be universal, and suggests that stress conducive to ill-health and early death - for instance, by cardiovascular disease - is to be expected among not executives but lower grade workers, non-manual and manual. Psycho-social accounts have played some part in how the results of the 'Whitehall' and 'Whitehall II' longitudinal studies of occupational health in the British civil service have been interpreted.

The Whitehall studies of the health of British civil servants The Whitehall studies have handled far larger numbers than I did in the pottery study, but there has been no ethnography to complement their more medically orientated measures of health, for the approach has been epidemiological not sociological, and concerned more with disease than illness or sickness.

In the first Whitehall study, a cohort of men (only) aged 40-69 years had its initial screening between September 1967 and January 1970. As many as 18,000 men were identified and flagged at the NHS Central Registry, which informed the investigators of any deaths, and, by 1995, they had been followed up for at least 25 years - beyond retirement age. Their jobs had been graded into the four broad civil service categories: administrative, professional and executive (by far the largest), clerical and 'other', mostly messengers and other manual workers. When the data were adjusted for age and length of follow-up, it was found, among those who died before retirement age, that the ratio of the risk of the top grade to the bottom grade was just over 1:3 (Marmot and Shipley, 1996). This is similar to the result for class differentials in premature mortality derived from recent analysis of the Longitudinal Study (p.142), and is consistent with earlier analysis of the Whitehall study (Marmot *et al.*, 1984), and comparable work on health outcomes other than death in the Whitehall II study (Marmot *et al.* 1991).

The association between civil service grade and mortality may be attributed to any one or more of several factors, such as: health selection for grade, whether initially or with promotion or demotion; 'way of life' outside work; and features of the work each grade does, either physical or organizational.

Marmot and Shipley (1996) apply a similar test to their data for health selection effects as do Fox *et al.* (1990) in using the Longitudinal Study. Fox *et al.* find that class differentials in mortality changed rapidly in the first five years of follow up, but reached a steady state after that. More than 90% of deaths in the Whitehall cohort occurred after five years of follow up. However, this test allows for promotion and demotion by health *after* the age of 40-69 (the ages of men at the start of the study), not for possible health selection for grade before that age was reached. Health selection for grade in the civil service remains a possible cause of the differentials found.

The first Whitehall study paid much less attention to the various dimensions of socio-economic status than did the second. Thus Marmot and Shipley (1996) are obliged to use car ownership as an indicator of SES in dealing with the possibility that mortality differences by grade might be attributable to way of life rather than work (raised by Fox and Adelstein, 1978). Car ownership represented relative affluence in 1967-70. They find that car ownership and grade contribute independently of each other to the estimation of mortality among civil servants: higher grades and car owners have lower mortality than lower grades and people without cars. Moreover, differentials attributable to grade diminish among those who die after 69 and before 90, whereas differentials attributable to car ownership remain almost unchanged. Thus the element in grade that is related to work affects mortality while of working age more than if affects the deaths of those who survive into retirement.

The second Whitehall cohort was established between 1985 and 1988. While deaths will be followed up, the results to date are for various aspects of morbidity. The new cohort contains 3,400 women as well as 6,900 men. The design sets out to address the socio-economic differentials found in the first study in more depth, including a focus on stressful working environments and lack of social support. Cardiovascular disease is a major, though far from the only, outcome that is focused upon.

Marmot *et al.* (1991) report on morbidity differentials for six categories in hierarchical order, each a composite of current civil service grades. The following trends by grade test significant for both sexes at $p<.01$: probable/possible ischaemia (heart attack) as measured by ECG, and self-assessed health (average or worse); while pre-menstrual 'bloating' shows a similarly significant and particularly sharp gradient with lower grade for women. Many possible explanations of these differentials also produce significant trends. They include: health related behaviours (smoking, alcohol use, lack of vigorous exercise, diet); family history of heart attacks; and a range of psycho-social factors. Among the psycho-social factors, these *work characteristics* (measured by self-report) produce significant trends for both men and women, with health the better the higher the score: 'high control', 'varied work' and 'fast pace', while 'job satisfaction' has a significant trend for men, though not women. In each case, the higher the civil service grade the higher the score for work characteristics. The binary relations between grade on the one hand and both health and organizational patterns on the other suggest that health may be linked to grade through the differential organization of work at different levels in the civil service hierarchy.

The 'other' grade in the first Whitehall cohort is relatively small (18% of the total), by comparison with the proportion of manual workers in the general population. However, mortality differences between the upper, middle and lower non-manual grades are steep and progressive. This seems to favour an organizational explanation, rather than a physical one.

The second cohort has brought this out more clearly. Brunner *et al.* (1996) focus on determinants of plasma fibrinogen concentration (based on a blood test), which is associated with risk of coronary heart disease. They find two strong inverse relations: the first with childhood social circumstances (father's social class, their own education and their adult height), and the second with grade; that is, the poorer the childhood background and the lower the grade the greater the risk of coronary heart disease. The finding for grade replicates work on the first Whitehall study. In the second, it is shown that introducing childhood background, which might have selected for grade as well as influencing health, leaves intact the relation between grade and plasma fibrinogen concentration. This meets for Whitehall II my criticism that the follow-up on the first Whitehall cohort does not handle health selection for grade satisfactorily. Brunner *et al.* (1996) also show that 'high control', as measured by personnel officers, is inversely associated with plasma fibrinogen concentration. This is relatively firm ground for saying that the organization of work contributes to the risk of coronary heart disease. The determinant has something to do with the low grade jobs and the work characteristics that go with them.

Deficiencies of 'job strain' explanations One possible explanation for this link between ill-health and low grade in the civil services might be Karasek's (1979) 'demand-control' or 'job strain' model. Karasek proposes that stress is at its peak when workers do not have much control over the job (have low decision latitude) *and yet* have much demanded of them. It implies a common limit or breaking point to human capacities for coping with strain.

The authors of the Whitehall studies have tested the job strain theory on Whitehall II and found it wanting. Specifically, they found no support for the idea that heavy demands and low decision latitude have multiplicative effects, as Karasek argues (Stansfeld *et al.*, 1995). A further paper (Bosma *et al.*, 1998) corroborates this, showing that low decision latitude alone, not excessive demands, increase the risk of coronary heart disease.

The case from field notes in the pottery factory that came closest to affirming Karasek's job strain theory was that of several line supervisors who, finding that they were expected to reach a count each day, but that their machines were prone to breakdown simply because a conveyor became clogged with broken ware, surreptitiously left the guard unbolted so that they could free the flow without switching off the machine - until one man lost his fingers as a result and the HSE had to be alerted. These supervisors faced excessive demands and had middling decision latitude. However, mental stress was not necessarily the cause of their injuries, even though the men themselves referred to the pressures of their job in mitigation for breaking the rules. Their actions directly reflect the conflicting expectations to which they were subjected by superiors, and the fact that production targets were the priority.

The emphasis I have placed on workers' embodiment and the relations of power in employment, and, in particular, on the contest to control time, involve significant modifications to Karasek's model. On this basis, there are two main reasons for saying that Karasek's model is partial, not as it claims to be, universal. The first is that it neglects the extent to which human capacities are acquired and cultural, not just inherited and natural. It is, therefore, unrealistic to assume a fixed benchmark against which the stresses of 'civilized' existence can be assessed. As Part I (above) suggests, culture and social relations play a great part in shaping the worker. It is the worker so shaped who reacts to stressors. Moreover, workers are selected and made *differentially*, not out of the same mould. They must fit the requirements of different niches in the division of labour. Breakdowns in their health should be expected to reflect these differences, even though common humanity and its history to this point places limits on all of us.

The second point is that Karasek thinks of autonomy and control as a resource owned (or not owned) by the occupant of a role, rather than as a property of a relation of power, for example between employer and employee, and of power as negative only, rather than both negative and positive. Examples of how power is a relation are: the autonomy and control of a middle manager is not absolute, but conditional on being accountable to seniors; the employer is dependent to a degree on the efforts of particular employees, and sometimes their strategic position in production can give people who are low in the hierarchy, considerable power over those who are supposed to be their seniors. Power is positive, as well as negative, in a sense conveyed by the way that, especially in manual work, rhythm, which is acquired largely by imitating experienced workers, empowers workers to cope with repetitive jobs and exercise their minds on something else entirely.

Alternative explanations to job strain for explaining grade differences in health
Karasek's job-strain model apart, there are two other explanations to consider for the grade differentials in the Whitehall studies, each of which involves organizational patterns: first, relative exclusion from the organization's symbolic rewards and a consequent disproportion, in some cases, between effort put in and reward received (Peter and Siegrist 1997); and, second, frequent breakdowns of rhythm and failures to cope with deadlines, arising from lack of control of time in work (the approach outlined above, pp.19-21, 86-89).

The rewards and effort alternative to the job strain model has been developed macroscopically by Marmot (1994) and Wilkinson (1994). They have both argued that, where there is considerable social inequality in a country, premature mortality is more common than would be expected from average income and wealth alone, and contrasted the USA and UK unfavourably with Sweden and Japan in this respect. They infer that the greater relative deprivation where incomes are unequal, and lower social cohesion associated with it, are responsible for the greater levels of early death. Its near equivalent at the microscopic level of the employing organization is the idea, tested successfully in Bosma *et al.* (1998), that where the organization's symbolic rewards to individuals do not match the effort that they put in, stress and stress-related diseases will develop.

In its findings on the health effects of grades, the Whitehall II study tends to confirm that the civil service is 'bureaucratized' to a greater degree than many other work settings - so that what is expected of people is broadly in line with the discretion they are allowed. Moreover, employees are oriented, to a degree not found everywhere else, to the symbolic rewards that grade and promotion offers, and, perhaps as a result, are especially sensitive to what they see as unjust distribution of such rewards.

This does not ring true to the pottery factory. Not only were there mismatches between power and bureaucratic authority (compare Crozier 1964), but the symbolic rewards of the organization seemed to have little appeal to rank and file. Masspro was seeking to involve employees in the organization's reward system at several levels - for instance, decision-making in quality circles and

JCCs - but union activists suspected that this was a device to undermine collective bargaining, while rank and file workers showed little commitment to either management's plan or the union, and, when an industry wide agreement between employers and the union on pay and holidays was put to a vote, Masspro rank and file were unique in rejecting it, so defying both sides. To be sure they were interested in rewards and resentful when they seemed unfairly distributed (above, pp.50-51), but the rewards in question were not symbolic but material. The potters were relatively instrumental in their approach to employment. Most shop floor jobs were considered unrewarding in themselves - a means to an end that was enjoyed outside work. In such circumstances, it is unlikely that many felt excluded from the centre of decision-making or from the symbolic rewards that the company offered. This helps explain why a different explanation was developed to account for 'vulnerable bodies' in the pottery setting from the ones applied in the Whitehall studies.

This alternative links well with physical explanations for disease and injury at work, as reflection on repetitive strain injury in the pottery suggests. As was noted earlier (pp.81-2), RSI was coming to be seen as an 'epidemic' in pottery work. Physical and psycho-social explanations were vying with each other. According to the job strain model, for instance, the stressor producing the stress that induced RSI would be high demands in a low latitude job. However, the idea of 'broken rhythm' appears to fit the case better. Injury might arise when learned rhythm is no longer sustainable, either because of an increase in the pace of the work or because the worker is less fit than usual. The proximate cause is physical, specifically, ergonomic, rather than psycho-social. Indeed, those who presented with RSI and the district's senior orthopaedic surgeon, who had been to observe pottery work for himself, were convinced that RSI was a physical condition. Recent experimental evidence supports them, showing that affected tissues in cases of repetitive strain injury respond to mild cold shock in a distinctive way, quite differently from undamaged tissues, and tissues in cases of reflex sympathetic dystrophy, a degenerative disease with which RSI might be confused (Cooke *et al.*, 1993).

Might the 'broken rhythms and unmet deadlines' account also fit the civil service? At the lowest level of the civil services hierarchy, one would expect acquiring rhythm to be almost as important an accommodation as in repetitive manual labour. At the intermediate level, there would be more discretion and greater self-pacing. On the other hand, middle managers would be expected to lead their subordinates in achieving targets set from above and be held to deadlines. Their accommodation would, perhaps, be seen, in lay terms, as 'coping with stress', much as in the pottery context. In the factory, breakdowns in rhythm in repetitive work and threats of unmet deadlines among middle managers were quite common, because many factors were outside the control of any but the most senior management, and some not even within their control. These included machine breakdowns, the failure of supplies to appear on time, an unexpected number of absentees at the start of the day. Even if civil service workflow is smoother than it was in the factory, the effect of disruptions is likely to be least manageable at the lowest level, where employees have least control of time in work, and only just more so at the intermediate level, where managers can reschedule their short-term commitments in order to try and meet longer term deadlines that have more riding on them.

The alternative account, based on the pottery study, encompasses both organizational and physical effects on health and safety. It also covers a range of variations in social relations and culture at work that have to be understood if effective action is to be taken to stem the outcomes that all approaches seek to explain. On the first point, accommodations to repetitive work and to being accountable for meeting targets by deadlines are learned, and once learned actually reduce the risks associated with work in hazardous conditions. This observation sharpens attention further where occupations are hazardous, upon those who are ill-fitted to this type of work, inexperienced or have become unable to keep up with its demands. On the second point, the approach directs attention to a distinction between two forms of control of time in work that approximately distinguish between middle managers and rank and file employees. Both represent a potential threat to health. Moreover, rather than reducing variation in work organization to the conjunction and disjunction of two factors - demands and latitude or rewards and effort - the alternative model provides a view of the varieties of form of power relation and the cultures of risk that often grow up around those relations of power. From within occupational psychology, Kristensen (1998) has recently proposed quite a similar 'sociological' revision of the job strain model, arguing that psycho-social models neglect the context of organization and occupation in which ill-health arises, and should move towards 'triangulation' of methods of study rather than exclusive reliance on self-report questionnaires. The approach taken in the pottery study seems to fit both of Christensen's requirements.

Conclusion

Part III began with the point that life expectancy improved even as the economy industrialized and populations moved from country to town. At the same time, the social class gap in premature mortality continued, outliving not only economic development but also increasingly effective medical technology and health care delivery. I have been exploring aspects of why this class gap persists. In particular, I have argued that occupations and the varied exposure to hazards in the course of work that they involve, still affect health, can maim and may kill. This applies, as my own study in the pottery industry suggests, to manufacturing industry, and it applies, if in different ways and different circumstances, in the civil service.

Explanations for the effects of occupations on health, including premature mortality, might be physical or psycho-social. In either case, they should be put into a sociological context, for relations of power in employment and the cultures that emerge around work have a bearing on exposure to hazards. In the latter part of this chapter, I have compared the results of the important Whitehall studies of the British civil service with my much more modest study in the pottery industry. The comparison throws doubt on psycho-social accounts which abstract from the varied relations of power and cultures within which work takes place.

The mortality data for the pottery industry and for Whitehall reflect sudden injuries to a point, but more often long term illness, and thus lag behind the incidence of the conditions that gave rise to them. Employment and work patterns may have changed since the exposures that gave rise to current deaths. Extractive and manufacturing occupations have declined in numbers, and allegedly safer and healthier service jobs have taken their place. At the same time, however, labour markets have undergone significant changes, so that the jobs for life have become much less common. This is a trend in civil service employment as elsewhere and has recently been the subject of an extension to Whitehall II, in which it was shown that civil servants who lost tenure on being redeployed to First Step Agencies, suffered adverse effects on their health on a range of measures (Ferrie *et al.*, 1995, 1997). What impact might such changes have had on health in the population of working age at large, and what prospect do they open for the future?

9 Bodies at Risk: Weak Labour Markets may Damage your Health

> ... a transition is occurring ... from a uniform system of lifelong full-time work organized in a single industrial location, to a risk-fraught system of flexible, pluralized, decentralized underemployment ...
> Ulrich Beck, *The Risk Society,* (1992, p.143).

In the previous chapter, the main concern was the impact of specific *occupations* on health. In this chapter, I turn to the idea that *employment* and the labour markets that provide or withhold access to it, might have an important relation to health. Competing hypotheses have been advanced about what direction that relation takes. Both posit a correlation: the employed will be healthier than the unemployed and non-employed of similar age and sex. One side of the argument attributes this to the healthy worker effect, which implies that only the healthy get jobs and survive in them. The other says that employment is beneficial to health, and that not having a job causes a relative decline in health - it is known, accordingly, as the 'social causation' hypothesis, as opposed to the health causation or 'health selection' hypothesis (Elstad, 1995, Ross and Mirowsky, 1995).

Patently, while employment might be better for health than not having employment, how much benefit it can offer depends on the occupation and the conditions of work that accompany it. Whether employment confers an advantage depends also on the impact that it has on a worker's life outside work. The income it generates is one factor here. A debate over the relation between employment and women's health suggests that gender roles might be another: do women who work and have dependents carry a 'double burden' which affects their health adversely, or do they carry a 'double benefit' (Arber, 1991, Bartley *et al.*, 1992, Weatherall *et al.*, 1994, Martakainen, 1995) - is their health enhanced by having a job, perhaps as a release from the isolation that child-rearing or caring for the sick, infirm or disabled might impose?

Finally, whether employment benefits health is also likely to depend on the extent which employment is *stable*. Employment, non-employment and even unemployment (in spite of the fashionable idea of the 'underclass', Gallie 1994) are not permanent states. People move in and out of each of them in a life time. 'Stability' is measured by how often moves are made from employment. From the Second World War and the economic boom that followed on reconstruction after the war, employment was more stable for more occupations - but largely male - than at any time previously after early industrialization. Stable employment is a *late* modern phenomenon, indeed even more limited in historical span, for it has been on the wane from the point at which it peaked in the 1970s to the moment of writing (Brown, 1997).

Economic Instability and Health

The span of time covered by the studies discussed in the book overlaps with a secular decline in the numbers employed in manual work, and includes a recent period in which those employed in producing goods have fallen particularly sharply, while those employed in providing services have increased even more (pp.164-5, above). Some services are in distribution (such as shops), some in banking and insurance, some in education, health and welfare. To some extent there has been a shift to a knowledge-based economy, but by no means all the new jobs are knowledge-based. They vary from professional to cleaning services and in the educational and skill levels they require.

From the late 1970s, this restructuring of occupations has been accompanied by an overall *weakening* of demand in labour markets, and the post war commitment to government intervention to secure full employment (for men) has been all but abandoned. The trend has not been even. There has been a much higher level of unemployment for men in the UK than during the long postwar boom, and they have withdrawn from the labour market at earlier ages than before. Women's employment has risen to unprecedented levels, but, with it, the extent of part-time and temporary contracts, which fall mainly to women. 'Core' permanent, full-time jobs - long the province of white males of British descent - remain, but in smaller numbers.

The weakening of demand in labour markets has been uneven over time and by region of the country. Of particular interest is how the impact of two severe recessions - in the early 1980s and the early 1990s respectively - affected differently Britain north and south of a line drawn roughly between the estuaries of the Humber and the Severn rivers. In the early 1980s, unemployment rose rapidly where mining, steel-making, ship-building and manufacturing were concentrated - that is, in the north - whereas, in the early 1990s, unemployment rose rapidly where service employment was concentrated, especially financial services - that is, the south. In the event, this second recession appears to have been little more than a fluctuation. The flow of jobs from manufacturing to services has continued.

Changes in employment patterns and in occupational structure have been accompanied to a degree by changes in patterns of work. The most significant is that fewer people work in processes that carry high risks for health and safety. The near-disappearance of coal-mining is a major gain in occupational health terms. Not all high risk jobs have vanished. Construction remains in this category, as does off-shore gas and oil work, and these are less unionized and less effectively protected than coal-mining was. There are no doubt new risks in service jobs, but they are not of the same order as those in extractive and heavy industry and construction, or even as those in light manufacturing industry.

In an attempt to capture some of these recent and ongoing changes in employment, occupation and work patterns and their likely effects on health, I shall discuss analysis of a national sample survey conducted in two waves in 1984 and 1991: the Health and Lifestyle Survey or HALS (Cox *et al.*, 1993). This is secondary data analysis. It was not the primary purpose of this survey to examine employment, work and health, but I have used it for that purpose.[18]

HALS and the Changing Pattern of Employment, Work and Health between 1984 and 1991

The Health and Lifestyle Survey was based on a stratified random cluster sample of the population of Britain aged 18 and over in private households in 1984.[19] Initial contact with members of the sample was for interview, and subsequent data collection was by self completion questionnaires and measurements by health professionals. The first sweep in 1984/5 was repeated in 1991/2. There was some attenuation of numbers at each step. Of the 9003 who were interviewed in the first sweep, 6626 were alive and retraced at the second sweep, and 5352 were re-interviewed. They were asked additional questions about events in the

---

18   Mildred Blaxter and Judith Nickson have been generous with their knowledge of this data set, and the Health Promotion Research Trust in funding my use of it. Felix Bellaby with Susan Bailey, Margaret Fox and Jacquie White played a major part in analysing it.

19   England, Wales and Scotland were broken down by Parliamentary constituency, and 198 constituencies selected with probability proportional to the size of the electorate. One individual per household was selected from the electoral register by a standard sampling technique (Cox *et al.*, 1993, p.3).

intervening years (Cox, 1993 Ch.1). Most of the analysis that follows is restricted to the 4169 respondents at both sweeps of HALS, who were aged 18 to 60 in 1984 and hence 25 to 67 in 1991, and who were not already retired or permanently sick in 1984.

Health has many dimensions. HALS provides indicators for several. There is not space to consider all the measures actually included, and so I have made a selection of those with differing characteristics: job stress, death by 75, respiratory function and self-assessed health. Job stress and self-assessed health derive from reports by the respondents of how they felt. Though they may indicate underlying *disease*, they signify *illness* first and foremost. Respiratory function (FEV1) was measured by health professionals. Poor respiratory function is symptomatic of several diseases, affecting not only the lungs but often the heart as well. Death was recorded by cause (certified by a qualified medical practitioner) for those who died between interview in 1991/2 and the end of 1995. HALS contains no measure of sickness absence.

In order to use HALS for assessing the possible impact of weak labour markets on the health of the population of working age, unemployment rates for the local labour markets of respondents - that is, travel to work areas - were appended to the existing data set. Travel to work areas are defined at the decennial censuses of population as areas with a working population of at least 3,500, in which at least 75% of residents work and at least 75% of workers live.

The greater increases in unemployment in travel to work areas in 1991/2 were where unemployment was low in 1984 (r = -.40). Relative levels of unemployment in 1991 were positively and yet more strongly correlated with relative levels in 1984 (r = +.84). *Within* each of the divisions - North and South, 1991 levels of unemployment in TTWAs were strongly mapped onto 1984 levels, but there was no significant relation between rates of increase in 1991/2 and level of unemployment in 1984. Thus, the significant negative correlation between rates of increase of unemployment in 1991/2 and levels of unemployment in 1984 for the country as a whole is to be explained quite simply - by the switch of *rising* unemployment from North to South and the fact that *levels* of unemployment remained higher in the North than the South.

Do Weak Labour Markets Produce Ill Health and, if so, How?

The effect of labour market fluctuations on the health of the workforce and their dependents has long been a matter of controversy (Marsh, 1938, Bartley, 1992). There is evidence that individual unemployment produces ill-health (Marsh, 1938, Warr, 1987, Jinn *et al.*, 1995). There is also growing evidence that individual insecurity while in employment has an adverse effect (Arnetz *et al.*,

1995, Brooker *et al.*, 1997, Ferrie *et al.*, 1995, 1997, Heaney *et al.*, 1994, Siegrist *et al.* 1990). Results like these have often been controversial, because they may be confounded by the extent to which health selects individuals for employment (Arrow, 1996, Elstad, 1995, 1996, Bartley, 1988, 1994, 1996, Elkeles and Seifert, 1996).

Brenner's work with time series data sidesteps the healthy worker effect, by suggesting that economic instability precedes and has a lagged effect on ill-health in populations (Brenner, 1979, 1983, 1987a, 1987b, Brenner and Mooney, 1982, 1983). However, it steps into a different problem, for, from a coincidence between two trends at the aggregate level - such as mortality statistics and unemployment rates - one cannot reliably infer that individuals who are unemployed or insecure in their employment suffer ill-health (Gravelle *et al.*, 1981, Gravelle and Backhouse, 1987, Stern, 1983, Kasl, 1982).

A way forward lies in exploring the effects of labour market fluctuations on *individual* health, while holding employment status constant (Arrighi and Hertz-Picciotti, 1994, 1996). If health selection alone takes place, ill-health will be concentrated among those ejected from employment, and, of course, there will be proportionally more of them where unemployment is high than where it is low. However, if everyone's health - whether unemployed, non-employed or employed - varies with the rate of unemployment in their local labour market, there are good grounds for saying that labour markets do affect health.

The investigation is in two stages. The first asks which features of unemployment rates - their level or their rate of increase - affect the various forms of ill-health. The second singles out self-reported health and seeks factors that might account for why weak labour markets influence the health of populations of working age.

Stage 1: Demonstrating that Weak Labour Markets Produce Ill-Health[20]

In the first stage, there are two questions to answer: first, do weak labour markets produce ill health in their working age populations; second, does a sustained high level of unemployment have a different effect on health than a recent sharp rise in unemployment?

There is also a number of factors that might confound any relation there may be between weak labour markets and ill-health. I shall seek to control these in the analysis:

---

20   For further discussion, see Bellaby and Bellaby, 1999a.

- To some extent, health selects for employment and for keeping jobs - to control for health selection, employment status will be held constant and the effects of rate of unemployment on each status will be examined
- The gender and age compositions of the working population are correlated with both employment patterns (Walby and Bagguley, 1989) and ill health and so age and gender need to be controlled
- A preponderance of lower classes in an area will be associated with social disadvantage and ill health, and, if their labour is no longer in demand as the economy restructures, high unemployment will result (Bartley and Owen, 1996), creating the false impression that unemployment level accounts for ill-health - social class will be controlled by using the six-point scale of the Registrar General's scheme
- Region may affect health independently of unemployment rates, for it has long been the case that morbidity and mortality differ quite sharply from one part of the country to another (Langford and Bentham, 1996, Illsley and LeGrand, 1993) reflecting, among other things, the degree of urbanization (Blaxter, 1990) - this will be controlled by including standard region in the analysis and (in order to make region a linear variable) measuring variations in urban/rural composition from the Census 1991 classification (*Key Statistics for Urban and Rural Areas*, HMSO, 1997), which depicts as urban, built up areas with population of more than 2,000.

A Prima Facie Case

Figures 9.1 and 9.2 (below) are drawn from analysis of HALS, to which have been added unemployment rates in the local labour markets in which respondents lived. They make a *prima-facie* case for the argument that weak labour markets affect the health of working populations. To be in line with the social causation hypothesis, relatively full employment should produce relatively good health in the population of working age.

As Figure 9.1 illustrates, the higher the *level* of unemployment in local labour markets in 1991, the more likely were people of working age in all employment statuses - except unemployed - to assess their health as fair or poor rather than excellent or good. It applies to those in employment (part time and full time) and the economically inactive alike (home-makers, the retired and the permanently sick) and as much to women as to men. For the *unemployed*, however, there is a suggestion that the trend is reversed, possibly because of countervailing effects on their average health produced by selection.

Figure 9.1 Levels of unemployment in local labour markets and percentage of individuals reporting fair/poor health by employment status in the population of working age

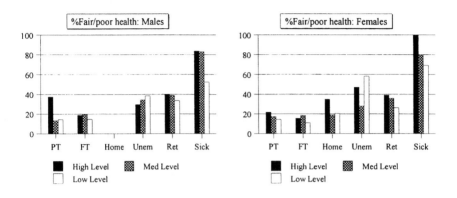

PT = part-time employee; FT = full-time employee; Home = home-maker/full-time education; Unem = unemployed; Ret = retired; Sick = permanently sick

In so far as health selects for employment[21], the unemployed are more likely to be rejected on health grounds when unemployment is low, for, when it is high, the unemployed will include many in good health. People of marginal health are more likely to have jobs when unemployment is low, and so the average health of the employed will be lower than in conditions of high unemployment. In addition, in areas of relatively full employment, there is less reason for the unemployed to abandon the search for work and opt for permanent sickness. Indeed, among males of working age in the HALS sample in 1991, only 2.8% were permanently sick in areas of low unemployment, but 6.1% were so in areas of high unemployment, while 13.8% who were unemployed in 1984 became permanently sick by 1991 in areas of high unemployment and only 5% did so in areas of low unemployment. Taken together, these selection effects mean - paradoxical as it may seem - that the unemployed are the least likely of all employment statuses to reflect the impact that high or rising rates of unemployment may have on the health of the population of working age.

21   See Chapter 2, where this argument is accepted as an approximate description, but heavily qualified as an explanation of what takes place.

Figure 9.2 Rate of increase in unemployment:
percentage of the employed having work stress

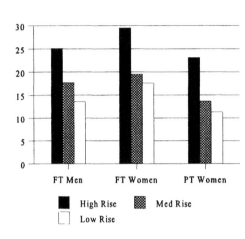

Figure 9.2 suggests a link between *rising rates* of unemployment and self-reported work stress among men and women in employment. The relatively few part-time men are left out here, but the more numerous part-time women and full-time workers, whether men or women, all tended to report stress in greater numbers when they worked in labour markets where unemployment levels were rising at the time of interview in 1991/2.

Modelling the Production of Ill Health

It remains to consider whether sustained high levels of unemployment and rising rates of unemployment in the short term have different effects on health, and whether these relations persist when factors that seem likely to confound them are allowed for: health selection for employment status; class, age and gender variations between small areas; and region of the country.

Table 9.1 shows the simple effects of unemployment rates on four measures

Table 9.1 Simple effects of unemployment rates on various
measures of ill health

Measure of ill health	Unemployment rate	Odds ratio	Significance
For 1991 sweep:			
Job stress	Level	0.980	19.8%
	Increase 91/92	1.359	0.0%
Death before age 75	Level	1.094	0.1%
For both sweeps:			
Respiratory flow	Level	1.013	10.0%
Self assessed health	Level	1.053	0.0%
	Increase 84/85	1.012	71.9%
	Increase 91/92	0.859	0.0%

of ill health: job stress, death by 75, respiratory function and self assessed health. Odds ratios are used to express relations in the tables: positive effects on the measure of health have odds ratios greater than 1 and negative effects odds ratios with values less than 1. Significance levels are also cited.

The method used in estimating the various measures of ill-health is logistic regression (Gilbert, 1993), which is useful when many variables are involved in an attempt to estimate a single outcome, say premature death, because it enables the main effects to be highlighted. The output of this procedure will be given in two forms: an odds ratio showing the independent effect of each factor upon the measure of ill-health in question, and the significance level of the estimate. When an odds ratio is close to 1, there is little or no difference from the average effect. When it is over 1, the relation is positive; but when it is under 1, it is negative.

Job stress and unemployment rates In 1991 HALS respondents were asked to complete a life events schedule, including six items about work in the previous year. The measure of job stress is based on reports of worry and stress arising out of job change, retirement, loss or fear of loss of job and any other crisis involving work, including a respondent's experience of a partner losing a job or retiring. Job stress has been related to TTWA unemployment levels and their increases in the year of the second interview (1991-2). Increases in unemployment have a significant relation to job stress but levels of unemployment do not. Among those who had *no* unemployment between 1984 and 1991, the proportion reporting job stress rises step by step with the rate of increase of unemployment, from 8.5% in the lowest quintile,

Table 9.2 Effects of unemployment rates and confounding factors on job stress

Estimated effect	Odds Ratio	Significance
Social class	1.092	2.0%
Age in years	0.991	5.4%
Gender		
Male	0.844	11.6%
Female	1.000	-
Employment status		
Full time	1.345	2.4%
Part time	1.000	-
Unemployment rate		
Level	0.991	64.3%
Increase 91/92	1.364	0.0%
Rurality of standard region	0.938	5.3%

through 10.0%, 15.7%, and 19.6% to 21.3% in the highest.

Table 9.2 reports the multivariate analysis. Among the statistically significant findings (p<.05) are that full time workers, employees of higher class and younger people are more likely to report high job stress than those who work part time, are lower class and older. The tendency for males to report less job stress than females may lose significance because the greater numbers of part time workers who are women is controlled for. Region also has a significant effect that is largely attributable to variations in rural population. The more rural the standard region within which TTWAs are to be found, the lower the job stress reported. The South East and West Midlands, the one adjacent to the metropolis, the other including Britain's second city, have job stress levels which are significantly higher than this model predicts.

However, the crucial result of this multivariate model is to suggest that rising rates of unemployment have an independent effect on job stress, over-riding the healthy worker effect, age, sex and social class, and region.

Death before aged 75 and unemployment rates   Deaths of respondents have been appended to the HALS data when they occurred after the second sweep of HALS and up to 1995. In all, 122 people of working age in 1984 who were interviewed again in 1991 had died before reaching 75 by 1995. Clearly, not everyone in the cross sectional sample had an equal chance of death by 75 within this calendar period. This must be borne in mind when appraising the results.

In Table 9.3, death by 75 is predicted by *level* of unemployment in local labour markets in 1991. Death cannot select for employment. If one assumes, as here, that premature death is

Table 9.3 Effects of unemployment rates and confounding factors on death before age 75

Estimated effect	Odds ratio	Significance
Social class	0.833	1.5%
Age in years	1.043	0.0%
Gender		
Male	2.049	0.0%
Female	1.000	-
Employment status		
Permanently sick	6.427	0.0%
Non-employed	3.142	5.6%
Employed	1.000	-
Unemployment rate		
Level	1.084	2.4%
Rurality of standard region	0.989	88.0%

an index of ill health in life, this result must be subject to the same controls for confounding factors, including the healthy worker effect, as are applied to other health measures.

The inclusion of age and permanent sickness in the model helps to offset the inbuilt bias in the sample. As expected, males are more likely to die by this age than women, as are members of the lower class. The non-employed have a markedly greater average risk of death by 75 than the employed, but this just fails to reach significance when the permanently sick are excluded. Region makes no significant contribution to the likelihood of death by 75, whether reduced to rurality or not. This is unexpected, but it would appear that variations in age, gender, class, employment status and unemployment rate account for regional differences in mortality. Critically, level of unemployment in 1991 is significantly and positively associated with the likelihood of death by 75. It is notable that this effect of local unemployment level is independent of individuals' employment status, for which people may be presumed to be selected by ill health leading eventually to early death.

Respiratory function and unemployment rates Whereas job stress was based on respondents' own reports, the measure of respiratory function, like the certification of death, was performed by health professionals. Here the focus is FEV1 (Forced Expiratory Volume) as measured by portable electronic spirometer. There was a trial run and observations made when the respondent had an acute respiratory infection were recorded 'missing'. The HALS clinical researchers categorized FEV1 scores by standard deviations *below* the norm for sex, stature and age. Here the odds of falling more than

Table 9.4 Effects of unemployment rates and confounding factors on respiratory flow

Estimated effect	Odds ratio	Significance
Social class	0.833	0.0%
Age in years	1.021	0.0%
Gender		
Male	1.059	40.0%
Female	1.000	-
Employment status		
Permanently sick	3.483	0.0%
Non-employed	1.391	5.3%
Full time	1.252	0.0%
Part time	1.000	-
Unemployment rate		
Level	1.009	24.6%
Rurality of standard region	0.907	0.0%

one standard deviation below the norm have been estimated.

So measured, below normal respiratory function is a good predictor of premature death (odds ratio 3.368, p<.01). Death by 75 is associated with levels of unemployment in TTWAs, but respiratory function produces a non-significant, even if positive, relation with level of unemployment. The result is based on both measures of FEV1 and two measures of unemployment - at 1984 and 1991.

Respiratory function is influenced significantly by lower class, greater age, and the degree to which the region is urban rather than rural (as with job stress, the West Midlands and the South East have a significantly greater incidence of poor respiratory function than the model predicts). The worse respiratory function of the non employed than the employed just fails to reach significance at the 5% level when the permanently sick are excluded. It is intriguing that those in full time employment should more often have a below normal function than those in part time employment, especially in view of the fact that gender, the usual arbiter of hours of work, is controlled. It may reflect more prolonged exposure to pollution or less opportunity for exercise. Crucially, however, the main finding - about the link with unemployment rates - is negative, and cautions against assuming that all dimensions of health are affected by unemployment rates.

Self assessed health and unemployment rates Self assessed health is, of course, a self reported measure. Respondents were asked: 'Would you say that for someone of your age, your own health is generally excellent, good, fair or poor?' The odds of fair/poor health have been estimated.

In HALS, self- assessed health proved to be the strongest predictor among all health measures of death subsequent to 1991 within the sample but the nature of that link is problematic (Appels *et al.*, 1996, Moum, 1992).

Table 9.5 (below) shows that self assessed health displays quite a complex relation with unemployment rates in TTWAs. It is positively associated with average level of unemployment 1984-91, but also negatively associated with rising rates of unemployment in 1991-2. At first sight, the latter suggests that, when confronted with adversely changed expectations, respondents try to persuade themselves that they are in the best of health. However, the result is not repeated when self assessed health in 1984 is estimated from rate of increase in that year. It seems that level of unemployment estimates fair/poor health. It can be surmised that the result for rising rates of unemployment in 1991/2 reflects the peculiar circumstances discussed above, when recession hit the South, which had previously been little affected, so causing sharply rising rates where levels of unemployment remained low. The significant contributors, unemployment rates apart, are social class (lower class report more adversely than higher class), employment status and region. Neither gender nor age makes a significant independent difference to self assessed health. It may be that individuals compare themselves with others of the same gender as well as similar age when assessing their health. Each of the following employment statuses is significantly more likely to assess its health adversely than the ones below it: the permanently sick, the retired, the unemployed, homemakers and those in employment. The net result is support for the healthy worker effect, for those in employment report by far the best health on average.

Table 9.5 Effects of unemployment rates and confounding factors on self-assessed health

Estimated effect	Odds ratio	Significance
Social class	0.804	0.0%
Age in years	1.000	91.6%
Gender		
Male	1.110	7.9%
Female	1.000	-
Employment status		
Permanently sick	18.291	0.0%
Retired	2.854	1.7%
Unemployed	1.736	1.1%
Home or education	1.443	0.0%
Employed	1.000	-
Unemployment rate		
Level	1.031	0.0%
Increase 84/85	1.008	82.6%
Increase 91/92	0.866	0.2%
Rurality of standard region	0.937	0.1%

As is the case for job stress and respiratory function, the more rural the region the better is health.

However, neither region nor the healthy worker effect accounts for the contributions that variations in unemployment rates make to self assessed health.

Stage 2: Explaining How Weak Labour Markets Affect Health[22]

There is limited value in showing statistically significant relations unless

---

22   Further discussion is available in a working paper - Bellaby and Bellaby 1999b.

mechanisms can be found to account for them. So far, a difference has been identified between high levels and rising rates of unemployment, which suggests possible mechanisms. High levels may produce fair/poor self-assessed health and relatively early death. Rising rates do not have these effects where levels are relatively low, but seem to produce job stress.

'Stress' tends to be a catch-all explanation for the effects of economic instability on health (Bellaby, 1986), but its value may be more limited. At best it is part of a longer causal chain that begins with social processes - the effects of weak labour markets on material life and social relations. I hypothesize that these are of two main kinds: political-economic and socio-cultural. The political-economic can be summarized in terms of, first, *risky jobs* - in weak labour markets those who get or keep jobs must accept worse health and safety conditions than they would where labour markets favoured employees; and, second, *deprivation* - weak labour markets tend to reduce the income otherwise available to keep self and dependents, by depressing wages and salaries, and deprivation leads to ill-health. There are also two socio-cultural processes that might be involved: first, *individuation* - weak labour markets isolate people from communities and interpersonal relations and depress health; and, second, *anomie* - weak labour markets tend to divert and disrupt the life-course and prevent people from fulfilling expectations based on better economic conditions, so affecting their health.

There is not space to consider all four of the measures of ill-health. Instead, I shall focus on the self-reports - of job stress and health status. To what extent are the relations already found, first, between rising rates of unemployment and job stress and, second, high levels of unemployment and self-assessed health to be explained by any of the hypothesized processes?

A similar statistical technique will be used to that of the previous stage. However, since the main interest is now the difference that it makes to introduce an intervening factor, such as 'anomie', into the relations that have been indicated between unemployment rates and health, loglinear modelling will be preferred to logistic regression.

Risky Jobs

Most people earn a living for a major part of their lives by selling their labour to an employer. In principle, there are several ways in which weak labour markets may make work more of a risk to health: increasing the hours of work; causing work at unsocial hours, such as nights and weekends; increasing the physical effort required; and causing a worsening of the relation between autonomy and control or 'decision-latitude' and job-demands.

It is not a foregone conclusion that these worsen self-assessed health, far less that they explain the greater part of variation in health across a national sample. Unfortunately HALS has very limited measures of the nature of work. Hours, shifts and physical effort are the only issues of this type on which questions were asked. There is no measure of autonomy and control for instance. However, it is possible to make some inferences about stressors that remain unmeasured, because there are questions, involving 'the job' as a possible answer, about what respondents believe affects health, for better or worse, and how respondents would explain any changes in their health over the previous seven years.

Working hours According to the Labour Force Survey in Britain, hours of full-time employees rose from 38.3 (men 39.8) in Spring 1984 to 39.3 (men 41.2) in Spring 1991 and further to 39.4 (41.4) in Autumn 1992, which was out of step with the downward trend elsewhere in the European Community (Eurostat 1986-94). In the HALS sample, between 1984 and 1991, average hours of full-time employees increased from 43.7 to 45.1, and of part time from 16.3 to 18.5. However, there is no significant relation between self-assessed health and working hours. Nor is level of unemployment related to working hours.

Shifts Shifts were worked by a small minority of full-time workers (15.7%) and again bore no relation to self-assessed health or level of unemployment.

Physical Effort The greater the physical effort the worse is health. This bivariate relation is linear and significant at 5%. There is quite a strong linear relation between unemployment levels in 1991 and job effort. The number of respondents who report that their job needs a lot of physical effort goes up, and the number who says it requires none goes down the higher the level of unemployment.

At first, it seemed likely that this relation was in turn to be explained by the tendency of unemployment to be higher in areas where manual work is relatively common. Indeed physical effort is far more likely to be required of manual than non-manual workers: 53.3% of manual workers say their job involves a lot of effort, but only 18.4% of non-manual workers say this. However, when both unemployment level and manual/non-manual are included in a log linear model to estimate physical effort, the two factors have independent effects. The manual/non-manual factor appears to mediate some of the effect of unemployment levels on the physical effort required but not much of it.

A log linear design based on assumed independent relations of self-assessed health to both physical effort and manual/non-manual jobs fits well, but the relation of job effort to self-assessed health ceases to be linear or indeed to have any shape. There is, then, a hint that the physical effort jobs require where labour

200 Sick From Work

markets are at their weakest is involved in producing self-reported ill-health, but on this evidence it cannot be concluded that physical effort *explains* the relation.

Otherwise hidden stressors? The relations between level of unemployment and the respondents' own reports that there was a link between their health and their work can be quickly summarized: there is no relation between level of unemployment and believing one's job/work makes one healthy; there is no relation between level of unemployment and wanting to change one's job or indeed get a job to improve one's health; there is no relation between level of unemployment and saying that one's job was one of the three main factors in becoming more healthy over the last seven years; there is a relation, significant at the 5% level, between level of unemployment and implicating one's job in worsening health over the last seven years, but it is inverse, i.e. the lower the level of unemployment the more likely is the job to be blamed.

This last relation becomes insignificant when employment status is introduced. Then the difference between those in work and others emerges as highly significant. The full time workers, in particular, are more likely to implicate their jobs in explaining worsening health, and they do so consistently more often the lower is the level of unemployment. There is also a strong relation between self-assessed health and implicating the job in worsening health, but, paradoxically, it is negative: i.e. the more likely employees are to blame the job for worsening health, the more healthy they are likely to report themselves.

The changes in average working hours that were detected for the whole sample who were in work in both 1984 and 1991, are higher for both full-time and part-time workers who implicate their job in their worsening health: for full-timers, weekly hours were 47.7 in 1991 as against 44.1 in 1984, and for part-timers the corresponding figures were 22.9 and 17.7. It seems that those in work were working harder in the trough of the 1991/2 recession than they had done in 1984, and were likely to think that this intensification of labour was worsening their health. However, when health is viewed across all categories, even by using self-reports of a parallel kind (the self-assessed health measure), it is clear that the people who said they were put under greater stress at work felt on the whole much healthier than those who did not experience this intensification.

Thus, whether because of the limitations of HALS or because of the facts of the matter, the *risky job* mechanism does not convincingly connect rates of unemployment to perceived ill-health. In evaluating this rather unexpected finding, it has to be borne in mind that 1984-91 was a period of change in the occupational structure, that extractive and manufacturing industry continued to decline, construction was in recession, and service and non-manual jobs were on the increase. This would have reduced the overall risk in jobs.

Deprivation

In a money economy, one's standard of living depends on purchasing power, and that in turn on income, which, for the overwhelming majority, derives directly or indirectly from earnings in employment. Few have capital, except for what is tied up in such necessities as a house, and many have neither liquidity nor a means of earning money that is independent of the labour market. Individuals may also have dependents or themselves be dependent. In households of more than one person what is earned in employment by any of their number is usually shared. Therefore per capita household income is a decent approximation to prosperity/deprivation.

Table 9.6 estimates self-assessed health from per capita household income allowing for the effects of employment status and *level* of unemployment. Should

Table 9.6 Log linear model estimating poor self-assessed health in 1991 from average household income, employment status and unemployment levels in 1991

Hypotheses	Odds ratios	Model fit
Every £10 increase improves health	**1.57**	
Every £10 increase decreases the first effect	*0.77*	$\chi^2 = 139.8$
Employment Status: Permanently sick	**14.41**	DF = 137
Employed	**0.55**	P = .417
Actively non-employed	**0.48**	
1% higher unemployment	**1.07**	

Notes: for odds ratios, emboldened p<.001; plain p<.01; italics p<.05; for model fit, the higher the probability the better the fit. Estimates based on employment status in successive rows exclude the employment status already addressed: thus, 'employed' contrasts those in employment with those out of it, excepting the permanently sick, and so on. 'Actively non-employed' are full-time students and home-makers, and inactively non-employed, the unemployed and retired

deprivation act directly on the health of individuals, by making their subsistence inadequate, increases in per capita household income on health would be beneficial but produce diminishing benefits for higher levels of income. This prediction is confirmed in HALS when self-assessed health is modelled using per capita household income: each £10 increase in per capita household income per week produces a growth in the odds of good/excellent health, and each £10 increase produces an identical decrease in the growth rate of these odds. The model produces a good fit in which income, employment status and level of unemployment have significant independent effects on self-assessed health and there are diminishing returns to self-assessed health from income. There is support for the healthy worker effect: unsurprisingly the permanently sick report least good health, the employed the best and those who are active in non-employment (that is home-makers or students) better health than those who are retired or unemployed. Yet, even when the healthy worker effect is allowed for, by controlling employment status, level of unemployment has an independent effect on self-assessed health.

Deprivation, its causes and its effects on health are the subject of a larger literature (Macintyre, 1994) than any of the other possible mechanisms to explain the link between weak labour markets and health. There is not scope in this chapter or indeed perhaps in HALS to do justice to the issue. Nevertheless, the findings show that by far the greater part of the effect of employment status and unemployment levels on self-assessed health remains when income is introduced, and that income exerts an effect independent of labour markets. Thus deprivation is implicated in the process that leads from weak labour markets to perceiving one's health to be poor, but it is not the only missing link.

Individuation

Durkheim (1984) thought of the transformation of Western society in the late nineteenth century as the long term break up of local communities, each with a simple division of labour and ready solidarity, and their merger to form a larger, inchoate mass of interdependency based on a complex division of labour and having a tendency to 'egoism'. In a word, the process could be characterized as 'individuation'.

In the course of the transformation, individuals would also lose their roots in a shared belief system and moral code and become relatively rule-free or 'anomic'. For Durkheim individuation was irreversible, but anomie could be overcome. A stable form of solidarity could emerge that moralized individualism, building a new code upon the interdependence that the complex division of labour had created.

Durkheim also expected anomie in the temporary conditions of economic instability - slump and boom alike - to which capitalism was prone. Later writers have often (in effect) linked individuation, anomie and deprivation together, arguing that, because employment (or employing others) is the crux of participating in all aspects of a capitalist society, those who are unemployed, underemployed and on low incomes tend to be 'relatively deprived' and may become 'socially excluded' (Marmot, 1994, Wilkinson, 1994). It is these analyses of the short-run that seem most relevant to the search for mechanisms to account for the effects of weak labour markets on health.

The hypothesis tested in this section is that weak labour markets tend to exclude people from communities and interpersonal relations and in so doing produce ill-health. The assumption (true or false) is that social integration is based on secure employment and the lifestyle a steady income supports.

HALS offers a number of possible indicators of social integration. Three are objective states: how often respondents see relatives of any kind to speak to, how often they speak to their neighbours, and whether they are married or in a stable partnership and have remained so between 1984 and 1991. A fourth is subjective - the individual's sense that they get personal social support. The index of personal social support (PSSI) is based on seven questions inviting the respondent to assess the quality of the support he or she can rely on.

Table 9.7 models the relations between unemployment rates, employment status, self-assessed health and the various indicators of social integration. As the first column of odds ratios shows, when employment status and level of unemployment are controlled, only weekly contact with relatives produces a significant relation between social integration and health. However, it is the reverse of what an 'exclusion' argument would expect, for contact with relatives predicts *poorer* health not better.

Moreover, the introduction of this variable leaves intact relations that are found without it. The permanently sick are (unsurprisingly) most likely of all employment statuses to report poor health, followed by other non-employed and in particular the unemployed and retired rather than homemakers and people in full-time education. By inference, those in best health are the employed, which is consistent with the healthy worker effect. The higher the unemployment, the poorer the self-assessed health, showing that unemployment levels have an effect on perceived health that over-rides the healthy worker effect. Yet social integration plainly does *not* mediate the effect of unemployment rates on self-assessed health.

The second column of odds ratios depicts the relations found between weekly contact with relatives and employment status and level of unemployment. High levels of unemployment predict frequent contact with relatives (not the reverse as expected). Moreover, the permanently sick have most frequent contact and other non-employed have more frequent contact than the employed. What may be consistent with the exclusion hypothesis is that, in spite of having the time to do so, the unemployed and retired (inactive non-employed) are less likely than homemakers and students (active non-employed) to see relatives frequently.

Table 9.7   Log linear model estimating self-assessed health from levels of unemployment, employment status, kin relations and neighbourliness

	Odds Ratio of Outcomes		
	Poor Health	Kin Relations	Neighbour-liness
Employment status:			
Permanently sick	**12.82**	1.57	*1.64*
Employed	**0.48**	**1.53**	**1.53**
Active non-employed	**0.56**	*0.77*	NS
1% higher unemp. level	**1.07**	**1.08**	**1.05**
Weekly contact - relatives	1.29		
Weekly contact - neighbours	NS		

Notes: for odds ratios, emboldened p<.001; plain p<.01; italics p<.05; for model fit, the higher the probability the better the fit. Estimates based on employment status in successive rows exclude the employment status already addressed: thus, 'employed' contrasts those in employment with those out of it, excepting the permanently sick, and so on. 'Actively non-employed' are full-time students and home-makers, and inactively non-employed, the unemployed and retired

The third column repeats the pattern for chats with neighbours. The results are similar to those for contact with relatives. They do not support the exclusion hypothesis: even the distinction between active and inactive non-employed found for kin relations fails to reach significance here. As has already been seen in the first column, neighbourliness has no independent relation to self-assessed health.

Not the least surprising aspect of these findings is that neighbourliness, unstable partnerships and perceptions of personal social support have no independent relation to self-assessed health. At the zero order level chats with neighbours and a high score for personal social support *are* associated with reports of good health, as the literature suggests (Blaxter, 1990, Cohen and Syme, 1985). However, these relations disappear when employment status and level of unemployment are controlled. Unstable partnerships are not associated either with unemployment level or self-assessed health, though the unemployed are more prone to them than other employment statuses.

It is notable that contact with kin and relatives is stronger in areas of high than low unemployment. Unemployment levels remained high, even in 1991, by and large where they had been high in 1984. It may be supposed that - faced with a weak labour market and its consequences for household income - people in areas of longstanding relatively high unemployment would have been obliged to turn to neighbours and relatives for support. However, the benefits have not proved sufficient to outweigh the otherwise adverse consequences of underemployment.

It should be stressed again that, unlike neighbourliness, frequent relations with kin appear to kick in when one is already ill and requires care, even in this sample of people of working age, for the relation between self-assessed health and seeing relatives to speak to is negative, not positive.

In sum, while the findings for individuation and exclusion are intelligible in their own right, they lend no support to the idea that unemployment produces ill-health by breaking down established social relationships. It would seem that (as Durkheim argued) individuation is a long term consequence of *successful* capitalism, and that exclusion is much less germane to health where capitalism fails than has been generally supposed.

Anomie

When HALS respondents of 1984 were interviewed a second time in 1991, they provided reports of life events in the year before their second interview. In the two years spanning the recall of the first interviewees and the time of the last interviews, Britain was in sharp recession again. An index of 'shocks' or anomie was constructed by adding up life events that were adverse but logically independent of both weak labour markets and health. These items were included: divorce/separation, row with partner, difficulty with child, row with relative, lost contact with close tie, assault or robbery, major financial problems, serious brush with law and other serious upsets. Only the *events* were recorded, not how disruptive the respondents found them or the stress they attributed to them.

Anomie and self-assessed health Table 9.8 (lighter portion) introduces the variable 'shocks' into a design to estimate self-assessed health from employment status and level of unemployment. Shocks are independently associated with reports of fair/poor health. Their inclusion strengthens the model as a whole, but does not diminish the strength of associations between self-assessed health and either employment status or level of unemployment.

Anomie and rising rates of unemployment If shocks or anomie do not account for how *level* of unemployment influences self-assessed health might they be the mechanism by which *rising rates* of unemployment affect health? There are good grounds to make this distinction, because in 1991/2 areas with historically low levels of unemployment were more sharply affected by the new recession than those with historically high levels. The darker shaded section of Table 9.8 estimates shocks themselves from rising rates of unemployment.

Employment status is included in the usual way, but different contrasts than those associated with levels of unemployment now produce a stronger model. In particular, it is the unemployed (not the permanently sick) who are most likely to have had such a shock, while the (relatively early) retired are the best protected, followed by those in full time jobs.

Table 9.8 Log linear models estimating A) self-assessed health from levels
of unemployment, employment status and 'shocks', and B)
probability of incurring at least one shock, from employment
status and *rises* in the rate of unemployment

A)	Fair/ Poor Health		B)	Shocks	
Permanently sick	13.51		Unemployed	2.50	
Employed	0.47	$\chi^2 =$ 149.5	Retired	0.66	$\chi^2 =$ 30.0
Active non-employed	0.54	DF = 143	FT employed	0.74	DF = 25
1% higher unem- ployment. level	1.08	P = .338	1% rise in unem- ployment. rate	1.25	P = .225
Each added shock	1.23				

Notes: for odds ratios, emboldened p<.001; plain p<.01; italics p<.05; for model fit, the higher the probability the better the fit. Estimates based on employment status in successive rows exclude the employment status already addressed: thus, in 9.8A, 'employed' contrasts those in employment with those out of it, excepting the permanently sick, and so on; and, in 9.8B,.'retired' contrasts them with all the non-retired, excepting the unemployed, and so on

Anomie, job stress and rising rates of unemployment Self-assessed health is not associated with rising rates of unemployment. Rather, it is areas with historically high levels of unemployment in which fair/poor health is reported most often. On the other hand, rising rates of unemployment provide a good estimate of levels of stress associated with life events at the workplace in the previous year among the employed. Table 9.9 shows this estimate (1) and also how it is affected by the inclusion of the shocks or anomie measure (2).

Here, unlike shocks, job stress is measured by respondents' reports of worry and stress, not the mere occurrence of life events. The items included are: changed jobs, loss of job, job crisis, retirement, partner's job loss/crisis, partner's retirement.

Table 9.9 Logistic regression models estimating job stress among the employed from unemployment rates in 1991 and 1992, age, gender, occupational class and working hours

	Odds Ratio	
Variable	**1) With anomie**	**2) Without anomie**
FT *versus* PT employed	*1.34*	*1.35*
Age	NS	*0.99*
Gender	NS	NS
Manual *vs* Non-manual	*0.91*	*0.92*
Unemployment Aug 91	**0.72**	**0.70**
Unemployment Aug 92	**1.38**	**1.43**
Contribution of anomie	**1.67**	-
Model χ^2	203.8, DF=7, P=.0000	60.3, DF=6, P=.0000

Notes: for odds ratios, emboldened p<.001; plain p<.01; italics p<.05

1992 unemployment rates are positively associated, but 1991 unemployment rates are negatively associated with job stress, an indicator that rise in rates, not historically high rates, account for job stress, which is the mirror image of the results for self-assessed health. These conditions were distinctive of the South at that time. Job stress is also more likely in non-manual than manual employees and among full time than part time employees.

There is a strong and significant positive association between anomie and job stress. It seems that many aspects of people's lives fall apart when employment becomes insecure: indeed serious financial problems, problems with kids, disputes with friend or relative, legal problems, housing worries and marital quarrels were all referred to in the same context as job worries, though not more long term outcomes, such as divorce, or events more associated with a background of deprivation, such as the death of family and friends and being the victim of robbery.

Introducing anomie into the logistic regression model considerably increases its overall power and makes the contribution of being young to having job stress insignificant. It also reduces the odds ratio for unemployment rate in 1992 slightly, suggesting that anomie mediates some of the effect of insecurity in employment on job stress.

Weak labour markets and self-assessed health revisited The contribution of health can be tested further by focusing on the one life-events item that is explicitly concerned with job loss: 'Have you lost a job or thought that you would soon lose your job in the last year?'

Table 9.10 Log linear model estimating self-assessed health in 1991 from employment status in 1991 and job-loss in the year preceding

Lost or feared loss of job in previous year, now:-	Odds Ratio	Model Fit
Permanently sick	**9.52**	
Employed	2.16	$\chi^2 = 3.98$
Actively non- employed	1.58	DF = 7
Remainder	0.41	P = 0.783

Notes: for odds ratios, emboldened p<.001; plain p<.01; italics p<.05; for model fit, the higher the probability the better the fit. Estimates based on employment status in successive rows exclude the employment status already addressed: thus, 'employed' contrasts those in employment with those out of it, excepting the permanently sick, and so on. 'Actively non-employed' are full-time students and home-makers, and 'remainder' the unemployed and retired

The results in Table 9.10 can be summarized in this way: first, permanently sick, employed and active non-employed are less healthy than the average person in their new status following job loss experiences; and, second, other respondents, including the retired and unemployed, are healthier than the average person in their status following job loss experiences. The two findings can be reconciled in an account that focuses on the interaction over time of weak labour markets and perceived ill-health. In this account, periods of unemployment and retirement lead to a gradual decline in health. Thus, recently unemployed and retired will be healthier than the average person already unemployed and retired. However, those who have recently left the labour market for 'active' non-employed statuses, such as home-making and full-time education and for permanent sickness, together with people who have had job loss experiences but remain employed, will be less healthy than the average person already within these relatively sheltered statuses. The influence of weak labour markets on self-assessed health thus appears to be long term rather than short term, which contrasts with how rising unemployment and associated anomie lead to job-stress.

Conclusion

There is a sense in which Chapter 8 dealt with the archaeology of the relation between employment and ill-health, teasing out the prospects for death before 65 or 75 of people who may have been incapacitated or had their long term health impaired decades before. In this chapter, evidence of the effects on health of comparatively recent changes in British labour markets has been reviewed.

High levels of unemployment appear to have the major effect on self-assessed health and eclipse the impact of rising rates of unemployment, so seeming to affirm the long term impact of economic and social conditions on health (Kuh and Davey Smith, 1993). Rising rates of unemployment seem to produce job stress among those made insecure in their employment. These suggestive results have come to light because the geographical distribution of unemployment was changing sharply in 1991/2, and HALS captured the moment.

It is not surprising in work of this kind to find that no one of the political-economic and socio-cultural mechanisms that has been examined fully mediates the effect of unemployment rates on perceived health. Yet even the negative results might steer future investigation: there is no consistent support for the idea that high rates of unemployment damage health by causing people to take or remain in more risky jobs; nor do the results favour the idea that ill-health arises from the social isolation that might accompany relative deprivation in a consumer society and may be expected to follow from high unemployment.

One direction that needs to be pursued is suggested by the extent to which rising rates of unemployment eventually become high levels. There may be a larger process than has been glimpsed, which joins the effects of rising rates and of higher levels of unemployment. Disruptions to everyday life delivered by actual or imminent job-loss cause immediate stress, but contribute in the end, partly through the material deprivation that is associated with low demand, to worse health where unemployment eventually becomes high than where it is low. Greater social integration develops in areas of already high unemployment and comes to offer an element of social support from both neighbours and kin, but social integration is not enough to offset the ill-effects of high unemployment.

As Beck foretold (1992), the emerging 'flexibility' in labour markets is probably beginning to mask the weakness of demand for labour by substituting underemployment in part-time, temporary jobs for unemployment fom full-time, permanent jobs (Dex and McCulloch 1997). In due course, people may adapt to this changed pattern. The evidence to date suggests, however, that flexible labour markets may damage their health.

Conclusion

In my beginning is my end.
T.S.Eliot (1888-1965), *East Coker*

The argument of *Sick From Work* has pivoted on two distinctive claims: first, that employment is an asymmetrical relation of power, with which workers usually comply, but which also gives rise to conflict and resistance, because employers must exploit labour power and employees must conserve it; second, that workers are embodied selves, who are made useful to capital by a social process of selection, and docile by accommodating to the demands of their jobs. I have developed from these premises, hypotheses about health in work and employment, and have looked for evidence to test them. Most of the investigation has been my own, with particular emphasis on an anthropological-style study in 'Masspro', a pottery factory, but I have also drawn on less intensive studies of disability and employment, risk behaviour among employees of the National Health Service, and the impact of changes in labour markets from 1984 to 1991 on the health of the population of working age. The findings of these original studies have been compared with those of published research, including, for example, research on health and work in Whitehall and on occupational injuries.

Humans are adaptable to the environment and adapt it to their needs, but neither bodies nor the environment are indefinitely malleable. Thus, the process of selecting bodies has outcomes that are approximately similar to those of 'natural selection', with the labour market as habitat. The chronically ill and disabled are indeed marginalised. However, there is too much divergence from what 'natural selection' would predict, to permit any other conclusion than that selection is a *social* process, which sometimes involves discrimination, and is usually 'fair' only because it follows rules that are generally accepted, but also open to challenge - for example, about the employment of people past retirement age, and the frequent exclusion of disabled people from the workplace.

This selection process allocates people to slots in the division of labour and shapes them to fit. In doing so, it accentuates some and suppresses other qualities in individuals. It is where accentuated qualities are stretched to breaking point and/or other qualities are habitually under-used, that individual health is vulnerable. However, ill-health manifests only when ways of coping break down. Novice workers learn how to cope with the distinctive time demands jobs make - they develop a rhythm and/or a way of managing the stress that being

211

accountable for meeting deadlines imposes. Further, when workers lack control of time internal to work but have control over time external to it, ill-health is likely to lead to absence from work. It is less likely to do so where external control is lacking, as in recession, and/or internal control is present, as for many managers and professionals. Notwithstanding these regular links with the organization of work, sickness absence makes ill-health social and a morally ambiguous action. Workplace culture offers a constraining set of acceptable reasons for absence, which differ in some respects for women and men, younger and older and manager and worker.

Workers' embodied selves become adapted to a lived (physical-cum-symbolic) space in which they work habitually, but these spaces have varied symbolic properties, some threatening, some strengthening. The relation is experienced in different ways in differing work groups - as containing manageable risk, as making workers immune to abnormal risk, as exposing them to risk normally, or as requiring them to take risks. Crucially, many health-related behaviours, including smoking as well as encounters with hazards in the workplace, have to be included in what is to be explained, rather than treated as preferences which exert an independent effect on health. Workplace culture is part of that explanation, but it, in turn, requires explanation.

On balance, employees have risks imposed upon them by the employment relation, rather than *taking* the risks they incur, whether individually or in following the rules of risk cultures. Occupations can still kill, and published statistics tend to understate the extent to which they do so, and more still, the extent to which they impair workers' health. The study of Masspro offers an unusual opportunity to identify the characteristics of fairly specific occupations that might lie behind the occupational mortality statistics and to try and disentangle the effects of jobs from those of gender, class and environment outside work. I conclude from this that these manual occupations do leave physical 'footprints', if not quite as distinct as those Ramazzini claimed to find. This is not to deny that other factors, among them gender roles and both class and environment beyond the workplace, have an impact.

The restructuring of occupations in recent years has removed some of the more physically dangerous jobs (including many in the pottery industry). The changes were accompanied by a sharp rise in unemployment in the early 1980s. The jobs that were lost included many in the core manual sector of the labour market, where unions and internal labour markets were established. In the wake of the destruction has come a new beginning, the so-called 'flexible' labour market. In the last chapter of the book, I drew on the nation-wide Health and Lifestyles Survey in a novel way, to try and establish whether the changes that occurred in local labour markets during the span of the survey (1984 to 1991) might have threatened the health not just of the unemployed, but the population of working age as a whole, in work and out of work. The results suggest that labour markets do affect the health of those retaining employment and the non-employed who depend on them, in spite of health selection for survival in employment. Sharply rising unemployment seems to give rise to stress among those in employment, while sustained high levels of unemployment are associated with relatively poor self-assessed health and may predict premature death. The analysis did not give a full explanation, though anomie - the shattering of stable expectations - accounted, in part, for the link between rising unemployment and stress, and deprivation of income, in part, for the relation between high levels of unemployment and adverse self-assessed health.

Sociology, Psychology and Epidemiology - Division of Labour or Collision Course?

The sociological approach I have taken inevitably implies some modifications to the interdisciplinary study of the relation between work and health. As Figure 10.1 suggests, the prevailing epidemiological and psycho-social approaches focus on explaining health outcomes, that is disease. However, to

Figure 10.1 Approaches to employment and health

	Individual	Collective	
The Body	1) Internal	2) External	⟩ **Disease**
The Mind	3) Stress	4) Stressors	
Social Action	5) Choices	6) Rules, Roles & Power Relations	⟹ **Illness/ Sickness**

understand ill-health fully in any context, it is necessary to distinguish *disease*, as biological process, *illness* as individual experience of ill-health, which is informed by culture, and *sickness* as the making social of ill-health. Though disease may be present in the background, culture and social relations play the main part in illness and sickness, and so it is misleading, for instance, to treat sickness absence as an index of morbidity in working populations. The distribution of disease in populations, its course in individuals and how it is understood and treated, are medicine's territory and benefit also from the psycho-social approach, but even they need supplementary attention from sociology.

Internal and *external* approaches to the effects of occupations upon the health of the body are represented here. For example, the clinician usually encounters the effects of work on health as internal diseases which require individual treatment, and may be unaware of their occupational basis. Health and safety inspectors interpret them as an index of collective phenomena: the workplace and working practices may have to change to prevent other cases occurring. Again, social action involves choices (internal), but these are both constrained and enabled by rules, roles and relations of power (external).

Divisions of labour protect professional and academic interests from each other. However, the concept of embodiment and the use made of it here have implications for epidemiology and psychology as well as sociology. Three elements are brought together in embodiment - body, mind and self. So much attention has been devoted to the relation between mind and body within medicine and psychology, that the more significant dualism between self and the couple, body and mind - both conceived as 'other'- has passed unnoticed. Thus, it is falsely claimed that psycho-somatic medicine resolves the deep dualism in human sciences. So much attention has been devoted within social and cultural studies to the self and its constitution in culture and social relations, that the dualism of self and mind/body has passed unnoticed in the humanities too. In claiming to have resolved the dualisms, medicine and psychology as 'natural science' often seek to reduce the self to body or mind or both. Similarly, sociology often seeks to reduce body and mind to a culturally and socially constituted self - this has applied from Durkheim to post-modernism. Thus, it may be falsely claimed that sociology can encompass everything.

To take embodiment seriously one has to think of body, mind and self as three facets of the same thing, or, better, three moments in the same process. The limits and possibilities of the human body and mind affect what the self can be. Yet, in shaping selves, culture and social relations also tune or discipline bodies and minds through the self. How body and mind are tuned also determines their breaking points. In training, an athlete accentuates qualities of body and mind which enable a certain distance to be run at a competitive speed and does so as part of a culture which gives sport value, and in relations of interdependence and power that realize that value. Similarly each occupation shapes the body, the mind and the identity of the one who performs it. Just as an athlete can only press at the limits of what is biologically *and* historically possible for the body and mind and the identity of the one who performs it. Just as an athlete can only press at the limits of what is biologically *and* historically possible for the body and mind, so too the worker. Both have histories that began with a communal form of religious asceticism and continued with the modern army. However, capitalism has generalized these disciplines of work, to such an extent that no one escapes them, and they begin no later in life than school age and are relaxed only when one ceases to have the potential to produce value for exchange and profit.

It is such a concept of employment and work, as historically specific social forms that construct fitness and make bodies that become vulnerable to ill-health and injury, that should take the place of an individual universal body or mind or mind/body, in those disciplines which seek to understand and explain the relation between health and work.

The Future of the Body and Employment

The studies in a pottery factory, the NHS and changing labour markets from the mid 1980s to the early 1990s throw light on the recent past. Given the trends, what can be expected to change?

The demographic trend can be extrapolated more reliably than any other. The large generation born in the 1950s and 1960s will reach retirement age around 2020/2030. They have fewer children than their parents. Assuming that there is the same level of demand for labour as in the late 1990s, there will be shortages, and so early retirement will become less common and there may well be a return to the pattern of working beyond retirement that prevailed in the immediate post war era, indeed until the late 1950s. There appear to be many who could cope with work to a greater age than is at present the norm.

For the time being, the trend is against jobs for life. The recent insecurity of jobs is problematic for those who have been educated for and worked in a period when more jobs have been secure than at a previous point in the history of employment in Britain. The effect of sudden insecurity which we saw in the South in the 1990/2 recession may not recur, because new entrants may become inured to it and expect nothing else. It does not necessarily imply low wages or salaries, even if earnings are sporadic.

However, flexible labour markets make unionisation less likely than it was in the relatively stable employment of the 1960s and 1970s, especially in the now largely dismantled public sector. Since unions have an important part to play in making workplaces healthy and safe for their members, this could have knock on effects for injuries and diseases at work. So far any such effects may have been masked by the sharp decline in employment in coalmining (where injury and low).

One of the main reasons why secure employment has become less common is the break up of larger employing organizations and their replacement by smaller units. Like the decline of unionisation, this is likely to have the effect of imperilling the regulation of health and safety in the workplace. Health and safety inspectors are small in numbers and unable to make regular visits especially to the smallest units of employment. Self-regulation is not a viable substitute. The reporting of accidents, for instance, declines sharply as size of establishment decreases.

Finally, there has been speculation for some years about a revival of home-working, this time centred upon the use of IT networking employees' or sub-contractors' home-based work stations to the employer's server. It does not appear to be extensive as yet. If it were to become so, it would remove many workers from face to face exposure to colleagues and supervisors, though it would not be difficult for employers to monitor performance through computer networks - in detail over short intervals of time if they chose. 'Telework' appears to individuate the worker socially without necessarily increasing his or her autonomy or decision-latitude. One would expect health and safety when at work to be very difficult to regulate. Telework also has implications for the spatial and temporal boundaries that factory and office work traditionally draw around paid work and the home respectively, and may consequently change how workers approach illness and the issue of having time off work to recover.

Consumers who are also Producers

In the late twentieth century, people in developed countries have - in a specific sense - become divided against themselves: they are *consumers* and are, have been or will be *producers*, but these facets are separated by the division of labour and markets. Few produce what they consume, even in the limited sphere of preparing the food that they eat. Most consume in different places and times than those in which they produce, and in the company of different people. Most are employees and, even if self-employed, many are subordinated by their contracts. They naturally see themselves as working in order to live - that is, earning a wage or salary in order to buy consumer goods for themselves and their families. From a bird's eye view, however, they live in order to produce *and* consume goods and services on which businesses make a profit.

This state of affairs has arisen with mass consumption. Mass consumption began in the United States even before the Second World War, and followed in Britain in the 1950s and in the other countries that now form the European

Union, Australia and New Zealand and Japan and some of the rest of East Asia, at various times from then until the present. Elsewhere in the world it has barely begun, so mass consumption in one place is coeval with mass poverty in another.

Self identity and social standing have come to reflect patterns of consumption. In such a context it may seem as if each person makes and remakes themselves, changing not only their outward trappings, but even their minds and their bodies at will. They do not seem to be products of their inheritance or even of what they do for a living. Yet, from the bird's eye view, fewer - including women with dependent children - go through life without spending a large part of their most active mature years in employment as producers than did so before mass consumption became the norm. When people only consume and do not produce, it is chiefly as potential producers in the making (children) who are dependents of current producers, or as producers who have provided for their own withdrawal in old age out of earnings when employed. Each is a unity of the two sides: one can be a consumer because one is, has been or will be a producer.

The Consumer and Health

In the prevailing view, what applies in general to the consumer, applies in particular to health, even ageing. It is the individual's responsibility not to let themselves go. This idea has both long and short histories. Its short history is how consumerism emerged from the austerity of the reconstruction of Britain after the Second World War.

In the immediate post war period, reviving extractive and manufacturing industries took precedence; high male employment, including that of pensioners, was encouraged; consumer goods were rationed, both to keep down inflation and to divert money into capital investment; social security was extended to iron out pockets of poverty and poverty that was associated with such stages in the life cycle as child-rearing and old age; and, not least, there was a commitment to state health care provision. As in the war of mass mobilisation, so in peace, the accent was on collectivism.

The consumer boom of the 1950s left the austerity of the immediate post war period behind it. Rationing was ended. It had been an opportunity to influence the nation's diet with health in mind, from providing orange juice free to pre-school age children through adding vitamin D to margarine to restricting access to sweets and biscuits. Its removal was viewed with relief by most consumers, but the hedonism it permitted was taken on guiltily. Whereas poverty and ignorance had justified collective intervention in health promotion earlier, now poor health began to be attributed to individual over-indulgence and to advertising and profiteering by businesses. This attitude was partly attributable to the immediate antecedents, partly to a strain of Puritan self-denial with a much longer history. It was probably reinforced by the extent to which, even under the NHS, medicine and dentistry focused on cures of individual conditions by surgery and drugs, and made (free) health care seem a privilege not to be squandered by lack of care of self.

The collectivism of the Second World War and the immediate post war period was not new either. Sewage disposal in houses and under streets, refuse collection and clean water had been introduced in the last quarter of the nineteenth century. Schemes for improved working class housing began at the same time, as also did health and safety regulation of workplaces (employment of women and children had been regulated earlier in several industries, such as mining). This collective provision continued. However, it ceased to be seen as what health was about. Though once regarded as the cutting edge itself, it was taken for granted once the cutting edge appeared to be new medical technology.

The fact that an increasing number of people - especially women - depend on earnings in employment to maintain their consumption and that of dependents, exposes them to new risks. Attention to these has been partially eclipsed by recent official campaigns to change individual consumption in order to improve health and the fear of remote risks in the food chain and from the environment. In the prevailing view, at one extreme there are risks any individual can control by a change of lifestyle, and, at the other, risks which seem to stem from global capitalism and lie beyond the control even of governments. However, risks in the workplace are local and could be controlled.

There is some scope for individual action, but - given the extent to which risks arise from the employment relation itself - collective intervention is needed. The state - local, national or supra-national - has to set a common agenda for health and safety and enforce it punitively, because individual employers are unlikely to incur the extra costs of good practice for fear of becoming uncompetitive. At the workplace level, workers need to be able to act together to protect their interests, for official inspection is unlikely to be sufficiently frequent to deter abuse of regulations by employers. These were the lessons learned in the early industrial revolution. They remain valid.

Redressing the Balance

A number of trends have begun to redress the balance in favour of making the relation between employment, work and health focal.

The first has been renewed recognition over the last twenty years of a strong link between social disadvantage and ill-health. Not having employment is a disadvantage in itself - the longer that status lasts the more so. In addition, demand for manual work, especially of low skill, has been falling, as a secular trend and of course whenever there is recession. As a result unskilled workers are largely underemployed and, when they do get work, the jobs are low paid. As we saw in Chapter 9, local labour markets with high levels of unemployment not only have more unemployed people, especially men, they also seem to push more men into permanent sickness status and to deter more women from entering or re-entering the competition for jobs. Those affected are overwhelmingly in manual work. The health of all of working age but the unemployed themselves - even of those who retain employment - appears to be adversely affected by high levels of unemployment, which cause general material deprivation in an area. It may need other measures than reflation of demand, such as improved education and training, to remedy social disadvantage, but reflation - perhaps on a regional basis - seems to be the *sine qua non*. Adequate levels of employment are thus a health issue.

A second factor that propels employment and health up the agenda is the demand for equitable access to employment by disabled people. This has been inadequately addressed by government for many years. In Chapter 2, we saw evidence of discrimination in employment on several grounds - ethnicity, age, gender, and, not least, being disabled. Above all, it is only approximately true that *health* selects people for survival in employment, and disability by no means necessarily makes people unemployable. Though there are sometimes costs associated with employing disabled people, there is scope to modify jobs to fit potential workers. The Americans with Disabilities Act in the United States, the Disabilities and Discrimination Act in Britain and similar measures in other countries, put some of the onus on employers to explain why they should *not* employ a disabled applicant. In many cases, employing disabled people will carry a special duty of care, including implications it may have for their health and proneness to injury.

Thirdly, in Britain and the United States in particular, governments' commitment to retrenching spending on social security causes them to seek jobs for those not in work, including the non-employed who draw benefit - not only disabled people, but also lone parents. Employing lone parents carries with it potential risks to their health and that of their children alike. In general, a policy which seeks to off-load responsibility for the upkeep of those currently on social security and their dependents implies special responsibility for ensuring their health and well-being in employment.

To name a fourth factor, some spheres of production - livestock rearing, egg production and food processing among them - are hazardous to *consumers*, and this has been borne in upon the public by a series of epidemics including listeria, E-coli and new variant CJD. It also involves the use of organophosphates, oestrogen and antibiotics in managing livestock, pesticides and herbicides in managing crops. Effective regulation of these is as important to those employed in the processes as to consumers, and can usually only be achieved by simultaneous attention to health in employment. A similar point can be made about radiation hazards - even in the nuclear industry, where (for lack of alternative jobs in some areas, such as Sellafield) employees have often been ranged against environmental lobbies.

Finally, as a member of the European Community (now European Union) since 1972, Britain is bound by the terms of its Treaties - including the Social Chapter of the Maastricht Treaty of 1992, with provisions for health and safety at work, including maximum working hours. In any common market there is pressure from members, not only to reduce tariffs and avoid discrepancies between currencies, but also to bring taxes or subsidies on business and consumption and any other cost that affects trade to a similar level. Thus, Britain is being obliged to pay similar attention to employment and health as its partners in the EU, and that obligation is enforceable in law. In the long term, it can only avoid this effect of 'harmonisation' by withdrawing its membership.

In short, health in work and employment is not only *theoretically* a more significant topic than the trend towards linking health to consumer behaviour alone makes it seem, it is also becoming *practically* more important for government and employers.

References

Adams, J. (1995), *Risk*, London: UCL Press.

Alexander, L. (1982), Illness maintenance and the new American sick role, In Chrisman N.J. and Maretski, T.W. (eds), *Clinically Applied Anthropology*, Dordrecht: D.Reidel.

Alfredsson, L., Spetz, C-L. and Theorell, T. (1985), Type of occupation and near-future hospitalization for myocardial infarction and some other diagnoses, *International Journal of Epidemiology*, 14: 378-88

Alonzo, A.A., Acute illness behavior - a conceptual exploration and specification, *Social Science and Medicine*, A14: 515-26.

Appels, A., Bosma, H., Grabauskas, V., Gostautas, A. and Sturmans, F. (1996),Self-rated health and mortality in a Lithuanian and a Dutch population, *Social Science and Medicine*, 42: 681-9.

Arber, S. (1991), Class, paid employment and family roles - making sense of structural disadvantage, gender and health status, *Social Science and Medicine*, 32: 425-36.

Arber, S. and Lahelma, E. (1993), Inequalities in women's and men's ill-health: Britain and Finland compared, *Social Science and Medicine*, 37: 1055-68.

Arnetz, B.B., Brenner, S.O., Levi, L., Hjelm, R. *et al.* (1991), Neuroendocrine and immunologic effects of unemployment and job insecurity, 18th European Conference on Psychosomatic Research (1990, Helsinki, Finland), *Psychotherapy and Psychosomatics,* 55: 76-80.

Arrighi, H.M. and Hertz-Picciotti, I. (1994), The evolving concept of the healthy worker survivor effect, *Epidemiology*, 5: 189-96.

Arrighi, H.M. and Hertz-Picciotti, I. (1996), Controlling the healthy worker effect: an example of arsenic exposure and respiratory cancer, *Occupational and Environmental Medicine*, 53: 455-62.

Arrow, J.O. (1996), Estimating the influence of health as a risk factor on unemployment: a survival analysis of employment durations for workers surveyed in the German Socio-Economic Panel (1984-1990), *Social Science and Medicine* 42: 1651-9.

Augé, M. (1995), *Non-Places*, Translated by Howe, J., London: Verso.

Baldamus, W. (1961), *Efficiency and Effort*, London: Tavistock Publications.

Barnes, C. and Mercer, G. (eds) (1996), *Exploring the Divide*, Leeds: The Disability Press.

Barrows, S. and Room, R. (1991) *Alcohol, Behavior and Belief in Modern History*, Berkeley: University of California Press.

Bartley, M. (1985), Coronary heart disease and the public health 1850-1983, *Sociology of Health and Illness*, 7: 289-313.

Bartley, M. (1988), Unemployment and health: selection or causation - a false antithesis? *Sociology of Health and Illness*, 10: 41-67.

221

Bartley, M. (1992), *Authorities and Partisans*, Edinburgh: Edinburgh University Press.

Bartley, M. (1994), Unemployment and ill-health: understanding the relationship. *Journal of Epidemiology and Community Health* 48: 333-7.

Bartley, M. (1996), Unemployment and health selection. *Lancet* 348: 904.

Bartley, M., Popay, J. and Plewis, I. (1992), Domestic conditions, paid employment and women's experience of ill-health, *Sociology of Health and Illness*, 14: 313-43.

Bartley, M. and Owen, C. (1996), The relation between socio-economic status, employment and health during economic change, *British Medical Journal*, 313: 445-49.

Bartley, M., Carpenter, L., Dunnell, K. and Fitzpatrick, R. (1996), Measuring inequalities in health: an analysis of mortality patterns using two social classifications, *Sociology of Health and Illness*, 18: 455-75.

Bates, I. (1993), A job which is 'right for me'? Social class, gender and individualization, In Bates, I. And Riseborough, G. (eds), *Youth and Inequality*, Buckingham: Open University Press.

Beck, U. (1992), *The Risk Society*, Sage.

Bellaby, P. (1985), *Experiments in Changing Work Organization*, London: ESRC.

Bellaby, P. (1986), 'Please boss, can I leave the line?' A sociological alternative to stress and coping discourse in explaining sickness at work. *International Journal of Sociology and Social Policy* 6: 52-68.

Bellaby, P. (1987a), *The Relation between Work Organization and Sickness Absence in the Pottery Industry*. London: ESRC.

Bellaby, P. (1987b), The perpetuation of a folk model of the life cycle and kinship in a pottery factory, In Bryman, A., Bytheway, W., Allatt, P. and Keil, T. (eds), *Rethinking the Life Cycle*, Basingstoke: Macmillan.

Bellaby, P. (1989), The social meanings of time off work: a case study from a pottery factory, *Annals of Occupational Hygiene*, 33: 423-38.

Bellaby, P. (1990a), What is a genuine sickness? The relation between work-discipline and the sick role in a pottery factory, *Sociology of Health and Illness*, 12: 47-68.

Bellaby, P. (1990b), To risk or not to risk? Uses and limitations of Mary Douglas on risk-acceptability for understanding health and safety at work and road accidents, *Sociological Review*, 38: 465-83.

Bellaby, P. (1992), Broken rhythms and unmet deadlines: workers' and managers' time-perspectives, In Frankenberg (1992).

Bellaby, P. (1999), Spatiality, embodiment and risks encountered in the making of pots, *Social Science and Medicine*, 48: 1321-32.

Bellaby, P. (1999), New rules for old: a comparison of smoking and drinking among employees of the UK National Health Service and how these might be explained, *University of East Anglia*, mimeo.

Bellaby, P. and Bellaby, F.N.W. (1999), Unemployment and ill health: local labour markets and ill health in Britain 1984-1991, *Work, Employment and Society*, forthcoming.

Bellaby, P. and Bellaby ,F.N.W. (1999), Political-economic and socio-cultural process that might link weak labour markets to adverse self -assessed health, *University of East Anglia*, mimeo.

Bellaby, P. and Oribabor, P.E. (1980), 'The history of the present' - contradiction and struggle in nursing, In Davies, C. (ed) *Rewriting Nursing History*, London: Croom Helm.

Bendelow, G. and Williams, S. (1995), Transcending the dualisms, *Sociology of Health and Illness*, 17: 139-65.

Best, M.H. (1990), *The New Competition*, Cambridge: Polity Press.

Bethune, A., Harding, S., Scott, A. and Filakti, H. (1995), Mortality and the Longitudinal Study 1971 and 1981 Census cohorts, In Drever (1995), Chapter 8.

Blanck, P.D. (1995), Resolving disputes under the Americans with Disabilities Act. A case example of an employee with a back impairment, *Spine* 20: 853-9.

Blane, D., Davey Smith, G. and Bartley, M. (1993), Social selection: what does it contribute to class differences in health? *Sociology of Health and Illness*, 15: 1-15.

Blaxter, M. (1990), *Health and Lifestyles,* London: Routledge.

Blauner, R. (1964), *Alienation and Freedom, Chicago:* Chicago University Press.

Bloor, M., Samphier, P. and Prior, L. (1987), Artifact explanations of inequalities in health: an assessment of the evidence, *Sociology of Health and Illness*, 9: 231-64.

Boris, E. (1986), *Art and Labor*, Philadelphia: Temple University Press.

Bound, J., Schoenbaum, M. and Waidmann T. (1996), Race differences in labor force attachment and disability status, *Gerontologist*. 36: 311-21.

Brenner, M.H. (1979), Mortality and the national economy: a review and the experience of England and Wales 1936-1976, *Lancet*, ii: 568-73.

Brenner, M.H. (1983), Mortality and economic instability: a detailed analysis for Britain and comparative analyses for selected industrialized countries, *International Journal of Health Services*, 13: 475-87.

Brenner, M.H. (1987a), Economic instability, unemployment rates, behavioral risks, and mortality rates in Scotland, 1952-1983, *International Journal of Health Services*, 17: 563-620.

Brenner, M.H. (1987b), Relation of economic change to Swedish health and social well-being, 1950-1980, *Social Science and Medicine*, 25: 183-95.

Brenner, M.H. and Mooney, A. (1982), Economic change and sex-specific cardio-vascular mortality in Britain, *Social Science and Medicine*, 16:.431-42.

Brenner, M.H. and Mooney, A. (1983), Unemployment and health in the context of economic change, *Social Science and Medicine*, 17: 1125-38.

Breuer, J. And Freud, S. (1974), *Studies on Hysteria*, Translated Strachey, J. & A., Harmondsworth: Penguin.

Brooker, A.S., Frank, J.W., Tarasuk, V.S. (1997), Back pain claim rates and the business cycle. *Social Science and Medicine* 45: 429-39.

Brown, R.K. (1997), Flexibility and security: contradictions in the contemporary labour market, In *The Changing Shape of Work*, Basingstoke: Macmillan, 69-86.

Brunner, E., Davey Smith, G., Marmot, M., Canner, R., Beksinska, M. and O'Brien, J. (1996), Childhood social circumstances and psychosocial and behavioural factors as determinants of plasma fibrinogen, *Lancet*, 347: 1008-13.

Bryder, L. (1988), *Below the Magic Mountain*, Oxford: Clarendon Press.

Bury, M. (1996), Defining and researching disability: challenges and responses, In Barnes and Mercer (1996).

Canto-Klein, M. (1975), La représentation de l'espace et du temps: étude sur un type de voyage en chemin de fer, *Cahiers Internationaux de Sociologie*, 59: 355-66.

Chapireau, F. and Colvey, A. (1998) Social disadvantage in the International Classification of Impairments, Disabilities and Handicaps, *Social Science and Medicine*, 47: 59-66.

Clarke, S, Elliott, R. and Osman, J. (1995), Occupation and sickness absence, In Drever (1995), Chapter 13.

Coggon, D., Barker, D.J. and Cole, R.B. (1990), Stomach cancer and work in dusty industry, *British Journal of Industrial Medicine*, 47: 298-301.

Cohen, S., and Syme, SL. (eds) (1985*), Social Support and Health,* New York: Academic Press.

Cooper, J. (1995), Occupational injuries at work, In Drever (ed) (1995), Chapter 11.

Corrigan, P. and Sayer, D. (1985), *The Great Arch*, Oxford: Blackwell.

Cousins, C., Jenkins, J. And Laux, R. (1998), Disability data from the LFS: comparing 1997-98 with the past, *Labour Market Trends*, 106: 321-35.

Cox, BD, Huppert, FA, and Whichelow, M.J. (1993), *The Health and Lifestyle Survey,* Aldershot: Dartmouth Publishing.

Crow, S. (1996), Including all of our lives: renewing the social model of disability, In Barnes and Mercer (1996).

Crozier, M. (1964), *The Bureaucratic Phenomenon,* London: Tavistock.

Dahl, E. (1993), Social inequality in health - the role of the healthy worker effect, *Social Science and Medicine*, 36: 1077-86.

Davey Smith, G., Shipley, M.J. and Rose, G. (1990), Magnitude and causes of socio-economic differentials in mortality: further evidence from the Whitehall Study, *Journal of Epidemiology and Community Health*, 44: 265-70.

Dean, H. and Taylor-Gooby, P. (1990), Statutory sick pay and the control of sickness absence, *Journal of Social Policy,* 19: 47-67.

Department of Social Security (1992), *Departmental Report*, London: HMSO.

Dex, S. And McCulloch, A. (1997), *Flexible Employment*, Basingstoke: Macmillan.

Dodier, N. (1985), Social uses of illness at the workplace: sick leave and moral evaluation, *Social Science and Medicine*, 20.2: 123-8.

Doeringer, P. And Piore, M. (19971), *Internal Labour Markets and Manpower Analysis*, Lexington: D.C.Heath.

Doll, R. (1976), Mortality in relation to smoking: 20 years of observations on male British doctors, *British Medical Journal*, 25 December, 1976: 1525-36.

Douglas, M. (1970), *Purity and Danger*, Harmondsworth: Penguin.

Douglas, M. (1986), *Risk Acceptability According to the Social Sciences*, London: Routledge and Kegan Paul.

Douglas, M. (1987), *How Institutions Think*, London: Routledge.

Douglas, M. (1992), *Risk and Blame*, London: Routledge.

Douglas, M. and Wildavsky, A. (1982), Risk and Culture, Berkeley: University of California Press.

Drever, F. (ed) (1995), *Occupational Health - Decennial Supplement*, OPCS/HSE, London: HMSO.

Drever, F. and Bunting, J. (1997), Patterns and trends in male mortality, In Drever and Whitehead (1997), Chapter 8.

Drever, F. and Whitehead, M. (eds) (1997), *Health Inequalities*, Office of National Statistics: Decennial Supplement, London: HMSO.

Duprée, M.R. (1995), *Family Structure in the Staffordshire Potteries, 1840-1880*, Oxford: Clarendon Press.

Durkheim, E. (1984), *The Division of Labour in Society*, Translated Halls, W.D., Basingstoke: Macmillan.

Eagleton, T. (1991) *Ideology*, London: Verso.

Edwards, P. and Scullion, H. (1982), *The Social Organization of Industrial Conflict*, Oxford: Blackwell.

Elkeles, T. and Seifert, W. (1996), Immigrants and health: unemployment and health-risks of labour migrants in the Federal Republic of Germany, 1984-1992, *Social Science and Medicine* 43: 1035-47.

Elstad, J.I. (1995), Employment status and women's health - exploring the dynamics, *Acta Sociologica*, 38: 231-49.

Elstad, J.I. (1996), Inequalities in health related to women's marital, parental, and employment status - a comparison between the early 70s and the late 80s, Norway, *Social Science and Medicine*, 42: 75-89.

Esping-Andersen, G. (1990), *Three Worlds of Welfare Capitalism*, Cambridge: Polity.

Eurostat: Labour Force Survey Results, 1984-1992, Luxembourg: Office des publications officielles des communautés européenes, 1986, 1988, 1990, 1991, 1992, 1993, 1994.

Evans, R.G., Barer, M.L. and Marmor, T.R. (eds) (1994), *Why are Some People Healthy and Others Not?* Berlin: de Gruyter.

Ferrie, J.E., Shipley, M.J., Marmot, M.G., Stansfeld, S. and Davey Smith, G. (1995), Health effects of anticipation of job-change and non-employment: longitudinal data from the Whitehall II study,. *British Medical Journal*, 311: 1264-1269.

Ferrie, J.E., Shipley, M.J., Marmot M.G., Stansfeld, S., and Davey Smith, G. (1997), The health effects of major organizational change and job insecurity, *Social Science and Medicine*, 46: 243-254.

Figlio, K. (1985), What is an accident? Medico-legal practices and the causes of occupational illness in the 19th and 20th centuries, In Weindling (1985).

Fletcher, B.C. (1991), *Work, Stress, Disease and Life Expectancy*, Chichester: Wiley.

Foucault, M. (1977), *Discipline and Punish*, London: Allen Lane.

Fox, A. (1974), *Beyond Contract,* London: Faber and Faber.

Fox, A.J. and Adelstein, A.M. (1978), Occupational mortality: work or way of life? *Journal of Epidemiology and Community Health,* 32: 73-8.

Fox, A.J., Goldblatt, P. and Jones, D. (1990), Social class mortality differentials: artifact, selection or life circumstances? In Goldblatt, P. (ed), *Longitudinal Study: Mortality and Social Organization,* London: HMSO.

Fox, N. (1993), *Post-Modernism, Sociology and Health,* Buckingham: Open University Press.

Frankenberg, R.J. (1986), Sickness as cultural performance: drama, trajectory and pilgrimage. Root metaphors and the making social of disease, *International Journal of Health Services,* 16: 603-26.

Frankenberg, R.J. (1992), 'Your time or mine?' Temporal contradictions in biomedical practice, In Frankenberg (1992).

Frankenberg, R.J. (ed) (1992), *Time, Health and Medicine,* London: Sage.

French, J.R., Caplan, R.D. and Harrison, R.V. (1982), *The Mechanisms of Job Stress and Strain,* Chichester: Wiley.

Friedman, A.L. (1977), *Industry and Labour,* Basingstoke: Macmillan.

Gallie, D. (1994). Are the unemployed an underclass? Some evidence from the Social Change and Economic Life Initiative. *Sociology,* 28.3: 737-57.

Garfinkel, H. (1967), *Studies in Ethnomethodology,* Englewood Cliff NY: Prentice-Hall.

Garfinkel, H. (ed) (1986), *Ethnomethodological Studies of Work,* London: Routledge and Kegan Paul.

Gay, P.W. and Smith, R.L. (1974), *The British Pottery Industry,* London: Butterworth.

Geertz, C. (1973), *The Interpretation of Cultures,* New York: Basic Books.

Giddens, A. (1984), *The Constitution of Society,* Cambridge: Polity Press.

Gilbert, N. (1993), *Analyzing Tabular Data,.* London: UCL Press.

Gilman, SL. (1988), *Disease and Representation,* NewYork: Cornell University Press.

Glozier, N. (1998), Workplace effects of the stigmatization of depression, *Journal of Occupational and Environmental Medicine,* 40: 793-800.

Gouldner, A. (1954), *Patterns of Industrial Bureaucracy,* Glencoe: Free Press.

Gouldner, A. (1965), *Wildcat Strike,* New York: Harper Torchbooks.

Gravelle, H.S.E., Hutchinson, J. and Stern, J. (1981), Mortality and unemployment: a critique of Brenner's time-series analysis, *Lancet,* ii: 675-9.

Gravelle, H.S.E. and Backhouse, M.E. (1987), International cross-section analysis of the determination of mortality, *Social Science and Medicine,* 25: 427-41.

Green, J. (1997), *Risk and Misfortune,* London: UCL Press.

Greenhow, E.H. (1858), *Papers Relating to the Sanitary Condition of the People of England,* London: General Board of Health.

Griffin, C. (1985), *Typical Girls,* London: Routledge and Kegan Paul.

Grint, K. (1991), *The Sociology of Work,* Cambridge: Polity Press.

Hakim, C. (1995), Five feminist myths about women's employment, *British Journal of Sociology,* 46: 429-55.

Hakim, C. (1996), *Key Issues in Women's Work*, London: Athlone Press.

Harding, S., Bethune, A., Maxwell, R. and Brown, J. (1997), Mortality trends using the Longitudinal Study, In Drever and Whitehead (1997).

Hawkesworth, M. (1998), Spatiality and the presentation of facial acne, Paper read at the British Sociological Association Annual Conference.

Haynes R,, Bentham G, Lovett A, Eimermann J.N.A. (1997), Effect of labour market conditions on reporting of limiting long term illness and permanent sickness in England and Wales, *Journal of Epidemiology and Community Health* 51: 283-8.

Heaney, C.A., Israel, B.A. and House, J.S. (1994), Chronic job insecurity among automobile workers - effects in job satisfaction and health, *Social Science and Medicine* 38: 1431-7.

Herzlich, C. (1973), *Health and Illness,* Translated by Graham, D., London: Academic Press.

Herzlich, C. And Pierret, J. (1987), *Illness and Self in Society*, Translated by Forster, E., Baltimore: Johns Hopkins University Press.

Hyde, M. (1998), Sheltered and supported employment in the 1990s: the experiences of disabled workers in the UK, *Disability and Society*, 13: 199-215.

Illsley, R. and LeGrand, J. (1993), Regional inequalities in mortality, *Journal of Epidemiology and Community Health*, 47: 444-9.

Jahoda, M. (1982), *Employment and Unemployment*, Cambridge: Cambridge University Press.

Jaques, E. (1982), *The Forms of Time*, London: Heinemann.

Jinn, R.L., Shah, C.P. and Svoboda, T.J. (1995), The impact of unemployment on health - a review of the evidence, *Canadian Medical Association Journal*, 153: 529-40.

Johansson, P. and Palme, M. (1996), Do economic incentives affect work absence? Empirical evidence using Swedish micro data, *Journal of Public Economics*, 59: 195-218.

Johns, G. and Xie, J.L. (1998), Perceptions of absence from work: People's Republic of China versus Canada, *Journal of Applied Psychology* 83: 515-30.

Karasek, R.A. (1979), Job demands, job decision latitude, and mental strain: implications for job redesign, *Administrative Science Quarterly* 24: 285-307.

Karasek, R.A. and Theorell, T. (1990), *Healthy Work,* New York: Basic Books.

Kasl, C.V. (1982), Strategies of research on economic instability and health, *Psychological Medicine*, 123: 637-49.

Kivimaki, M., Vahtera, J., Thomson, L., Griffiths, A., Cox, T. and Pentti, J. (1997), Psychosocial factors predicting employee sickness absence during economic decline, *Journal of Applied Psychology*, 82: 858-72.

Kleinman, A. (1980), *Patients and Healers in a Context of Culture,* Berkeley: University of California Press.

Knutsson, A. and Goine, H. (1998), Occupation and unemployment rates as predictors of long term sickness absence in two Swedish counties, *Social Science and Medicine,* 47: 25-31.

Kristensen, T.S. (1991), Sickness absence and work strain among Danish slaughterhouse workers: an analysis of absence from work regarded as coping behaviour, *Social Science and Medicine,* 32: 15-27.

Kristensen, T.S. (1998), Job stress and cardiovascular disease: a theoretic critical review, *Journal of Occupational Health and Psychology,* 1: 226-60.

Kuh, D. and Davey Smith, G. (1993), When is mortality risk determined? Historical insights into a contemporary debate, *Journal of the Social History of Medicine,* 6: 101-2.

Kumar, K. (1988), From work to employment and unemployment: the English experience, In Pahl, R.E. (ed), *Work,* Oxford: Blackwell.

Kumar, K. (1995), *From Post-Industrial to Post-Modern Society,* Oxford: Blackwell.

Laban, R. and Lawrence, F.C. (1947), *Effort,* London: McDonald and Evans.

Langford, I.H. and Bentham, G. (1996), Regional variations in mortality -rates in England and Wales - an analysis using multilevel modelling, *Social Science and Medicine,* 42: 897-908.

Leder, D. (1990), *The Absent Body,* Chicago: Chicago University Press.

Lefebvre, H. (1991), *The Production of Space,* Translated by Nicholson-Smith, D. Oxford: Blackwell.

Lewis, G. (1975), *Knowledge of Illness in Sepik Society,* London: Athlone Press.

Littler, C.R. (1982*), The Development of the Labour Process in Capitalist Societies,* London: Heinemann.

Macintyre, S. (1994), Understanding the social patterning of health: the role of the social sciences, *Journal of Public Health Medicine* 16: 53-9.

Maletic, V. (1987*), Body - Space - Expression,* Berlin: Mouton de Gruyter.

Marmot, M.G. (1994), Social differentials in health within and between populations, *Daedalus,* 123: 197-216.

Marmot, M. and Theorell, T. (1988), Social class and cardiovascular disease: the contribution of work, *International Journal of Health Services,* 18: 659-74.

Marmot, M.G., Shipley, M.J. and Rose, G. (1984), Inequalities in death - specific explanations of a general pattern? *Lancet,* xx.(I): 1003-6.

Marmot, M.G., Davey Smith, G., Stanfeld, S., Patel, C., North, F., Head, J., White, I., Brunner, E. and Feeney, A. (1991), Health inequalities among British civil servants: the Whitehall II study, *Lancet,* 337: 1387-93.

Marmot, M., Feeney, A., Shipley, M., North, F. and Syme, SL. (1995), Sickness absence as a measure of health status and functioning: from the UK Whitehall II study, *Journal of Epidemiology and Community Health,* 49: 124-30.

Marmot, M.G. and Shipley, M.J. (1996), Do socioeconomic differences in mortality persist after retirement? 25 Year follow up of civil servants from the first Whitehall study, *British Medical Journal,* 313: 1177-80.

Marsh, L.C., Fleming, A.G. and Blackler, C.F. (1938), *Health and Unemployment,* Oxford: Oxford University Press.

Marshall, G., Rose, D., Newby, H. and Vogler, C. (1988), *Social Class in Modern Britain,* London: Unwin Hyman.

Martakainen, P. (1995), Women's employment, marriage, motherhood and mortality - a test of the multiple role and role accumulation hypotheses, *Social Science and Medicine*, 40: 199-212.

Martin, J. and Roberts, C. (1984), *Women and Employment*, London: HMSO.

Martin, J., Meltzer, H. and Elliot, D. (1988), *The Prevalence of Disablility Among Adults*, OPCS surveys of disability in Great Britain, Report 1. London: HMSO.

Martin, J., White, A. and Meltzer, H. (1989), *Disabled Adults: services, transport and employment*, OPCS surveys of disability in Great Britain, Report 4, London: HMSO.

Marx, K. 1975), Economic and Philosophical Manuscripts (1844), In Karl Marx: *Early Writings*, Harmondsworth: Penguin Books, 279-400.

Marx, K. (1976), *Capital*, Vol 1, Translated by Ben Fowkes, Harmondsworth: Penguin Books.

Maslow, A. (1970), *Motivation and Personality*, 2nd edition, New York: Harper and Row.

McDowell, L. and Court, G. (1994), Performing work: bodily representations in merchant banks, *Planning and Environment*, D, 12: 727-50.

McKay, S. (1998), Older workers in the labour market, *Labour Market Trends,* 106: 365-9.

McKendrick, N. (1961), Josiah Wedgwood and factory discipline, *Historical Journal*, 1: 30-55.

Meijers, J.M.M., Swaen, G.M.H., Volovics, A., Slangen, J.J.M. and van Vliet, K. (1990), Silica Exposure and lung cancer in ceramic workers: a case-control study, *International Journal of Epidemiology*, 19.1: 19-25.

Messing, K., Tissot, F., Saurel-Cubozolles, M-J., Kaminski, M. and Bourgine, M. (1996), Sex as a variable can be a surrogate for some working conditions: factors associated with sickness absence, *Journal of Occupational and Environmental Medicine* 40: 250-60.

Mills, C.Wright (1970), *The Sociological Imagination*, Harmondsworth: Penguin.

Moum, T. (1992), Self-assessed health among Norwegian adults, *Social Science and Medicine*, 35: 935-47.

Navarro, V. and Berman, B.M. (eds) (1983), *Health and Work under Capitalism*, Baltimore: Baywood Publishing.

Nichols, T. (1997), *The Sociology of Industrial Injury*, London: Mansell.

North, F., Syme, SL., Feeney, A., Head, J., Shipley, M.J. and Marmot M.G. (1993), Explaining socio-economic differences in sickness absence, *British Medical Journal,* 306: 361-6.

Ohnuki-Tierney, E. (1984), *Illness and Culture in Contemporary Japan*, Cambridge: Cambridge University Press.

Oliver, M. (1996a), *Understanding Disability,* Basingstoke: Macmillan.

Oliver, M. (1996b), Defining impairment and disability, In Barnes and Mercer (1996).

Ollman, B. (1976), *Alienation*, 2nd edition, Cambridge: Cambridge University Press.

Parsons, T. (1954), *The Social System*, Glencoe: Free Press.

Parsons, T. (1958), Definitions of health and illness in the light of American values and social structure, In Jaco, E.G. (ed), *Patients, Physicians and Illness*, Glencoe: Free Press.

Peter, R. and Siegrist, J. (1997), Chronic work stress, sickness absence, and hypertension in middle managers: general or specific sociological explanations? *Social Science and Medicine*, 45: 1111-20.

Pheasant, S. (1991), *Ergonomics, Work and Health*, London: Macmillan.

Pheasant, S. (1996), *Bodyspace: Anthropometry, Ergonomics and the Design of Work*, 2nd edition, London: Taylor and Francis.

Pilcher, W. (1972), *The Portland Longshoremen*, New York: Holt, Rinehart and Winston.

Polanyi, K. (1957), *The Great Transformation: The Political and Economic Origins of Our Time*, Boston: Beacon Press.

Pollard, S. (1968), *The Genesis of Modern Management*, Harmondsworth: Penguin.

Radcliffe-Brown, A.R. (1952), On joking relationships, and, A further note on joking relationships, *Structure and Function in Primitive Society*, London: Cohen and West.

Ramazzini, B. (1940), De Morbis Artificium Diatriba, Padua, 1713 (2nd edition), Translated by Wright, W.C., Chicago: Chicago University Press.

Ravaud, J.F., Madiot, B. and Ville, I. (1992), Discrimination towards disabled people seeking employment, *Social Science and Medicine*, 35: 951-8.

Reilly, P.A. (1995), Repetitive strain injury: from Australia to UK, *Journal of Psychosomatic Research*, 39: 783-8.

Reinberg, A., Andlauer, P., De Prins, J., Malbecq, W., Vieux,N. And Laporte, A. (1984), Desynchronisation of the oral temperature circadian rhythm and intolerance to shift work, *Nature*, 308 (5956): 272-4.

Ross, C.E. and Mirowsky, J. (1995), Does employment affect health? *Journal of Health and Social Behavior*, 36: 230-43.

Roy, D. (1952), 'Banana time', job satisfaction and informal interaction, *Human Organization*, 18: 158-68.

Sacker, A. (1990), Smoking habits of nurses and midwives, *Journal of Advanced Nursing*, 15: 1341-6.

Sahlins, M. (1974), *Stone Age Economics*, London: Tavistock.

Samuel, R. (1977), Workshop of the world, *History Workshop*, 3: 6-72.

Santiago, A.M. and Muschkin C.G. (1996), Disentangling the effects of disability status and gender on the labor supply of Anglo, black, and Latino older workers, *Gerontologist*, 36: 299-310.

Savage, M. and Egerton, M. (1997), Social mobility, individual ability and the inheritance of class inequality. *Sociology*, 31.4: 645-72 (1997).

Selye, H. (1956), *The Stress of Life*, New York: McGraw-Hill.

Shakespeare, T. (1996), In Barnes and Mercer (1996).

Shakespeare, T. (1998), Choices and rights: eugenics, genetics and disability equality, *Disability and Society*, 13: 665-81.

Shaw, C. (1969), *When I was a Child*, Facsimile reprint, London: S.R. Publishers.

Siegrist P.R., Junge, A., Cremer, P. *et al.* (1990), Low status control, high effort at work and ischemic heart disease: prospective evidence from blue collar men, *Social Science and Medicine*, 31: 1127-34.

Sly, F. (1996), Ethnic minority participation in the labour market: trends from the Labour Force Survey 1984-1995, *Labour Market Trends*, 104: 259-70.

Sly, F., Duxbury, R. and Tillsley, C. (1995), Disability and the labour market: findings from the Labour Force Survey,. *Labour Market Trends*, 103: 439-57.

Sly, F., Thair, T. And Risdon, A. (1998), Women in the labour force: results from the spring 1997 Labour Force Survey, *Labour Market Trends*, 106: 97-117.

Soja, E.W. (1996), *Thirdspace*, Oxford: Blackwell.

Sontag, S. (1991), *Illness as Metaphor* and *AIDS and its Metaphors*, London: Penguin.

Stansfeld, S., Feeney, A., Head, J., Canner, R., North, F., and Marmot, M. (1995), Sickness absence for psychiatric illness: the Whitehall II study, *Social Science and Medicine*, 40: 189-97.

Stansfeld, S., North, F.M., White, I. and Marmot, M.G. (1995), Work characteristics and psychiatric disorder in civil servants in London, *Journal of Epidemiology and Community Health*, 49: 48-53.

Sterling, T. (1978), Does smoking kill workers or working kill smokers? *International Journal of Health Services*, 8: 437-52.

Stern, J. (1983), The relationship between unemployment, morbidity and mortality in Britain, *Population Studies*, 37: 31-64.

Stevens, G. (1992), Work injury: a view from HSE's trailer to the 1990 Labour Force Survey, *Employment Gazette*: 621-38.

Steward, B. (1998), Telework and the social process of sickness, Paper read to the *British Sociological Association Medical Sociology Group*, Annual Conference at University of York.

Stronks, K., van de Mheen, H., van den Bos, J. and Mackenbach, J.P. (1995), Smaller socio-economic inequalities in health among women: the role of employment status, *International Journal of Epidemiology*, 24.3: 559-68.

Sykes, A.J.M. (1966), Joking relationships in an industrial setting, *American Anthropologist*, 68: 188-93.

Thompson, D., Rawlings, A.J. and Harrington, J.M. (1987) Repetition strain injuries. In Harrington, J.M. (Ed) *Recent Advances in Occupational Health*, Vol 3.

Till, A. (1987), New tableware production methods, Paper read to the *Joint Symposium on Health and Safety in the Pottery Industry*, British Occupational Health Society and North Staffordshire Medical Institute (Arlidge Section), Stoke-on-Trent.

Townsend, P. and Davidson, N. (eds) (1988), *Inequalities in Health*, Harmondsworth: Penguin.

Trist, E.L., Higgins, G.W., Murray, H. And Pollock, A.B. (1963), *Organizational Choice*, London: Tavistock.

Turner, B.S. (1996), *The Body and Society*, 2nd edition, London: Sage.

Turner, B.S. and Sampson, C. (1995), *Medical Power and Social Knowledge,* 2nd edition. London: Sage.

Turner, V. (1970), *The Forest of Symbols,*

Turner, V. (1982), Liminal and liminoid in play, flow and ritual: an essay in comparative symbology, *From Ritual to Theatre,* New York: Performing Arts Journal Publications.

Vahtera, J., Kivimaki, M. and Pentti, J. (1997), Effect of organizational downsizing on health of employees, *Lancet* 350: 1124-8.

van Gennep, A. (1960), *The Rites of Passage,* Translated Vizedom, C.K. and Caffee, G.L., London: Routledge and Kegan Paul.

Walby, S. and Bagguley, P. (1989), Gender restructuring: five labour markets compared, *Environment and Planning,* D, 7: 277-92.

Wald, N. and Nicolaidis-Bouman, A. (1991), *UK Smoking Statistics,* 2nd edition, Oxford: Oxford University Press.

Walsh, D.C. (1987), *Corporate Physicians,* New Haven: Yale University Press.

Warr, P. (1987), *Work, Unemployment and Mental Health,* Oxford: Oxford University Press.

Waterhouse, J.M., Minors, D.S. and Scott, A.R. (1987), Circadian rhythms, intercontinental travel and shift work, in W.Gardner (ed), *Occupational Health,* Vol. 3, London: Wright.

Weatherall, R., Joshi, H. and Macran, S. (1994), Double burden or double blessing - employment, motherhood and mortality in the Longitudinal Study of England and Wales, *Social Science and Medicine,* 38: 285-97.

Weber, M. (1968), *Economy and Society,* Vol. 1, Translated by G.Roth and C.Wittich, New York: Bedminster Press.

Weindling, P. (ed) (1985), *The Social History of Occupational Health,* London: Croom Helm.

Whipp, R. (1990), *Patterns of Labour,* London: Routledge.

Wilkinson, R.G. (1994), Inequalities and health, *Lancet* 343: 538-x.

Willis, P. (1977), *Learning to Labour,* Farnborough: Saxon House.

Willis, P. (1978), *Profane Culture,* London: Routledge and Kegan Paul.

Wilson, G.B. (1940), *Alcohol and the Nation,* London: Nicolson and Watson.

World Health Organization (1980), *International Classification of Impairments, Disabilities and Handicaps,* Geneva: WHO.

Wray L.A. (1996), The role of ethnicity in the disability and work experience of preretirement-age Americans, *Gerontologist,* 36.3: 287-98.

Young, A. (1980), The discourse on stress and the reproduction of conventional knowledge *Social Science and Medicine,* 14B: 133.

Young, A. (1993), A description of how ideology shapes knowledge of mental disorder (post-traumatic stress disorder), In Lindenbaum, S. And Lock, M (eds), *Knowledge, Power and Practice,* Berkeley: University of California Press.

Young, I.M. (1990), *Throwing Like a Girl and Other Essays in Feminist Philosophy and Social Theory,* Bloomington: Indiana University Press.

Zerubavel, E. (1981), *Hidden Rhythms*, Chicago: Chicago University Press.

Zola, I. (1966), Culture and symptoms - an analysis of patients' presenting complaints, *American Sociological Review*, 31: 615-30.

Zola, I. (1972), Medicine as an institution of social control: the medicalizing of society, *Sociological Review*, 20: 487-504.

Index

absence 20, 115
careers 84
control 8, 19
cyclical 8, 83
deadlines 20, 21, 60, 86
decision latitude 19, 21
external 9, 10, 20, 84, 114
flexible hours 135
internal 9, 10 20, 84, 114
line-paced 10, 83, 116, 117
linear 9, 83
relations of power 114
rhythm 19, 20, 59, 60, 84, 85
self-pacing 9, 115
shift work 85
Townsend, P. 140, 141
Trist, E. 86
Turner, B. 6, 62-64, 101
Turner, V. 9, 68

US Health and Retirement Survey 39

Vahtera, J. 132
van Gennep, A .68, 101
Vulnerability
broken rhythm 84-86
coping 83, 84
coping breakdowns 83
gender 90
qualities accentuated 81
qualities depreciated 82
unmet deadlines 86-88

Walby, S. 191
Wald, N. 154
Walsh, D. 15
Warr, P. 188
Waterhouse, J. 85
Weatherall, J. 186
Weber, M. 51, 87
Wedgwood, Josiah I, 84
Well-being
quality of life 15
Whipp, R. 64
White, J. 187n
Whitehall studies 18, 162, 177-182, 184
Whitehead, M. 140, 141, 165
Wilkinson, R. 181, 203
Willis, P. 44, 148
Wilson, G. 153
Work and play 9
Work groups
effort 86
World Health Organization 15, 29
Wray, L. 39

Young , A. 18
Young, I.M. 63
Youth 19
men 102
women 102, 103

Zerubavel, E. 9, 83
Zola 12, 154